Building Research Establishment Report

CW00590473

Solar heating systems for the UK:
design, installation, and economic aspects

S J Wozniak BA PhD

Department of the Environment
Building Research Establishment

London: Her Majesty's Stationery Office

Full details of all new BRE
Publications are published
quarterly in BRE News. Requests
for BRE News or for placing on
the mailing list should be
addressed to:
Distribution Unit
Publications and Publicity Unit
Building Research Establishment
Garston, Watford WD2 7JR

Cover photograph
The BRE low energy house
laboratories with the solar
laboratory in the foreground

ISBN 0 11 670762 3
© *Crown copyright* 1979
    First published 1979

Contents list

Note: In general, SI units are used in this book. Other units compatible with the metric system (for example, bar and litre) are used extensively in the sections dealing with plumbing design and water supply. In particular, litres rather than kilograms are used for flow rates and both kilowatt-hours and joules are used for energy.

Summary

The book deals with many of the practical problems of design, installation and operation of solar water heating equipment for use in the UK.

Detailed information is presented on systems for pre-heating domestic hot water in single-family dwellings since this is one of the major areas where there is likely to be a continuing interest in solar technology; other potential applications ranging from simple swimming pool systems to those designed for industrial or commercial premises are briefly discussed.

In addition to a consideration of the plumbing components and circuits that are used for solar water heating in the UK the book also contains information on specialised aspects such as electronic differential controllers, heat transfer fluids, and the possible future application of high performance collectors. Some of these aspects are however still the subject of research and it has therefore not proved possible to give a complete set of definitive design solutions.

An indication is given of the probable energy savings that may be realised from many types of systems and the present and possible future cost-effectiveness of solar energy is discussed within a framework of internal rate of return. It is shown that solar space or water heating is unlikely to show a good return on investment in most situations.

The final chapter outlines some of the pitfalls that should be avoided when designing experiments intended to assess the thermal performance of solar equipment installed in buildings.

1 Introduction

The energy crisis of the early 1970s brought in its wake a much increased awareness of the possibilities of utilising 'soft' or 'alternative' energy technologies such as wind, wave and solar power. The advantage of such energy supply systems is that they are fuelled from a source whose continued existence is virtually assured and not easily subject to political or military interference. The principal disadvantage of such technologies is, at present, that the capital investment required is often far in excess of the level at which either national or private concerns could consider widespread replacement of existing supply systems by those utilising 'renewable' energy: the underlying problem is often not the collection but the storage of this energy.

Prominent amongst the alternative technologies that have been considered for application in the UK is the use of solar energy for low temperature water heating. The technology is not new; solar water heating systems have been in widespread use for over 20 years in countries having an abundance of sunshine and, whilst their construction and performance has been the subject of continuing scientific research, the basic components have remained substantially unchanged.

The situation in the UK at present is that more than 50 companies are manufacturing solar water heating equipment. Some of these companies are small and their activities unregulated, and unfortunately some of the systems that have been sold are unlikely to last the 10–30 years, without incurring substantial maintenance costs, which are necessary if they are to approach economic viability.

Previous BRE publications[1, 2, 3] have outlined the economics and possible scale of the future exploitation of solar energy for domestic water heating in the UK and have dealt briefly with some of the practical problems that it was thought might arise. This book deals in more detail with these practical aspects: the examples of unsatisfactory practice are not imaginary, and many come from inspections that the author has carried out on systems that have been installed in private houses.

It has been evident for some time that a few companies in the solar energy business make over-optimistic claims for their equipment, and some of these have recently been high-lighted[4, 5, 6]. Section 6 of this book presents a guide to what might be considered reasonable costs for the components of small solar systems and outlines briefly methods for calculating the likely fuel savings. Unless otherwise specified all component and fuel costs are at early 1978 levels.

2 System design

2.1 General

As noted above this book deals principally with the design and installation of solar systems for supplying domestic hot water in individual dwelling houses or similar premises. A basic knowledge of plumbing practice is assumed; there are available many texts on the subject that give introductory information[7, 8]. An essential point about all the systems described in Section 2.2.2 is that they are designed for preheating domestic hot water; it will only be during hot sunny summer weather that a household can expect its hot water requirements to be totally solar heated.

The only 'novel' parts in a solar collector system are the collector itself and its fixing to the roof of a building (one of the most usual locations). The rest of the system is fairly conventional plumbing, and if ordinary good practice is followed there should be few problems if the components are all carefully selected so as to be compatible with one another and with the chosen heat transfer fluid.

Solar collectors of standard design comprise the following:

1 A blackened or otherwise treated collector plate whose principal function is to convert the incident solar radiation into heat.

2 Fluid passages through which a water or oil-based heat transfer fluid flows. Heat generated on the collector plate is transferred to this fluid which subsequently transfers it to water contained in a storage vessel.

3 One or more transparent or translucent covers (usually a single sheet of glass) whose principal functions are to help to insulate the collector plate from the cooler ambient air, and to provide weather-proofing.

4 Insulation material behind the collector plate whose function is often one of providing some mechanical support for the collector plate as well as helping to prevent heat loss. Sometimes a reflective metal foil is placed immediately behind the collector plate, and may prove useful in designs having only a small thickness of insulation material.

5 An enclosing box whose principal functions are to hold the other components of the collector in their correct respective positions and to protect the plate and insulation material from the weather.

The basic operation of solar collectors of this type is covered in numerous texts (for example references 9, 10, 11 and 12) as well as in the BRE literature already cited[1, 3]. A detailed description of these devices is given in Section 3.1; it may be noted that the terms solar collector and solar panel are synonymous, but the latter is sometimes used to describe photovoltaic cells also.

2.2 Systems for preheating domestic hot water

2.2.1 General

Solar collector systems for domestic hot water application may be grouped into 2 distinct categories, *direct* and *indirect*.

Direct systems are those in which the water that ultimately is drawn from the hot taps passes through the collectors.

Indirect systems are those in which a fluid other than the water ultimately drawn from the taps passes through the collectors. This fluid may or may not be water-based and such systems will of necessity incorporate a heat exchanger, the primary working fluid being on one side and the tap water on the other.

There are two distinct ways in which the heat transfer fluid can be circulated round the system; either natural thermosyphon action can be used or, often more conveniently, a small pump can be employed. These systems are called *gravity* (sometimes 'thermosyphon') and *pumped*, respectively.

Containment of the primary fluid in an indirect system may be achieved in several ways but, depending upon the degree to which the fluid is exposed to atmospheric oxygen and airborne contaminants they may be classified as *open*, *vented* or *sealed*.

In an *open* system atmospheric gases and contaminants are freely mixed with the primary fluid and frequently the fluid passages in the collector plates are alternately filled with air and fluid as the plates drain and refill.

In a *vented* system the design of the primary circuit resembles that of many central heating installations in the UK. A small cistern is placed sufficiently above the highest point of the circuit so as to provide a positive gauge pressure at all points in the circuit even when the pump is running. The concentration of atmospheric gases in the primary fluid may not be zero but should certainly be far less than in an open system. It should be noted that in central heating nomenclature this type of system is termed 'open vented'.

In *sealed* systems the primary fluid loop is completely sealed from the atmosphere and provision for expansion is usually made by incorporating a diaphragm expansion vessel. This type of device is sometimes incorporated into central heating installations where microbore tubing is used – the pump heads are here often higher than in a 'conventional' vented system and use of sealed system equipment can lead to increased flexibility of component layout.

Several typical system layouts are shown in Section 2.2.2; these cover most of the standard ways in which solar collectors are currently coupled to water supply systems. A few notes are given with each diagram detailing the special design and operating precautions that should be taken with systems of that particular type. The characteristics of the various component parts and their suitability for any given duty are detailed in Section 3.

As noted in Appendix I it is a requirement in the UK that prior to the installation of a solar water heating system the details of the proposed system be notified to both the local water undertaking and the local planning department*. It must not be assumed that any system described herein will automatically meet with approval. In addition, Building Regulations must be complied with.

There are several aspects of ordinary good plumbing practice which apply to all the solar collector systems described in this section and for any given system the following check list should be consulted to make certain that no basic necessities have been overlooked.

1 All systems should have provision for drainage of both primary and secondary fluid should repair be necessary. Primary circuits incorporating check valves may need more than one draining point.

2 All indirect systems must incorporate provision for expansion of the fluid in the primary circuit and provision for venting and overflow or other safe discharge in the event of boiling.

3 All components should be compatible with the fluid in contact with them. This is particularly important for primary circuits filled with non-aqueous fluids, and for mixed-metal systems: more details are given in Section 3.

4 All components should be suitable for continuous operation at the maximum working temperature of the system; for most circuits using aqueous fluids this can be taken to be near 100°C (slightly higher for sealed pressurised primary circuits). For systems using non-aqueous heat transfer fluids dangerously high temperatures could conceivably be reached using high performance flat plate collectors if the secondary system were drained. At these temperatures pumps

and other components designed primarily for central heating or similar duty may fail. Consideration should also be given to the likely effects of the high stagnation temperatures that may be attained under fault conditions.

5 The solar system should be connected to the existing system in such a way that preheated water is supplied to the hot cylinder and taps only: there is a possibility with some solar system designs that preheated water could be supplied to the WC or cold taps if these are not already supplied at mains pressure. Since both standard and hybrid water service systems have been used in UK houses a thorough preliminary check is advisable to ascertain the layout of the existing pipework.

6 Wherever possible all components should meet the requirements of the appropriate British Standard; both the recently published HVCA Guide and the British Standards Institution draft Code of Practice for solar water heating systems contain details of relevant Standards and Codes [13, 14]. In areas where dezincification is known to occur gunmetal fittings (or other approved dezincification-resistant fittings) should be specified for use in direct circuits [15]. If there is any doubt as to the suitability of a particular type of fitting the local water undertaking could be consulted.

In the diagrams of indirect systems that follow the heat exchangers are all shown with the supply to the solar panels taken from the lower connection; it might be thought that the alternative method of connection would be preferable but this is incorrect. Since this point often causes some confusion a brief explanation will be given.

Simple heat exchangers are often operated in what may be termed 'parallel flow' or 'counterflow' modes. The basic difference between these situations is illustrated in Figure 1. When the temperature difference between inlet and outlet on one side of the exchanger is very small then the performance of parallel flow and counterflow designs is very similar but under more general conditions a counterflow heat exchanger will usually exhibit higher efficiency. However, heat exchangers in solar storage vessels cannot be analysed using the formulae applicable to these idealised cases because if severe store stratification exists then a portion of the exchanger may be operating in reverse – extracting heat from a hot region of the store and transferring it to a cooler region whilst at the same time transferring a small amount of solar heat to the store. The occurrence of these phenomena is intimately

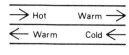

Figure 1 Basic modes of heat exchange: (a) Counterflow, (b) Parallel flow

(a)

(b)

---

* Strictly, it is necessary to inform the water undertaking only when the house or premises is served with mains water.

linked with both control system characteristics and sensor positions and will not be treated in detail in this book. An example will however be used for illustrative purposes.

The principal aim of the solar system should be to transfer the maximum quantity of solar heat into the storage vessel. Since the thermal efficiency of solar collectors decreases as their temperature rises it would seem logical to supply them with the coldest possible fluid; the collectors' efficiency will then be at the maximum possible and the heat input to the storage vessel (calculated under steady state conditions as the product of the flow rate and the temperature difference across the collector) will also be a maximum. A boundary condition in this steady state analysis is that the temperature difference across the collector equals that across the heat exchanger, assuming no heat loss in the connecting pipework. The thermal behaviour of the heat exchanger and the relevant analysis are not straightforward because the stratification (if any) of the store is unknown but it seems intuitively obvious that the inlet temperature of the collectors in the system shown in Figure 2a will always be less than or equal to that shown in Figure 2b. The equality occurs with zero stratification in the store and in this situation the systems are thermally identical if it is assumed that the convection currents set up by the heat input from the exchangers are the same in both cases – this is in fact an unreasonable assumption the invalidity of which should however have little effect on an idealised heat exchanger where it will be assumed that each segment sees only the local store temperature.

In an idealised example of severe store stratification – which could occur if a quarter of the contents of a previously uniformly-hot store were drawn off – either of the systems depicted in Figure 2 may exhibit undesirable characteristics. Suppose that the system temperatures were as shown in Figure 3a but that the pump was then caused to operate by a period of high intensity irradiation. Suppose also that the control system sensors are positioned as shown at points X and record the local store temperature and the collector outlet temperature. Finally, suppose that

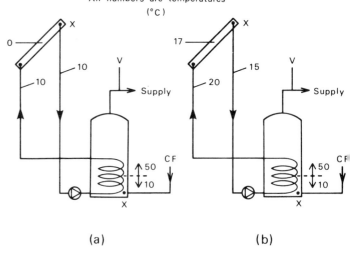

X = position of temperature sensors
All numbers are temperatures
(°C)

(a)   (b)

Figure 3 Conditions for lock-on of a differential temperature controller under zero or low solar irradiance. Severe store stratification and parallel flow heat exchange are assumed: (a) Before switch-on, (b) After switch-on

after the pump switches on the sun disappears behind a cloud or night falls. The pump will continue to function until the temperature recorded by the panel sensor falls close to that of the store sensor; this may however not happen for some time because the panel is being supplied with hot fluid (via the coil which has its top half immersed in water at 50°C) and the net result is that a significant quantity of heat may be lost. Figure 3b shows conceivable system temperatures during the time that the pump continues to operate and the only safe places for the store sensor are therefore at or above the uppermost level of the heat exchanger: it is shown in Section 3.7 that these may be considered undesirable. Systems using counterflow heat exchangers (as shown in Figure 2a) are less likely to suffer from the type of problem outlined above.

It would be appropriate to note in this introductory section that pumps should if possible be located so that they heat up the transfer fluid before it flows into the store, and not immediately before it returns to the panels. The effect on overall performance is however likely to be small, and in some systems it is not possible to site the pump in this preferred position.

It would be worthwhile developing a simple test that would tell the householder whether his system was functioning correctly; this matter is currently the subject of debate but a possible method might be to have *for any given system*, a 'characteristic temperature' that the solar storage vessel should reach on 'a good summer's day' with no draw-off of water. Unfortunately, both this and similar tests that rely on temperature measurement alone can be insensitive to minor system faults.

At this point it may be appropriate to give a serious warning concerning the use of mercury-in-glass thermometers near copper plumbing components. If by accident the thermometer were broken, and mercury were spilled on to the copper (or worse still lodged in crevices in contact with copper), embrittlement could occur as

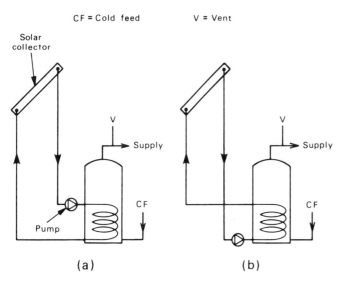

CF = Cold feed   V = Vent

Solar collector

Supply   Supply

CF   CF

Pump

(a)   (b)

Figure 2 Connection of heat exchangers in simple solar water heating systems: (a) Counterflow, (b) Parallel flow

mercury diffused into grain boundaries in the copper; the net result over a period of time could be seriously to weaken an area of copper. It is recommended that mercury thermometers should never be used to measure temperatures in a domestic water system containing copper or brass components.

Another possible approach would be to install an hour-run counter on the pump: work at BRE has shown that both control system faults and air-locking can substantially alter the run-time.

In cases of complete air-locking, where no circulation at all occurs, the pump will, under favourable weather conditions, run continuously and become hot while the connecting pipework remote from the pump will remain cool. This may be used as a simple go/no-go indication in pumped systems.

2.2.2 System types

The guidance notes given below are intended to high-light the areas in which mistakes are most likely to occur in the design or installation of a particular system type.

SYSTEM TYPE 1: direct, gravity-circulation

The 'direct gravity' system is perhaps the simplest that can be envisaged in which the collectors and storage vessel are separate entities; see Figure 4. It might be thought that these types of systems are unlikely to find widespread application in the UK, except perhaps in situations such as holiday chalets where only summertime hot water is required. One of the fundamental problems for winter-time operation is that many types of collectors are susceptible to frost damage unless they are drained in very cold weather; draining by automatic valves seems likely to be unacceptable to local water undertakings since repeated cycling of these devices perhaps several times daily would lead to undue waste of potable water. Similarly, protection against excessive system temperatures

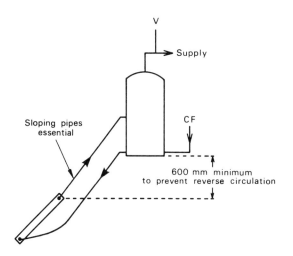

Figure 4 System type 1: Direct, gravity-circulation

by running hot water to waste may not be allowed, and the most practicable safeguard may be a fan-coil unit in the circulation pipework. The necessary power-output rating of such a device would be equal to the maximum possible power retention of the collectors at the highest allowable system temperature.

Another problem, common to all direct systems, is the possibility that in areas where the water has a high temporary hardness furring of the waterways could occur over a period of years, thus degrading the thermal performance of the collector plate.

Despite these drawbacks however it is not unlikely that this type of system may find increased use: there are many areas in the UK where deposition of temporary hardness is unlikely to be much of a problem (a good indication is provided by the degree of furring in kettles) and it is not difficult to envisage designs of collectors and systems which will withstand freeze-thaw cycles, thus obviating the problem of wintertime draining (see Section 3.1.9). It is considered that this type of system which is often dismissed as unworthy of further comment, can, if properly designed and installed, be inherently safe, self-regulating, and quite reasonably effective. However a long-term problem may arise in that the water quality in respect of the level of temporary hardness cannot be guaranteed, except in buildings where water softening equipment is installed.

Critical to successful operation are correct positioning of the collectors relative to the storage vessel and use of large bore pipework, which should never be less than 28 mm diameter except in very small systems and all of which *must* be sloped so as to preclude any possibility of air-locks being formed; this precaution is *absolutely essential*, and failure to observe good practice has been the reason for many a disappointment; nominally horizontal pipe runs are *not* acceptable in these systems, and sharp bends should be avoided wherever possible.

Another essential precaution with many types of collector plates is that they must slope so as to obviate any possibility of air-locks being formed in the headers. This is especially important in direct circuits where air will continually be released from solution. Failure to observe this precaution has resulted in unsatisfactory systems being installed overseas[16], and it is to be hoped that the same mistakes will not be repeated in the UK: Figure 5 shows several correct methods for installing solar collector plates of this type in gravity systems.

Additionally, the vertical distance shown in Figures 4 and 6 must exceed 600 mm: otherwise, according to work carried out in Australia and South Africa, reverse circulation can occur under some conditions, leading to unwarranted loss of stored heat. This same problem is encountered in boiler-fired hot water systems and 1200 mm is sometimes quoted as a minimum safe height[7]. It is likely that this type of solar system will prove suited to wall mounting because of the difficulty of achieving the correct relative position of the storage vessel with roof-mounted collectors. Section 5.3 should be consulted for further details of wall mounting.

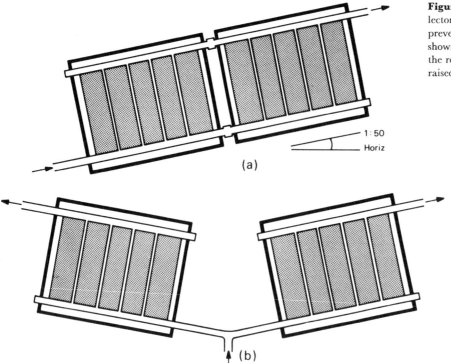

Figure 5 Two suitable methods of aligning collectors in gravity circulation systems so as to prevent air-locking. An alternative solution (not shown) is to mount the collectors 'square-on' to the roof but with either the left or right hand edge raised slightly relative to the roof surface

Only full-bore gate valves or other types having a very low flow resistance should be used in gravity circulation systems; use of any type of mechanical non-return valve cannot be advocated because of the very low circulation head available; this point is here stressed because of the contrary advice given by some other authors. A brief calculation is instructive. Water changes density by about 3 per cent over the range 0–80°C or 0·0375 per cent per °C. If the driving force for circulation is a solar collector 1 m in height with a temperature difference of 10°C across it and if the connecting pipework is an extra 2 m of vertical height the total driving force will be derived from the difference in density between two 3 m high water columns with a temperature difference of 10°C between them. The pressure head is therefore 11·2 mm of water or about 110 N/m² in this average case; at temperatures in the range 10–40°C however the pressure head would only be about 7·5 mm of water. The importance of correct design and installation of these systems cannot be over-emphasised since their performance can be most adversely affected by even minor faults.

SYSTEM TYPE 2: indirect, gravity-circulation

Indirect gravity systems operate in essentially the same manner as direct gravity systems and many of the precautions outlined for the latter apply equally here; see Figure 6. There are many variations on the general theme but the following basic rules, which to some extent summarise the text given with Type 1 systems, should always be observed.

1 The basic design should preclude all possibility of air or vapour locks in all parts of the system.

2 Provision should be made for expansion either with a cistern or sealed expansion vessel.

3 No horizontal pipe runs should be used – a minimum slope of about 1:40 would be an adequate design rule. Pipework should be 28 mm diameter or larger.

4 The solar collector plates should have a very low flow resistance.

Use of an indirect system means that there will always be a 'highest point' in the primary circuit (usually at the topmost level of the heat exchanger) and either a vent pipe or a reliable type of automatic air-release valve should be installed. Protection against overheating (if considered necessary) may be achieved by using a fan-coil unit.

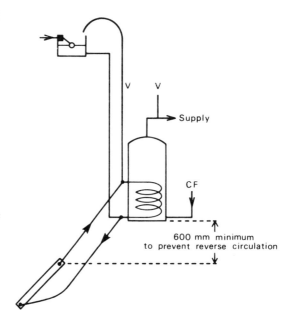

Figure 6 System type 2: Indirect, gravity-circulation

When compared to a direct system the obvious advantages of an indirect circuit are that antifreeze and/or corrosion inhibitors can in theory be used thus permitting the use of a wider range of collector plate materials. In addition, furring cannot occur in the collector plates even if the initial charge of water is high in temporary hardness. Non-aqueous heat transfer fluids should not be used unless their volume expansion coefficient is sufficiently large to compensate for their less favourable viscosity and specific heat. The simplest type of indirect gravity system is therefore one in which the primary fluid is water (perhaps with a little biocide added) and in which freeze-safe collectors are used; such a system would be suitable for use in any area of the UK, but it should be remembered that the thermal performance will be worse than that of a similar direct system because of the temperature drop across the heat exchanger; the latter can itself give rise to a substantial additional resistance to fluid flow. For this reason, low flow resistance heat exchangers should be used and these must be of a design that cannot be air-locked when correctly installed. The most suitable types of heat exchanger for these systems may be either annular or multi-tube bank designs: one possible disadvantage would appear to be a low heat transfer coefficient owing to the very low velocities, but the much reduced flow resistance of these units when compared to a single coil of tube may be the deciding factor. Insufficient information appears to be available concerning the performance of low-temperature-difference gravity circuits in the UK, and in view of the difficulty of constructing genuinely meaningful mathematical models of these systems it is considered that an experimental approach to optimisation might be more appropriate. The essential problem would appear to be a determination of the optimum size of pipework in view of the extremely low pressure heads that can be developed; oversized pipework will lead to a decreased performance for increased cost because of heat capacity and deadleg effects while the much reduced flow rates in smaller bore pipes may result in significantly lower thermal performance unless more expensive low U value collectors are used.

In the case of vented (as opposed to sealed) systems there exists the possibility that the primary pressure can be substantially less than that on the secondary side and this is one way of ensuring that any leaks in the heat exchanger cannot easily result in noxious substances present in the primary fluid being introduced into the tap water.

It would seem that sealed gravity systems can really only be justified where the choice of collector and/or fluid militates against using one of the simpler alternatives, but the final decision must rest with the designer after he has appraised all the available options. It should be mentioned that, in common with all sealed circuits, since the pressure in the primary is likely to be well in excess of that on the secondary side these systems may have to meet more rigorous conditions laid down by a local water undertaking in respect of the necessary design, strength and corrosion resistance of the heat exchanger.

An especial note of caution is appropriate in respect of systems using indirect-coil cylinders with a gravity-

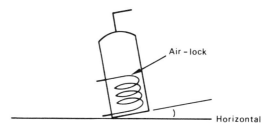

Figure 7 A possible cause of air-locking in indirect gravity systems using a coil heat exchanger

circulation primary. If the cylinder slopes slightly away from the uppermost coil connection then no air-locks can form in the coil but if an opposite slope is employed it is possible for a system of this type to become air-locked – this is illustrated in Figure 7. If indirect cylinders are used in gravity systems they should therefore be installed on a slope of approximately 1:50 (9 mm for a standard size cylinder of 450 mm diameter).

SYSTEM TYPE 3: direct, draindown, pumped-circulation

These systems comprise some of the simplest designs in which a pump is used to provide circulation of water through the solar collectors. Three systems, superficially different, are shown in Figure 8 but the basic operating principle is the same for each. The inclusion of a pump in a solar collector circuit immediately introduces the problem of controlling its operation since it is obvious that fluid should only be circulated when a useful amount of heat can be transferred to storage. This problem is treated in Section 3.7: it is here assumed that a suitable control system is incorporated.

Type 3a systems (Figure 8a) can have a very low capital cost since a suitable cistern, as opposed to a cylinder, can be used for the storage vessel, and in some cases even the existing cold water storage cistern can be utilised if it is of a suitable type.

This potential for low first cost and ease of fitting led to its use in a number of 'cheap and nasty' installations, giving the system type a bad name that is perhaps somewhat undeserved. Many of these ill-considered systems may cease to function after a few years because of the use of microbore pipework in areas of high temporary hardness; the basic design however may be potentially useful, and if properly installed could perform satisfactorily.

The pump may either be submerged in a cistern or (more conventionally) mounted externally and either arrangement is satisfactory if a suitable pump is used (see Section 3.4.1). In all cases the pump should be positioned so that it remains full of water at all times (except when the entire system is drained for repair or frost protection purposes), and should be suitable for use with supply water.

The essentials of operation are almost self explanatory from the diagrams – when the pump is switched on it forces water up through the collectors: when the pump stops the water drains from the collectors and from most

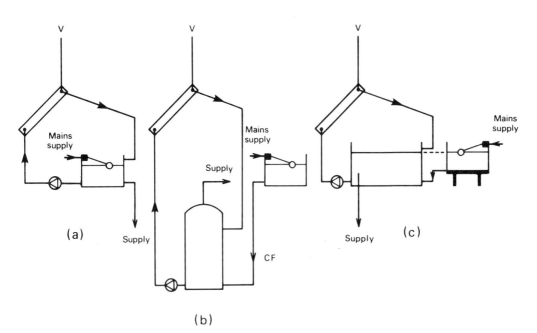

Figure 8 System type 3: Direct, draindown, pumped-circulation: (a) The existing feed cistern is used as the solar store, (b) A new cylinder is used as the solar store, (c) A new cistern is used as the solar store, with its water level controlled by the original cistern

of the pipework. It should be obvious that all the pipework in which water remains should be protected from frost since loft spaces can easily reach temperatures well below 0°C. As a general design rule therefore, any long lengths of pipe in the solar circuit should be positioned above the cistern overflow level and should slope so as to facilitate their draining. Care is also necessary in respect of the pump which if mounted outside the storage vessel should also be insulated; some protection will also be gained by situating it close to the storage vessel so that the two are thermally coupled by a short length of 22 or 28 mm pipe – this should reduce the risk of freezing provided that the storage vessel itself is well insulated and kept full of water.

Insulating a pump is of course not usual practice and it might be thought that this could introduce a risk of overheating. This may not be so for pumps that are sold principally for use in central heating systems since they are usually rated to work with water up to 100°C and in ambient temperatures up to 60°C: overheating is therefore unlikely to occur for two reasons. Firstly, there is in any case some thermal linkage between the pump and its motor which will tend always to equalise the temperatures of the two. The second reason, which is a consequence of the characteristics of most present-day solar panels, is the fact that the whole system could operate at water temperatures approaching the 90°C–100°C region only for a few hours per day. It is here concluded therefore that insulating a high-temperature-rated pump in this type of system is unlikely to cause overheating of the pump or its motor. This conclusion is restricted to pumps used in direct solar water heating systems using flat plate collectors, and should not be taken to be general. Because of the fire-risk of insulating any electrical apparatus only phenolic-resin-bonded glass fibre or other equally non-combustible material should be used.

These problems can however be avoided by using a control system that inhibits pump operation if the temperature at the base of the store rises above (say) 75°C, but both the collectors and the adjoining pipework must

be able to withstand severe thermal shock because the pump may subsequently be reactivated when the plate temperature is near 200°C.

It is important with systems of this type to ensure that they drain readily when switched off and so the pump should not incorporate non-return (check) valves of any type and draining should preferably not be dependent upon the correct operation of an electrically powered valve. For systems in which the flow pipe is submerged, an open vent should be fitted at the topmost point of the system; this is to ensure that water does not 'hang' in the pipes and collector. If a vent is incorporated then providing the head loss along this pipe can be kept small enough, 10 or 12 mm pipe can be used for systems comprising only a few square metres of collector. However these small pipe sizes are extremely prone to furring in hard water areas and unless the local water is very soft (and likely to remain so, which itself cannot be guaranteed because water is increasingly transferred around the country) the minimum pipe size should be 15 mm unless water softening equipment is installed. With Type 3a and 3b systems (Figures 8a and 8b) especially, care must be taken to ensure that sufficient excess capacity is provided in the storage cistern to accommodate the water that returns from the collector plates when they drain. If the plates have a high water content then this volume of water returning to a small cistern could result in undue force on the float valve assembly. This valve and its float should, in Type 3a systems, be suitable for use with hot water. An additional precaution for the basic Type 3a system is that the pipework connected to the float valve must not be of low-temperature-rated plastics: such material is used in many modern houses.

A slight modification is often used where the existing cistern is not big enough; this case is depicted in Figure 8c. The additional cistern is installed so as to provide a suitable volume of preheat storage and since its water level is controlled by the existing cistern (which may have to be raised slightly to suit) no additional float valve is necessary.

Types of collector

1

Plate 1 A selection of flat plate collectors displayed at the Centre for Alternative Technology, Machynlleth. Sizes range from 0.5 m² to 1.6 m² and weights from 7 kg/m² to 50 kg/m². Outdoor exposure testing of these collectors has already yielded useful information on their likely long term durability.

2

Plate 2 Although parabolic mirror concentrating collectors of this type can reach very high temperatures in full sunshine they are not ideally suited to the UK climate, and are unlikely to be widely used for heating domestic hot water.

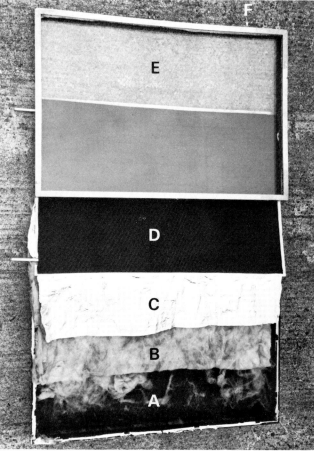

3

Plate 3 Component parts of a popular type of flat plate collector. The outer casing (A) is GRP and contains a 35 mm thickness of glass fibre insulation (B). A reflective metal foil (C) is laid between the insulation and the roll-bonded aluminium plate (D). The glass (E) is held in position by the aluminium angle frame (F) which is secured by aluminium screws to softwood strips laid inside the casing. There are many different types of flat plate collector but all utilise the same basic design principles.

Component failures

The photographs on this page illustrate the consequences of using a mineral-oil-based heat transfer fluid with off-the-shelf plumbing components.

4

5

Plate 4 All the items above were originally installed in a test rig at BRE filled with a heat transfer oil sold for use in solar water heating systems. Many of the internal rubber components have been attacked: both the pump isolating valves (A) and the small ball valve (B) jammed because of swollen internal seals. The pump was stripped before leakage occurred but from the condition of its internal seals (C, D, E) it is evident that failure was imminent. The only rubber components that survived were the 'O' ring seal on the pump air-bleed screw (F) and the length of silicone rubber hose (G). The hose is discoloured but appears still to be in sound condition. It is emphasised in Section 3.4 that many standard types of pumps and valves may not be suitable for use with mineral-oil-based fluids.

Plate 5 The automatic air-vent on the left was installed in an oil filled system and failed within 3 weeks. The valve on the right had been used for several months in a water filled system, and was still working satisfactorily before it was dismantled. The rubber sealing rings were originally the same size.

6

Plate 6 Deposition of scale on a 4 year old copper heat exchanger used in the hot water cylinder of a gas-fired central heating system. The thickness of the scale still adhering to the heat exchanger varies between 0 and 35 mm, and 7 kg of scale was removed from the bottom of the cylinder. The cylinder walls were coated with about 1 mm of scale, showing that deposition occurs elsewhere than on the heating surface. The temporary hardness of the supply water was about 250 ppm. Heat exchangers in indirect solar systems may be similarly affected over long time periods, and a significant decrease in the efficiency of the system might result. The inadvisability of using solar collectors in direct circuits for heating untreated hard water to high temperatures should need no further illustration.

Plate 7 Pitting corrosion failure of an 8 year old aluminium alloy valve used in a mixed-metal automotive cooling system; the body thickness is 4 mm compared with about 0.6 mm in a roll-bonded solar collector plate. As is typical of this type of corrosion the areas surrounding the corrosion pits have not been attacked.

7

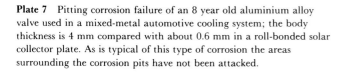

Plate 8 Pitting corrosion failure of a copper tube due to the presence of a carbon film produced by decomposition of pipe-drawing lubricants during annealing. Rapid failure of uncleaned copper tube may be expected if it is used with some supply waters (see Section 3.2).

8

Poor systems

9

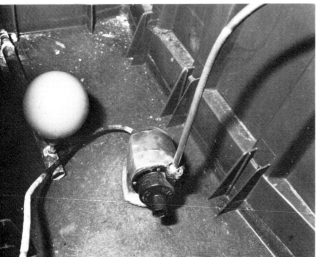

10

11

Plate 9 shows the interior components of a proprietary Type 3c system (see Figure 8c), typical of many installed in the UK since 1975. The two cisterns have been mounted on poor quality 12 mm chipboard which has deformed under the imposed loads. Most of the thermal insulation material that had been tied loosely round the solar store had fallen away, and the rest was removed for photographic purposes. This particular system had been out of action since the submersible pump (**Plate 10**) developed an electrical fault. The delivery pipe (with float attached) is showing evidence of both corrosion and slight scale formation. The methods used to attach the 32 × 3 mm aluminium straps to the roof (**Plate 11**) match the standard of workmanship that is evident in the rest of the system. Several repaired holes in the tiles on the north-facing roof slope bear witness to the original location of the collectors.

12

Plate 12 A 1.7 m² single-glazed 2-panel array of the type frequently used in the UK with poor Type 3 systems. The lower edges of the collectors are secured only by one 15 mm copper pipe. Both the pipes are let through the valleys of the tiles, so as to ensure a maximum potential rate of leakage. A large crack is just visible running down the glass in the left hand collector.

13

Plate 13 A 2.5 m² 3-panel array installed as part of a Type 3c system. A feature of this installation is that the collectors are secured by straps at both their upper and lower edges. Like others in the UK the system has now fallen into disuse because one of the collector plates has failed, and it may soon be removed completely.

14

Plate 14 Detail of the aluminium fixing straps pushed up underneath the roof tiles; lifting of the tile in the foreground is clearly visible. The thermocouple junction was found to be resting on the collector plate having been pushed through a hole in the collector casing. The steel screws used to secure the aluminium angle to the GRP casing are rusting badly after a few months' exposure.

15

Plate 15 Method used to secure the collectors to the roof; the sarking felt has been slashed and ripped aside, the straps pulled through and bent round an existing roof batten. In several systems of this type some of the straps were found not to be carrying any load – this being taken by the pipework.

Tunbridge Wells Girls' Grammar School project

16

17

Plate 16 Limited access to the roof from within the building necessitated using a crane to lift the collectors into position.

Plate 17 The collector support frameworks were bolted to steel joists themselves mounted on steel uprights passed through the roof membrane. Some leakage of rainwater through the roof has been experienced at these points. (See Section 5.2.)

18

Plate 18 After connection and pressure testing of the collector plates the gaps between the collectors and the rear, base, and end surfaces of the framework were clad with aluminium sheet so as to form a totally enclosed structure. Stainless steel screws were used to secure the cladding, the purpose of which was to limit wind loading whilst enhancing the appearance of the installation.

19

Plate 19 The completed installation viewed from an adjoining park. The thermal performance of the system was monitored by BRE, and the results have been published elsewhere (see reference 109).

BSRIA Project

The photographs on these two pages illustrate component parts of a system developed for mounting lightweight solar collectors to trussed rafter roofs. Photographs by courtesy of BSRIA. Details of this system are shown in Figure 41.

20

Plate 20   In order to provide some load distribution between the rafters underlying the collectors two seasoned timber binders 100 mm × 75 mm are secured to the rafters using steel connector brackets. Unfortunately no proprietary brackets long enough to span the entire width of the rafters could be found. Two brackets are used at each rafter-binder intersection – a total of 32 brackets per house.

21

Plate 21   All the loads due to the collectors are transmitted through the roof by six galvanised steel support posts secured to the timber binders. The sarking felt is raised by the metal collar, thus ensuring that any water penetrating higher up the roof is channelled to either side of the support posts.

22

Plate 22   Several ideas were tried before a satisfactory system for flashing the support posts to the roof tiles was found. Perhaps ironically, the only successful method is based on traditional lead flashing. An early prototype is shown here on the test roof at BSRIA; later models incorporate a steel skirt attached to the locking nut.

23

Plate 23 Sometimes it is not possible to manoeuvre timber binders of the required length into existing roof spaces. In this installation each binder is in 2 equal lengths with each length secured to 4 rafters.

24

Plate 24 Support posts and rails attached to the roof and ready to receive the collectors. The clearance between the roof tiles and the underside of the collectors should be sufficient for debris to be washed away.

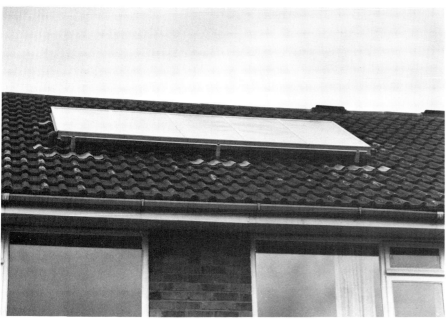

25

Plate 25 A 4.5 m² solar collector installed using the method shown above.

Swimming pool systems

26

27

Plate 26 A 15 m² unglazed polypropylene collector installed on a do-it-yourself basis; the 40 m² pool is situated behind the wooden trellis. The owner is very satisfied with the system, which maintains the pool at a comfortable temperature during the summer months. This system, situated in north Norfolk, withstood the severe winter of 1978–79 without any apparent damage, although the collectors are sagging slightly between their support rails. Apart from occasional cleaning no maintenance of polypropylene collectors should be required.

Plate 27 In this example of a seldom-used combination unglazed black-painted copper collector plates have been installed for heating an outdoor pool. The plates are almost inconspicuous, being fixed to wooden battens secured to the garage roof. Long-term durability of this type of collector plate may be expected to be high, with maintenance restricted to cleaning and occasional repainting.

28

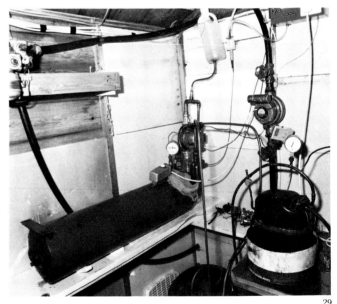

29

Plates 28 and 29 show an enthusiast's do-it-yourself solar space and water heating system using 18 m² of single glazed flat plate collector, a swimming pool as a heat store, and a heat pump (**Plate 29**). A strip of tiling either side of the collector might have improved its appearance.

Even if this area of collector were dedicated to water heating alone some conventional fuel would still be required, principally because of the low stagnation temperature of the collectors under most wintertime conditions.

Domestic hot water systems

30

31

Plates 30 and 31 Given sympathetic design, large areas of flat plate solar collector can be integrated successfully into most house types. In both these systems the collector plates are installed beneath patent glazing and serve to preheat the domestic hot water only.

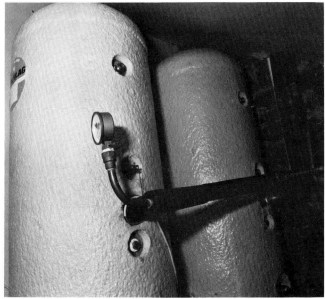

32

Plate 32 A significant problem in existing houses is often location of the preheat storage. One solution is to install two or more cylinders in parallel: if the secondary sides are connected top and bottom with short lengths of 22 or 28 mm pipe the cylinders will behave as one store, and coupling the heat exchangers in series ensures an adequate flow rate through each. If two or more 'preferred size' cylinders are used the total cost can be close to that of one large cylinder and with good thermal insulation there is little performance penalty. If the secondary sides of the cylinders are connected in series there is scope for increased 'stratification' – each cylinder acting as an isothermal store – but sophisticated controls and motorised valves are then required and the extra benefit may not justify the increased capital cost.

33

Plate 33 On some houses, if solar heating is required, there may be little option but to install wall-mounted collectors. Whilst the thermal performance may be adequate, there are often aesthetic disadvantages.

Sandringham project

34

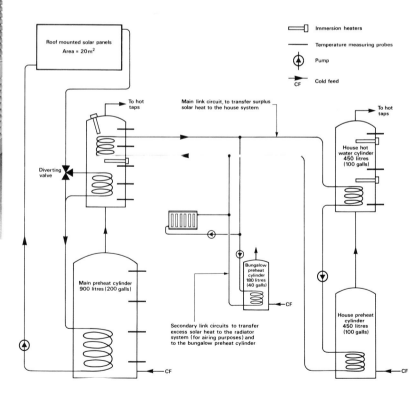

35

Designed with BRE assistance this is one of the most sophisticated solar water heating systems yet installed in the UK. 20 m² of flat plate collector (**Plate 34**) are used to heat 1350 l of water, and depending upon the system temperatures and the occupancy, excess heat can be diverted for use in adjoining buildings. The storage capacity required by large solar systems of this type is high-lighted by the size of the main preheat cylinder (**Plate 35**). If both the main cylinders overheat in midsummer the control system automatically transfers heat to one or more of the subsidiary stores. (See adjacent diagram.) After four years of operation the selectively coated copper collector plates are streaked with verdigris, and may soon require maintenance.

Often a float-operated delivery pipe is fitted, the idea being to ensure that the hottest preheated water is fed to the hot cylinder. Since the contents of the preheat vessel are usually stirred by the water returning from the collectors there is little stratification and it is doubtful whether this modification produces much net benefit; a seizure of the pivot could result in the *effective* volume of cold and preheat water storage being reduced to a low value and so the design of such devices needs to be sound. The feed may however be taken from a point about half way up the new cistern so long as the required minimum effective storage capacity is maintained, and provision for complete drainage incorporated.

SYSTEM TYPE 4: indirect, open, draindown, pumped-circulation

This type of system, see Figure 9, the design of which follows closely on those designated Type 3, might at first sight appear a little enigmatic since one of the principal reasons for using an indirect system is often that the choice is dictated by a desire to use collector plates or other system components that cannot be exposed to water containing dissolved gases and mineral salts.

In this system, which can clearly be classified as 'open' under the nomenclature adopted, the collector plates are exposed to a plentiful supply of oxygen and since the top-up to counter evaporative loss is often mains water, over a period of years the salt concentration may slowly increase up to and even beyond that present in the mains supply water, even if the initial charge were salt-free.

This increase in salt concentration may occur in any system that is not sealed and from which evaporation can occur, and the effect will be most serious in systems having a low ratio of water content to free surface area; conventional central heating systems containing 100 litres or more of water should suffer only a very slow increase in salt levels if the cistern is kept well covered. Solar systems,

however, can be more quickly affected, and for this reason alone renewal of aqueous-based primary fluids in areas where the water is even moderately hard might be advisable every few years.

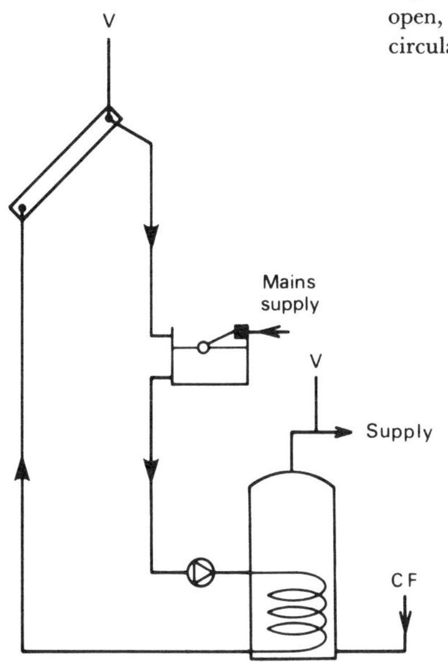

Over a long period of time, therefore, the potential for corrosion caused by either mineral salts, oxygen or both can become at least equal to that of mains water, and the overall advantages of this layout might appear questionable. The system may, however, be a very appropriate design if collectors which are not overly subject to corrosion problems (such as those with copper waterways) are used in an area of high temporary hardness; in these cases use of a direct system may be questioned (unless water softening equipment is installed) and an indirect system of some type may therefore be specified. The advantage over other types of pumped indirect systems is that, providing the cistern can be suitable positioned, no anti-freeze is required with any collector design which can be drained (some designs cannot, see Section 3.1.1) and the cost of periodic checks and possible replacement of fluids may be avoided. In addition, since only a small amount of biocide may be required as an additive if water is used as the primary fluid the heat exchanger may be of a type which might prove unacceptable to the local water undertaking if a more toxic fluid were to be used. This type of system has, however, been adopted in some instances for installations using roll-bonded* aluminium collector plates. The systems are filled with water dosed with a sodium benzoate-nitrite mixture (see Section 3.6.1) but the long-term effectiveness of this formulation when used in these systems is questionable, as is the likely lifetime of the collector plates; the oxygen-rich environment may however be able to induce the formation of an oxide layer capable of resisting further attack.

A few parts per million of chloride ions can give rise to greatly accelerated corrosion rates in some aluminium alloys and hence the use of this scheme in coastal areas, where salt spray and mist can carry inland, must be open to question since the collector plates draw in air every time the transfer fluid drains from them. Additionally, most mains water supplies contain chloride ions. Also sometimes advocated, however, is the use of ethylene glycol based antifreeze if the cistern cannot be positioned at a level sufficiently below the bottom of the collector plates. (In this case the plates only partially drain when the pump stops running and this may necessitate the use of antifreeze.)

Since glycol antifreezes are known to degrade by oxidation forming organic acids the advisability of their use in a system where high temperatures and plentiful oxygen are combined together may be questioned, especially as such degraded solutions can attack even copper. Protection against overheating of the store may be accomplished by inhibiting pump operation (as for Type 3 systems), but an added disadvantage here is that if the plate temperature is very high when the pump is subsequently reactivated some decomposition of the antifreeze or other additives may occur.

Figure 9 System type 4: Indirect, open, draindown, pumped-circulation.

---

* Roll-Bond is a process registered by Olin Brass but the term is used in this book to describe any collector plate manufactured in this way.

In summary therefore, systems of this general type may be adopted quite widely and may function satisfactorily, but they have several potential corrosion problems associated with them and particularly careful consideration should be given to the likely long-term behaviour of any proposed design.

SYSTEM TYPE 5: indirect, vented, pumped-circulation

Systems of this type follow to some extent standard UK central heating practice and since they can incorporate a wide range of solar collector plates their popularity at the present time is understandable; see Figure 10. However, the design of these systems is such that either the collectors and system must be 'freeze-safe' (Section 3.1.9) or a non-freezing fluid must be used in the primary circuit. One of the more common solutions to this problem to date has been simply to assume that a high concentration (about 25–30 per cent) of an ethylene glycol based antifreeze can be added to water and the resulting mixture used as the heat transfer fluid; this is common practice in motor vehicle engines and several standard formulations of antifreeze are available.

Unfortunately, all of these fluids have problems associated with them as may be shown by the attitude taken to them by a local water undertaking. The difference between the systems shown in Figures 10a and 10b is essentially only in the method of providing for expansion and venting in the primary circuit; in the latter case the cost is slightly reduced by having only one pipe serving as both the feed and vent and this requires a little explanation. Expansion and contraction of the primary fluid can obviously be accommodated satisfactorily by this system but if air or vapour accumulates in the top of the plates this has to push its way up the feed pipe before being discharged through the surface of the fluid in the cistern. It follows that the pipe should be well sloped to facilitate this action and that the cistern should be covered to prevent splashing as the gas or vapour exits. The pipe should also be of adequate diameter – preferably 22 mm or larger, and this may result in single-pipe circulation between the collectors and the cistern (see Section 2.3.6).

The behaviour of this system if the collectors boil is less easy to predict and considerable pressure oscillations could be produced which might result in damage unless all the pipework was well constructed. A slight modification to this design would obviate these potential sources of trouble, and is shown in Figure 10c.

In this modified scheme, which is really only a compromise between the two other designs, a separate vent pipe is fitted and this should ensure that boiling can proceed without an undue increase in pressure occurring. The feed pipe need not be taken to the lowest level but can be situated as shown; it is important, however, to ensure that the cistern is sufficiently far above the top of the panels to provide a positive gauge pressure in all parts of the circuit when the pump is running: it may prove difficult to design a satisfactory layout in houses having shallow-pitched roofs because of the lack of sufficient height if the collector panels are roof mounted. If air-lock problems are experienced during initial filling of these systems the most likely cause is the incorporation of a check valve; any difficulty can usually be overcome either by using the air bleed screw on the pump or by loosening one of the unions or drain valves. It is recognised that these air-lock problems may be troublesome during commissioning, but once all the air has been removed there would seem to be little reason to suppose that any problem will subsequently be encountered since those parts of the circuit at risk are at low level and run cooler than does the rest of the system. Since pumps can be damaged if

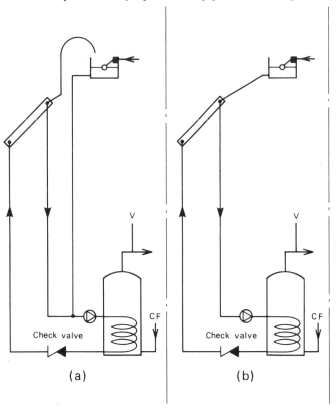

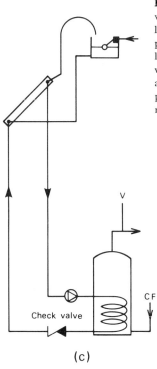

Figure 10 System type 5: Indirect, vented, pumped-circulation: (a) A layout following central heating practice with the feed taken to low level, (b) A frequently-used layout which may give problems, (c) An acceptable layout which minimises pipe lengths. The check valve prevents reverse circulation

they are energised whilst still filled with air some care must be exercised in commissioning these systems, and some authors recommend that the pump in Type 5 systems be installed in the vertical pipe that supplies fluid to the collectors, but thermally this is slightly disadvantageous. In time however it may prove to be the preferred location; an alternative solution is an automatic air vent at the top of the coil.

Protection against overheating may be accomplished by using a fan-coil unit in the collector circuit, and the control system should ensure that both the pump and the fan operate when the temperature at the base of the store becomes excessive: this control logic will also prevent excessive plate temperatures provided that the normal differential temperature control function is not inhibited.

The possible consequences of not installing these systems correctly should be noted; if pumpover occurs an excess of oxygen will be introduced into the circuit with probable dire results. If, with the pump running, any part of the circuit is under an effective negative pressure then air can be sucked in at any imperfect joint (or even at the pump itself) and oxygenation again occurs; serious cases of either of these maladies can result in both noisy operation and corrosion; Section 3.4.1 should be consulted for a detailed consideration.

It was partly to overcome similar difficulties in microbore central heating systems that sealed pressurised circuits were introduced to the UK some years ago. The use of this type of equipment is illustrated below and is fully described in Section 3.5.

SYSTEM TYPE 6: indirect, sealed, pumped-circulation

As noted above, systems of this type (see Figure 11) are derived from Type 5 systems but since expansion is accommodated in a diaphragm vessel no cistern or vent pipe is needed and this can give greatly increased flexibility of system layout; the essential point to realise is that these systems offer such flexibility simply because the static pressure in the primary circuit can be so high that no suitable type of pump could under normal circumstances produce a negative pressure at any point in the system. Vented domestic systems usually have static gauge pressures at their lowest points of about 0·5 bar (about 5 m of water or 50 kN/m²) whilst sealed systems can run at 1·5 to 2·5 bar, the relief valve operating at approximately 3·5 bar. This increase in normal running pressures has both advantages and disadvantages and some of the former are outlined above.

In addition however since the circuit is completely sealed from the atmosphere it is possible that many types of corrosion can no longer occur because of the lack of available oxygen, and heat transfer fluids, especially those containing ethylene or propylene glycol, may be used with a greater degree of confidence.

The disadvantages of these systems are principally that they require a high standard of workmanship and that all

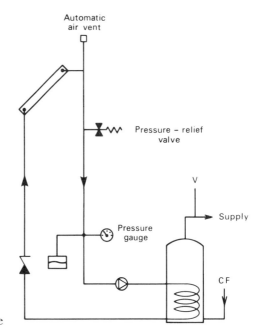

Figure 11 System type 6: Indirect, sealed, pumped-circulation. The check valve prevents reverse circulation

components of the circuit must be suitable for use at the maximum pressure that they could experience in service. Since the circuit is sealed and no provision is usually made for automatic fluid replenishment it follows that there must be no leaks, however small. These requirements are further discussed in Section 3.5.

The usual practice with central heating installations utilising sealed system equipment is to commission them by running the boiler and all the radiators at maximum temperature for about half an hour to release all the dissolved gases from solution and subsequently manually venting all the high points in the system.

Unfortunately, the sun will not necessarily be shining at maximum intensity on the collectors during the commissioning stage and so it will not be possible to vent all the dissolved gas contained in the initial water charge at once, even if the secondary water were drained so as to provide for a rapid temperature rise in the primary system. (If a non-aqueous heat transfer fluid is used and the system is both well designed and very carefully filled it may be possible to guarantee that no air pockets remain and so, assuming that the fluid contains no dissolved gas, this problem does not arise).

With water filled systems therefore an automatic air-release valve is almost a necessity since this will be able to operate whenever gas collects at the topmost point of the system. The penalty that may accrue as a result of not installing such a valve will depend to some extent upon the type and method of interconnection of the collector plates; if the array is of such a design that air-locking of a number of the risers can occur without the rest being affected then it is possible for the system to work at, for example, 'half power' – half the risers being inoperative.

It may seem a somewhat fanciful notion to suggest that this can actually happen but some of the author's earliest test rigs at BRE suffered from exactly this problem, and the clue came not from a decreased thermal performance (which was not at that time being monitored) but from noticing that the flow rate in the primary circuit had decreased, only to return to normal when the system was thoroughly vented manually. A permanent cure was effected by tilting the whole panel array slightly, in the manner depicted in Figure 5. In domestic installations neither flow rate nor heat-metering equipment will usually be available and so the householder will have to rely on the initial design of the system being sound.

The limitations of some currently produced automatic air-release valves and some of the precautions that must be taken in designing venting points are detailed in Section 3.4.2 and are of particular relevance to Type 6 systems.

Installations using an aqueous heat transfer fluid and high performance collectors may need protection against overheating if only because of the risk of losing fluid via the pressure-relief valve if boiling occurred. As with Type 5 systems a fan-coil unit should prove suitable. Installations using high-temperature-rated oils may be protected simply by inhibiting pump operation at store temperatures above (say) 75°C.

SYSTEM TYPE 7: indirect, sealed, draindown, pumped-circulation

A novel type of system has recently been introduced which incorporates a sealed circuit in which both frost and overtemperature protection are provided by draining the collectors; see Figure 12. The basic innovation in this system is the use of a purpose-built expansion vessel working on a principle similar to that of sealed vehicle-cooling systems. In order to ensure that the pump does

not run dry the expansion vessel should be large enough, and the end of the flow pipe should not become submerged unless alternative arrangements are made to ensure reliable draining. Additionally, the design of the expansion vessel should be such as to prevent air being introduced into its feed connection: inadequate design may result in both noisy operation and damage to the pump. Among the possible disadvantages of the system are that since the static pressures may be low it may be possible for negative pressures to be generated when the pump is running and under some fault conditions a partial vacuum might exist throughout the circuit even when the pump was switched off. It is recommended that a pressure gauge should be incorporated into these systems and the householder instructed as to its purpose. If a gauge pressure of (say) 50 kN/m² were maintained this would be indicative of a leak-free system in which, for example, iron and steel components might exhibit an adequate life.

Similar design concepts have been employed overseas for systems using either aluminium or steel collectors; in some systems de-aerated water and nitrogen gas are used (so as to exclude oxygen as much as possible) whilst in others a small initial concentration of oxygen is considered acceptable[17]. In all cases the gas pressure should be high enough to prevent negative pressures within the system and a pressure-relief (safety) valve must always be fitted (see Section 3.5). High standards of workmanship will be necessary to ensure that the initial pressure is retained, and it may be recommended that wherever possible soldered joints be used in those parts of the circuit that contain the gas charge. The collector plates and adjoining pipework should also be capable of withstanding thermal shock. It is the author's opinion that these designs merit further investigation since it may be possible to preclude both corrosion and freezing problems without the use of either antifreeze additives or non-aqueous fluids.

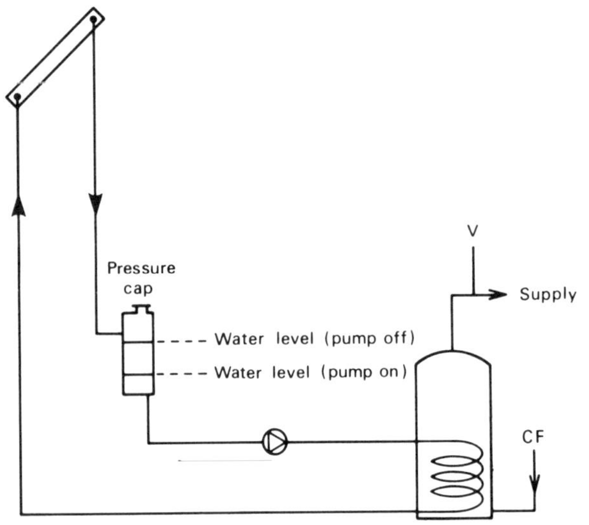

2.3 Design of secondary systems

2.3.1 General

The previous section discussed some possible designs for the primary circuits of solar collector systems for preheating domestic hot water but the utility of these systems may be impaired if the rest of the installation is not sensibly engineered; it should never be forgotten that attempting to use solar energy in the UK entails dealing with small energy inputs, and that engineering systems should be designed accordingly if any degree of final success (gauged by the amount of fossil fuel displaced) is to be achieved.

At a practical level, if a solar system is to be installed in an existing dwelling then the condition and design of the existing hot water service system should be competently assessed and if it transpires, as is likely, that there are deficiencies then these should be remedied in order that the solar system may have a chance to perform well.

Figure 12 System type 7: Indirect, sealed, draindown, pumped-circulation. A nominally fixed volume of gas is incorporated into the primary circuit

The most likely faults on existing systems will be insufficient insulation on the storage vessel (which itself can result in more heat loss than the solar system can supply) and an inefficient and/or expensive method of heating the water. It is outside the scope of this book to assess the primary energy savings that could result from, for example, changing an old, oversized and inefficient gas, coal or oil burner for a new and efficient unit but it can be stated that in many situations both the fuel and monetary savings to accrue from such action might be far greater when assessed as a fraction of the necessary capital investment than those resulting from the instal-lation of even a good solar system; in recognising these basic truths it will be appreciated that solar preheating of domestic hot water should really only be contemplated as an addition to an already thoroughly sound installation.

There are several possible designs for the secondary side of solar hot water systems; two of the most common that use cylinders are described below. Most of the principles outlined apply equally to systems using cisterns for hot water storage; types of storage vessels are detailed in Section 3.3.

2.3.2. Twin-store systems

In this system two separate stores are used to contain the solar heated and hot water respectively. These stores will be designated 'solar' and 'auxiliary', the labels being indicative of the type of energy used to heat them. The operation of the system is easy to understand from Figure 13a but the design is open to abuse if care is not taken to ensure that any particular installation is suited to the expected load pattern; a couple of examples will make this clear.

If the connecting pipe between the two storage vessels is excessively long or of large diameter and the demand is one of short intermittent peaks (for example, the supply to spray taps in a washroom) then volumes of warm water will be drawn into the connecting pipe but may cool to near room temperature before reaching the auxiliary cylinder. The effect of this will be to reduce the effective efficiency of the solar heating system and the heat lost to the building should not be assessed as useful because most of the loss will occur in summer when space heating is not required. In the example given it is clear that the connecting pipe should be kept as short as is practicable but for other installations where the demand is known to consist of a few periods of bulk usage this precaution is unnecessary, albeit still desirable merely to keep down the total length of pipework.

Another less-than-perfect aspect of this basic system is that the solar heated water must always pass via the auxiliary cylinder. This seems to cause considerable annoyance to many solar enthusiasts, who advocate the installation of various types of diverting valves and control equipment so that under suitable circumstances water may be drawn directly from the solar cylinder.

Although the aims are laudable there seems often to be some confusion as to how these more advanced systems

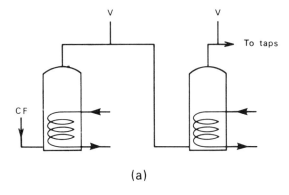

(a)

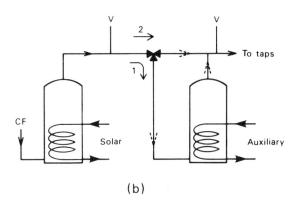

(b)

Figure 13 Twin-store secondary systems: (a) Basic layout of a twin-cylinder system, (b) A system incorporat-ing a diverter valve, showing alternative flow paths

are to operate; an example of a typical layout is shown in Figure 13b.

If, during midsummer, the temperature in the solar cylinder is adequate for washing purposes (say 45–50°C) then there is of course no reason why water should not be drawn directly from this store leaving the auxiliary cylinder undisturbed. Under these conditions it is advocated that the auxiliary fuel supply (assumed here to be an electric immersion heater) be switched off, thus saving energy at a rate equal to the rate of heat loss from the auxiliary cylinder (it is important to realise that the only penalty to accrue from storing heat is the inevitable loss), and these operations may be accomplished via a single thermostat if this incorporates a changeover switch. Alternatively, a single-contact thermostat may be used with a relay to give a changeover function, or the neces-sary circuitry may be incorporated into a differential temperature controller.

The valve is assumed to be a motorised type which can be switched by applying power to one lead and returned to its original position by applying power to another lead; these valves only draw current for the time that the motor is running and other types, where power loss is con-tinuous with the valve set in one of its positions, are not so suitable. Alternatively, and probably at less expense if a low flow resistance is important, a pair of 2-port valves may be used, one opening as the other closes and vice-versa. Two notes of caution must be entered here – it is possible to design these systems in such a way that a cylinder is prevented from venting by a closed valve and this is not good practice. In addition, each 2-port valve must normally be controlled by a separate change-over switch (see Section 3.4.3).

The principal advantage of either of these systems is that the immersion heater may be switched off for perhaps about 2 months in the year – this will be assumed to be the maximum for a domestic system and the period may well be very much less in a typical year. Assuming that a 160 l cylinder is insulated with a well-fitting 100 mm jacket and is kept at 50°C its loss rate may be estimated as about 80 W (see Section 2.3.7) and so the maximum saving could be about £3.00 per year based on a fuel cost of 2·5p per kWh. With cheaper fuels being used for the auxiliary the saving would of course be less and in view of the fact that the period of 2 months is probably not continuous (see below) the saving may be far less than £1 per year. The system is therefore unlikely to repay a capital investment of perhaps £40 especially as the valves may not function for more than a few years without maintenance.

These systems also have one disadvantage which is a result of the unpredictability of solar supply; whenever the thermostat in the solar store decides that water should no longer be drawn directly from that store the valves reverse and the auxiliary heater is switched on. If the auxiliary store has cooled down then no hot water can now be drawn off until the auxiliary heater has been on for (typically) half an hour, which could be annoying. A possible solution to this problem would be a second temperature sensor at lower level in the solar store to detect when this was becoming cool, and which could switch on the immersion heater before the valves changed over. This can be accomplished quite easily with a simple thermostat wired in series with the immersion heater thermostat; the original thermostat would now control only the valves. There is however a more subtle flaw in some of these systems as installed in the UK at present. It was noted above that the saving could be reduced from its calculated value of £3.00 if the period of operation of the valves was not continuous over 2 months. This is in fact likely, and in a worst case the valves switch over to auxiliary supply every evening because the solar store has cooled (as a result of water being used). The immersion heater then heats up the auxiliary store to full temperature overnight but before much water is drawn off (let us assume at midday) the system has switched back to direct-solar supply as the result of a morning's sunshine having brought the solar store back up to temperature. It may clearly be seen that since the auxiliary store is always at or near its maximum temperature (without much of this water being used) the reduction in heat losses (which give the savings) are so near zero as to be negligible. The valves are therefore technology for its own sake – no benefit results from their having been installed.

Use of a time switch with an on-peak immersion heater can show similarly small benefits if the off periods are so short that no appreciable decrease in water temperature occurs. It is also sometimes advocated that solar heated water be drawn off at (say) 40°C, using the same system of valves described above, whenever this is possible and that this will make the solar system more efficient because a larger volume of water will have been drawn off than if the demand had been satisfied by water from the auxiliary store (kept perhaps at 60°C). A similar principle applies to designs having a third tap at the kitchen sink, fed directly on solar heated water. There are two essentially different arguments here; one is true, the other probably false. It is true that if a greater volume of water is drawn off the efficiency of the collectors may be greater because the solar store may be cooler, and the 'third tap' systems use this basic logic.

It is, correspondingly, true as a general principle that if the final hot water delivery temperature (usually set by a thermostat controlling the auxiliary system) is lowered from the usual 60–65°C to 45–55°C there will be an increase in solar system efficiency simply because of the larger volume of water likely to be drawn from the hot taps. It has been the author's contention for some time that this lowering of water temperature is probably one of the most significant 'changes of lifestyle' that a house-holder could make to increase the effectiveness of a solar water heating system. The increase in output will how-ever not be large, probably less than 15 per cent; a further small improvement could be anticipated if a hot-fill washing machine or dishwasher were used instead of the corresponding cold-fill model.

It is not necessarily true however that setting the valves to switch at a solar store temperature of 40°C when the auxiliary temperature is kept at 60°C is a logical way of reducing a fuel bill. In this case the household has no option but to accept the water that comes from the hot tap (unless an override control is fitted) and if 40°C is ever acceptable then it might be considered to be always acceptable, and the auxiliary thermostat could also be set at 40 °C with provision for temporary boosting as described above. This will result in lower auxiliary losses and an increased throughput of water which will be equally beneficial to the solar collectors regardless of from which cylinder the draw-off occurred. It is possible that a reduction in draw-off temperature could lead to a reduction in the total energy requirement but no data is yet available. It should be noted that some types of fossil fuel boilers must not be set to operate at less than 60°C because of flue-gas-condensation problems; if a cylinder-stat is fitted it may be used to limit the delivery temperature independently of the boiler thermostat.

It should be clear by now that installation of valves in the manner described is a procedure that the present author does not advocate despite the widespread accep-tance of these schemes by some solar enthusiasts and companies; only under special circumstances can they be justified on technical grounds and it is very doubtful whether in well designed and insulated domestic systems they will ever be justified on economic grounds especially when possible repair costs are taken into consideration.

It is therefore recommended that such valves be omitted from system designs unless due and proper consideration is given to their possible modes of operation.

2.3.3 Combined (dual-coil) cylinder systems

In these systems the functions of the solar and auxiliary stores are combined in one large cylinder. The principal disadvantage of this arrangement, especially for existing properties, is the physical size of the cylinder, but in other respects these systems can offer a superior performance to the twin-cylinder designs described above. A typical layout is shown in Figure 14 and it may be seen that thermally the storage is still in two parts.

The solar coil is situated in the lower half of the cylinder (in direct circuits the solar flow and return should be situated in this lower region) whilst the upper portion is heated by auxiliary fuel.

Since correct operation of the cylinder relies on successful thermal separation of the upper and lower volumes of water the auxiliary heater should be a type that will not create excessive velocities in the secondary water; this implies that it should either be an indirect coil or an immersion heater, and since the heating effect of either of these is likely to extend a few centimetres below the physical bottom of the heater element is is suggested that there should be a separation of 150 mm between the bottom of the auxiliary heater and the top of the solar coil. If the solar circuit is direct (which is unusual but possible with these cylinders) then the flow from the solar panels – usually a connection about half way up the cylinder wall – should be designed so that it does not encourage mixing with the upper layers. A satisfactory method of achieving this would be to employ large diameter pipe for the last half metre of this pipe-run so as to ensure that the entry velocity was small.

When the auxiliary system is operative and the top of the cylinder is hot then the effective preheat volume is that below the lowest level of the auxiliary heater; this follows from simple thermodynamics. If the top half of the cylinder is hotter than the solar heated water then it is not possible in this system for heat to be transferred from the lower to the upper layer. This does not exclude some interference with the upper layer due to convection currents being set up in the cylinder but in cases of sizeable disturbance the net transfer of heat will be downwards, to the detriment of the performance of the solar circuit. If however the temperature of the solar heated water at any time exceeds the temperature in the top of the

cylinder (or if the auxiliary is switched off altogether) then the effective preheat volume now becomes equal to the whole volume of the cylinder and this has a number of desirable consequences. Firstly, in cases where the building is left unoccupied for a period the whole volume of stored water will be available for solar heating and this may enable a small saving on auxiliary fuel to be made when the system is next used. More importantly however, this step-increase in the effective value of the number of litres of storage per square metre of collector as the solar collector temperature exceeds the temperature of the top part of the cylinder, has the desirable consequence that scalding hot water is less likely to be produced on hot summer days and the system is in this respect partly self-regulating. As an additional bonus, the heat losses from the whole system will be less than those from equally insulated twin cylinders. In conclusion, dual-coil cylinders offer a reliable and to some extent safer method of installing solar preheating of domestic hot water in housing than do twin-cylinder systems, but it must not be inferred from this that they will necessarily be the most appropriate design in every case (in some houses there will simply not be sufficient available space for, typically, a 280 l cylinder), nor must it be claimed that their overall thermal performance will be appreciably better than that of a well designed twin-cylinder system. At the present time these special cylinders are unfortunately rather expensive but it is to be hoped that increased production will to some extent be able to overcome this problem.

2.3.4 Twin-cylinder systems with gravity mixing

This brief note is included because these systems, sometimes advocated, offer a method of achieving some of the benefits of a dual-coil cylinder whilst using two separate stores. A typical layout is shown in Figure 15 and it may be seen that if the solar store becomes hotter than the auxiliary store then some heat transfer can occur, which can be beneficial especially as regards limiting summer-time temperatures.

However, the practical difficulties of installing this type of system in typical houses will probably preclude its widespread adoption. In order to prevent reverse gravity circulation the auxiliary store should be at least 600 mm and preferably 1200 mm above the solar store. This cannot easily be arranged without either the secondary system pipes becoming excessively long (if the auxiliary store is placed in the attic) or the solar primary circuit having to descend to the ground floor of the building (if the auxiliary store is located as is usual on the first floor).

In houses where the collectors are placed at first storey level (say on a garage roof) then the system might be considered more appropriate but in view of the losses that will occur in the longer pipe runs which are almost inevitable it is considered unlikely that the system will produce a greater financial benefit that that possible with a normal twin-cylinder system.

Since reverse gravity circulation is a somewhat unpredictable phenomenon these systems should be checked after

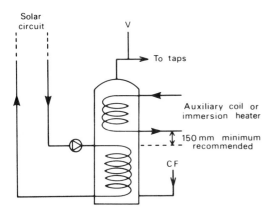

Figure 14 Layout of a system using a dual-coil cylinder

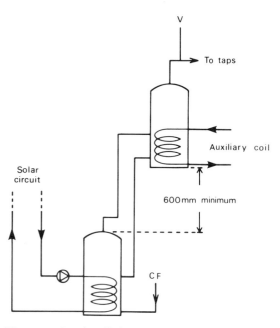

Figure 15 A twin-cylinder system incorporating gravity mixing. Some protection against summertime overheating may be achieved

installation to ensure that reverse flow does not occur, since this would be to the detriment of the solar collector's performance.

2.3.5 Secondary circulation systems

Secondary circulation systems are rarely if ever found in normal sized houses but are common in buildings where hot water must be transported from a central store to outlying areas.

Deadlegs in hot water service systems should be of limited length in order not only to ensure a satisfactory water service, but also to prevent undue wastage of water. The Model Water Byelaws[18] give the maximum length that is permissible with any given pipe size; most water undertakings have adopted these recommendations.

The circulation can either be by the action of gravity, in which case there must be some heat loss along the pipework to provide the necessary driving force, or a small pump may be included. The pump serves not only to circulate the water but, given a suitable system design, can also increase the pressure available at the outlets; this is often desirable with spray taps in single-storey buildings. In the past it has been common practice to specify over-sized heating equipment of all types and secondary circulation systems are no exception. In many cases the performance penalty is not large[19] but the cautionary note given here is that secondary circulation systems should be no bigger than is necessary and the heat losses should be calculated in advance so that an appropriate thickness of insulation may be specified. In pumped systems consideration should be given to switching the pump off when the building is unoccupied since even an 80 W pump operating for 16 excess hours per day wastes about 470 kWh of electricity annually, which in primary energy

terms is equivalent to the energy saved by 4·1 m² of solar panels (assuming an output of 300 kWh/m² year and gas as the auxiliary fuel with an energy overhead of zero and an efficiency at the point of use of 65 per cent). The situation is actually even worse than this because in addition there will be needless loss of heat from the secondary pipework, due to its being kept hot during the 16 excess hours per day. Gravity driven systems may benefit from a motorised valve operated by a time switch but this equipment must only be installed if it is known that the circuit will be out of use for the period during which the valve is to be closed: the local water undertaking should be notified of any intention to install such a system.

It should not be inferred from the above that in all cases specification of secondary circulation systems is to be avoided but the example given should serve as a warning of the magnitude of the inefficiences that can all too easily be designed into simple hot water systems.

2.3.6 Single-pipe circulation

A phenomenon that is often overlooked in the design of hot water systems is single-pipe circulation; this can occur whenever a vertical or near vertical pipe of diameter greater than about 15 mm is directly connected to a hot storage vessel. Figure 16a shows two of the most common design errors either of which can give rise to significant heat loss from an otherwise well designed system; a bad case of single-pipe circulation can in fact constitute the major portion of the total heat loss in a small very well insulated hot water system. Figure 16c shows how the system may be designed so as to reduce these losses, and Figure 16b shows the working principle of single-pipe circulation. Thermal insulation may be used to limit single-pipe circulation in poorly-designed existing systems.

2.3.7 Insulation of storage vessels

This section is included in order to illustrate the advantages that can accrue from thermal insulation and to provide substantiation of some of the heat loss figures used elsewhere in this book.

The substance of most of this section is taken from the results of previously unpublished research performed at BRE[20]. Table 1 shows both the heat loss and the cost of the heat loss from an uninsulated hot water cylinder in one year, assuming that the whole cylinder is kept uniformly hot and the ambient temperature remains at 21 °C. The cost of heat is assumed to be 2·5p/kWh. These heat loss rates are unlikely to be realised in practice because the cylinder would probably be situated in an enclosed airing cupboard, thus increasing the effective ambient temperature. Table 1 has been included principally so that comparison with Table 2 may be facilitated.

The heat loss data in Tables 1 and 2B were obtained experimentally and also theoretically, using a model that took account of the deficiences in real insulation jackets.

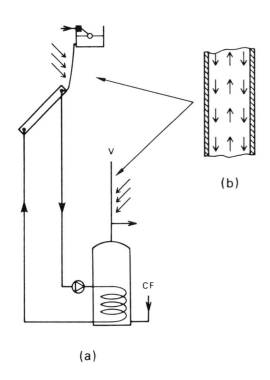

(b)

(a)

(c)

Figure 16 Occurrence of single-pipe circulation: (a) Poor design of system showing where single-pipe circulation may occur, (b) Working principle of single-pipe circulation, heat loss from the pipe provides the driving force, (c) Improved design

450mm < minimum >

Table 1 Heat loss data for uninsulated 120 litre cylinders

Storage temperature	Heat loss kWh/week	Cost £/year
50°C	63·4	82·4
60°C	86·4	112·3

Table 2 Heat loss data for insulated 120 litre cylinders

Storage temperature	Heat loss kWh/week		Cost £/year	
	A*	B*	A*	B*
50°C	4·8	13·7	6·2	17·8
60°C	6·1	18·1	7·9	23·5

* A: Theoretical, assuming use of a perfect 76 mm glass fibre insulation jacket
  B: Theoretical (and experimental) making allowances for the imperfections in a nominal 76 mm insulation jacket.

The discrepancy between experiment and theory never exceeded 5 per cent and so the two sets of values have not been tabulated separately.

It is of interest to note that the two principal causes of insulation jackets of the sectional type failing to meet their 'theoretical' performance were compression of the glass fibre (nominal 76 mm jackets were rarely more than 50 mm thick) and poor fitting on the top of the cylinder, combined with an average thickness of only 25 mm in this region. Since a substantial part of the heat loss occurs from the top surface of cylinders, the jackets tested were most unsatisfactory.

In practice, heat losses from cylinders will almost always exceed calculated values because of losses which will occur via the connecting pipework, and for this reason it is not sensible to provide excessive insulation levels. The maximum thickness of insulation that could be justified on a domestic hot water cylinder is probably between 100 mm and 200 mm of glass fibre or equivalent and that on the solar cylinder about half this because of the lower average temperatures (but see Section 4.1). The optima for any given system depend upon the relative costs of fuel and insulation material, the time for which the cylinders are kept hot, and also upon whether some heat loss is actually required for airing purposes, and so no exact figures can be given; the guidelines above may however be regarded as maxima for domestic use, and little benefit will result from increasing them. If the insulation on one cylinder is purposely reduced so that a heated airing cupboard may be constructed around it then this must of course be the auxiliary cylinder so that there will be some heat given off in wintertime.

It is hoped that these sections have served both to emphasise that installing solar equipment is only likely to be a sensible option when everything else has been done to ensure that the house is as thermally efficient as possible, and to point out some of the errors that can occur in the design of even the simplest solar systems.

2.4 Large solar systems

In the author's experience there is often some confusion in the minds of designers who are called upon to advise on the practicality either of straight-forward large solar installations or of specialised multi-purpose systems, and it is hoped that this short introduction to these subjects may at least clarify some of the basic principles involved. No attempt has been made to treat these subjects fully, and many detailed or quantitative questions must therefore go unanswered. However, it is anticipated that if the current interest in these topics is maintained a more specialised paper may subsequently be produced by BRE.

The topics to be covered in this section include swimming pools, space heating systems, and what may be termed multi-purpose systems in which an array of solar panels is used to provide heat for two or more loads and where the necessary switching and control is performed either manually or automatically. Systems for industrial and commercial premises are also discussed.

For any of the large systems described in this section it is important that the collector plates are connected together in such a way so as to ensure that each unit area will be supplied with heat transfer fluid at approximately the same rate. The latter part of Section 3.1.1 deals with the related topics of plate design and plate interconnection, and should be consulted.

2.4.1 Systems for swimming pools

There is already a considerable body of knowledge available in the UK[21] detailing how outdoor swimming pools may be heated during the summer months using solar energy, and the simple types of collectors which are all that are really required are discussed in Section 3.1.8.

The basic reason why this particular application can be successful is that a demand for a large quantity of heat at a low temperature coincides with the season of the year when there is often solar radiation in abundance. Simple unglazed panels are characterised by a rapidly decreasing thermal efficiency either as their temperature rises or as the level of solar irradiance falls and they work well only during the late spring to early autumn months, but if this is the only period of the year that the pool is in use the application is near to ideal; more detailed consideration will make this clear.

The pool will cool during the winter to very low temperatures and may be drained to protect it from frost damage. The suppliers' recommendations should always be followed since some types of pools may collapse if left drained for long periods. In early spring the pool may be refilled with mains water at approximately 5–10°C and because this is not a high temperature compared to the average daytime air temperatures in early spring (7.6°C in March at Kew) the solar panels can collect a useful amount of heat. As the average ambient temperature and pool temperature rise over the year so do irradiance levels and the panels will continue to work efficiently. In autumn there will be some inertia in the system, the pool 'remembering', via its temperature, the hot days of summer, and the panels will not be able to operate so efficiently at these higher temperatures as they might have done in spring under similar irradiance conditions.

The degree of inertia depends on the pool size and its

insulation but a decrease in collector efficiency as autumn approaches is not unexpected. These simple systems, if properly engineered and installed, should be able to deliver about 500 kWh/m² year taken over the 7 months March to September.

The principal precautions in designing an installation are to ensure that expansion is allowed for (polypropylene collectors have a particularly high coefficient of thermal expansion) and to attach the panels securely to a rigid framework or other structure which itself is well anchored to the ground. Additionally, the design must preclude air-locking of parts of the collector assembly and this is sometimes ignored in systems in which collectors are laid on the ground or on a flat roof. Ideally a south-facing slope of 20°–40° to the horizontal should be used so as to facilitate both venting in normal use and draining in winter. Often the systems are designed to drain whenever the pump stops and this is usually satisfactory, albeit control problems can occur (see Section 3.7.1).

Stratification in pools probably never exceeds 10°C but may have a significant effect on system performance: large water stores are well known for their ability to exhibit both stratification (layering) and channelling – where a stream of either heated or cooled water flows from inlet to outlet while leaving the bulk store temperature unchanged.

Sensible siting of the flow and return pipes is therefore likely to be important if optimum heat transfer from the collectors is to be realised. In some situations stratification may be desirable, for example, the top 1 m of a deep pool could be heated rapidly to comfort conditions before switching the system to all-pool heating. There will of course be a decrease in the total amount of heat added to the pool if this strategy is adopted.

Since collectors used for swimming pool applications will often be gaining energy at a rate exceeding 500 W/m² a high flow rate should be used, especially as any undue increase in collector temperature will have an adverse effect on the thermal efficiency because of the high U value of unglazed surfaces. For a temperature rise of 3°C with a retained power of 500 W/m² a flow rate of water of 0.04 l/m²s will be needed. Flow rates for water in excess of 0.08 l/m²s should rarely if ever be necessary and if used may incur a heavy penalty in pumping energy. Control difficulties may also occur (see Section 3.7.1).

The most significant source of heat loss from an outdoor pool is usually evaporation of water and use of a good pool cover, especially overnight, can result in much higher temperatures being maintained. It is important to note that the cover must actually *cover* the water surface and be a good fit so as to inhibit evaporation; if the cover is allowed to submerge its effect will become minimal. Another method of overcoming this source of heat loss is to add a compound to the pool water which spreads out in a thin surface layer, thus preventing some of the evaporation. Such chemicals are commercially available and whether their use is justified may easily be calculated from a knowledge of the rate of fall of the water level both with and without the chemical having been added.

Assuming that energy costs 2p/kWh (more for on-peak electricity, less for gas) the evaporation of 1 cm of water from 1 square metre results in an expenditure of about 13.5p. For a pool of size 10×8 m (80 m²) the cost of evaporation will be £10.80 for each centimetre drop in level.

In addition to these costs, if the pool is refilled with mains water at 15°C then an additional expenditure of about 9p will be necessary to bring this to the pool temperature of 20°C. The large difference between these figures (9p and £11) is a result of the enormously high latent heat of vapourisation of water (about 2.44 kJ/g at 20°C) and illustrates the importance of preventing evaporation. If the pool has a blackened base then it might be thought advantageous to remove the cover during sunny days so as to allow solar radiation to be absorbed; a dark coloured base is in fact not essential, especially in a deep pool, as significant absorption of the incident radiation occurs in water.

If the solar radiation absorbed by the pool is 500 W/m² then this gain can be balanced by an evaporation of 0.20 g of water per second per square metre of surface. This is equivalent to a rate of fall of water level of about 0.74 mm per hour and this rate of loss may occur especially with a hot pool on a windy day.

The rate of evaporation from a wet surface can be written
$$\theta = A K (P_w - P_i)$$
where θ = rate of evaporation (g/h)
A = area of wetted surface (m²)
K = constant
P_w = svp of water at the temperature of the water (mbar)
P_i = vapour pressure in the adjacent air (mbar)

At 20°C the svp of water is about 23 mbar, and P_i will be taken to be 18 mbar in this example. A value of $K = 16$ will be assumed, as advised by Milbank[22] for an air speed of 0.25 m/s.

Hence $\theta = 80$ g/m²h
$= 0.022$ g/m²s

This calculation shows that the rate of heat loss through evaporation is likely to be of the same order as the gain under average radiation conditions; on cloudy summer days the loss may however exceed the gain.

Other authors have considered heat losses from swimming pools in more detail, and McVeigh[23] gives the following formula for evaporation loss:
$$q_c = 9.15 \times h'_c (P_w - P_i) \quad \text{W/m}^2$$

With a wind speed of 4.5 m/s h'_c is given as 23 W/m² °C, and $P_w - P_i$ will be taken to be 5 mbar (see above). The calculated rate of heat loss is therefore 1.05 kW/m², corresponding to an evaporation rate of 0.43 g/m²s or a fall in water level of 1.5 mm/h (3.7 cm in 24 h).

These results seem abnormally high; Hassen[24] asserts that evaporation *and* convection losses from the surface of a pool may be calculated from the expression
$$(1.47(P_w - P_i) - (T_i - T_w)) \times 12.1 \ V^{0.8} \quad \text{W/m}^2$$

The temperature difference is significant if $P_w - P_i$ is small but will be taken as zero; if $P_w - P_i$ is again assumed to be 5 mbar and V is taken to be 4.5 m/s the loss rate is 300 W/m².

The discrepancies both in these figures, and in those cited by Milbank probably arise from boundary layer effects which could shield the water surface from both the high wind speeds and the lower humidity in the surrounding air. An inescapable conclusion however is that outdoor pools should if possible be sheltered and if massive heat losses are to be prevented must be covered when not in use.

The best solution therefore is probably to use a well fitting translucent cover that will both admit solar radiation and also prevent evaporative heat loss and with such a design the pool will gain energy during hot sunny weather not only from any solar collectors but also directly. In respect of thermal efficiency, one of the best types of pool cover would consist (typically) of two layers of a u-v stabilized* translucent plastic separated by an air gap of about 10–20 mm. If the cover were manufactured as a honeycomb structure in which every cell was sealed then the cover would float on the pool and form an effective 'blanket'; damage to a few cells would not impair the usefulness of the cover to a significant extent. It is however re-emphasised that a cover that becomes submerged with a free water surface above it is almost useless. Similarly, a cover installed above the pool which still allows air to pass over the water surface may give disappointing results.

The next case to consider is where the pool is heated (either during all but the winter months or year-round) by fossil fuel, and solar panels are installed merely as a boost. These systems have been purchased by a few private pool owners and some have been considered by public bodies as 'demonstration' projects. The essential result however is that the heat output from the panels per unit area per year can be far less than that obtainable in the simple case considered above. The reason is not hard to understand; the water is now kept (perhaps) at between 22 and 26°C (often higher for school pools intended for young children) and in order to deliver heat the panels must first reach this comparatively high temperature, which for unglazed panels in all but the best summer conditions is not an easy task, and their efficiencies drop rapidly.

In the limiting condition – say a pool kept at 30°C and with panels situated in a windy area – the solar heat supplied to the pool over the year could be small. It might with some justification be said that it is here that the laws of thermodynamics first make their presence felt; no matter how much solar heat is potentially available, if that heat cannot be collected at a high enough temperature then it cannot be collected and used at all. One numerical example will suffice: the March air temperature given above may be subtracted from the pool temperature to yield a result of 22.4°C. Assuming a U value of

_____

* Stabilized against attack by ultra-violet radiation.

20 W/m² °C the irradiance level would have to be at least 448 W/m² before heat collection could even begin. A 'combined' system using fossil fuel together with solar boosting is of course possible technically but less attractive economically, since more expensive glazed panels may have to be used and even here their output per unit area per year may be less than that of simple panels operating in a simple system. Detailed considerations of which type of panels to use, perhaps a combination of glazed and unglazed, are beyond the scope of this book principally because for any situation the optimum system design will depend upon, amongst other variables, the proposed location of the panels, the temperatures involved, and the relative costs of all the components. Such optimisations, sometimes rather amateurishly attempted, are not easy; in fact they are almost certainly difficult enough to require the use of computer simulation programmes.

2.4.2 Swimming pool and domestic hot water systems combined

In these systems, a few of which have been sold in the UK, an attempt is made to use one array of panels both for preheating domestic hot water and for heating (usually) an outdoor swimming pool.

If the pool is normally unheated and used only during summer then the optimum choice of panels will almost certainly be unglazed units, and the question that needs to be asked is whether it is likely to be worthwhile connecting these up to preheat the domestic hot water when they are not engaged in pool duty.

For very good engineering reasons pool-heating panels are usually used on a direct circuit; use of an indirect circuit can impose severe penalties because the temperature drop across the then necessary heat exchanger will result in a noticeable drop in performance of the panels. Alternatively, a very efficient (but expensive and bulky) heat exchanger may be used.

Assuming an efficient direct circuit for the pool water the obvious way to divert the solar heat to the domestic hot water preheat system is to close off the pipes to the pool and connect the panels to another circuit. This circuit may or may not run on chlorinated water; if not then the panels must be drained before the switchover. These operations, whilst technically quite possible arc not to be recommended for several reasons. (It is worth noting at this stage that almost anything is possible in domestic solar circuits if enough panels, valves, pumps, electronic control systems and heat exchangers are used. The question to be asked should not be 'is it possible?' but rather, 'is it sensible?').

Another way of preheating the domestic hot water is to pass it through a heat exchanger immersed in the pool water. It is instructive to calculate how much could possibly be gained by such a scheme (or different schemes using the same essential logic). In summer, when such a system could operate, the cold water supply temperature may be taken to be 15°C. The pool temperature, on average, during the period May–October may be about 20°C.

Thus the potential exists for heating the family's consumption of domestic hot water through 5°C for 6 months of the year. These are all reasonable assumptions and lead to the result, taking an average hot water usage of 170 litres per day, of about 180 kWh per year. This amount of energy is worth not more than £5 on domestic electric tariffs and if gas or oil is used for water heating perhaps about £2. The figures are approximate but justifiable and the question that should be asked is whether saving £2 a year is worth the trouble and expense of additional pipework, possibly a pump, diverter valves, a control system, and a heat exchanger costing together probably over £150 when installed. Maintenance costs must also be considered.

The ingenuity of a few designers does however not end here, unfortunately. It is sometimes proposed that complex control systems be installed which give a manually selectable 'priority' to either the pool or the domestic hot water system. The intricacies of some of the necessary electronics will not be described here; instead it will be shown that such devices may work considerably less well than a simple controller.

Using assumptions which will by now be familiar – a pool temperature of 20°C and an average water inlet temperature of 15°C, it is true that if the panels were switched to provide this 5°C rise in the domestic hot water the energy collected during this period could be greater than if the panels had remained connected to the pool circuit (this assumes however that the thermal transfer efficiencies of the two systems are not dissimilar).

As shown above, the amount of heat available (£2 worth) is small. However, these control systems, if having been told to heat the domestic hot water may continue to try to do so after this water has been raised to the pool temperature. (Other types of controllers may be more intelligent and refuse to obey their owners.) The net result of trying to preheat domestic hot water above 20°C (in this example) is that the temperature of the panels will increase slowly and their efficiency will decrease rapidly; a fair amount of the day's sunshine will have been wasted instead of finding its way into the pool.

It is now clear that the maximum extra gain from the system described (using all the assumptions) is £2 per year and cannot be greater. It can however be far less than £2 and can easily become negative. It is assumed above that the whole system will be shut down for the winter but even if it is not the answers are likely to be much the same.

2.4.3 Space heating systems

The use of solar energy for space heating of buildings in the UK seems even more fraught with the dangers of misinterpretation of ideas, concepts and results than other fields of solar utilisation.

The whole subject of solar energy for heating of buildings is certainly perennial and probably as old as recorded history. There are two basic approaches, which may be termed 'passive' and 'active'. In the passive approach areas of south facing glazing are used to admit solar radiation directly (or in a few designs indirectly) into the building interior. Some energy storage is usually accomplished in the fabric of the building itself, and the systems need no pumps, valves or other 'engineering' hardware. So much has already been written about passive collection of solar energy in buildings (see, for example, references 25, 26, 27) that no extensive repetition is necessary here.

The propensity of a few present-day UK solar enthusiasts to advocate large areas of south-facing glazing as an energy conservation measure must however be mentioned.

As a general principle it is true that in the UK the solar gains over the heating season through south-facing glazed areas (especially if double glazed and curtained at night) may outweigh the extra thermal losses that accrue as a result of the higher U value of glazed areas as compared to opaque walls, where U values of 0.4 W/m² °C or less may readily be achieved in standard constructions[28]. To these basic facts must be added a consideration of whether the building actually needs heat during all those periods when the solar gains exceed the heat losses. However, the most important factor that is sometimes omitted from consideration is the possibility that overheating in midsummer conditions may occur if excessive areas of glazing are used in south-facing walls; many modern UK buildings are a testimony to the neglect of these and similar design criteria.

An approach to design that attempts to balance wintertime benefits against both summertime discomforts and the cost of the solar control equipment (such as overhangs or external blinds) that may be necessary to alleviate these discomforts may be advocated to a few UK solar enthusiasts to whom wintertime use of solar energy appears to be an over-riding pre-occupation. These aspects of building design will be more fully discussed in another major BRE publication[29]. The 'active' approach to solar space heating in the UK is however relatively new, and is briefly discussed below.

The UK is situated at a comparatively high latitude and as a consequence would receive in winter only a fraction of the solar radiation incident at more favoured latitudes even if the skies were clear. It is a matter of common observation as well as of recorded fact that the UK winter climate is characterised by a large number of days having cloudy overcast skies and this limits the applicability of solar space heating since very little energy usable by present-day solar systems is incident in winter. The total amount of solar energy received is modest enough [about 475 MJ/m² (132 kWh/m²) on a south facing 45° surface and slightly less on the vertical during the 4 winter months November–February] but a significant fraction of this is incident at such a low power density as to make collection at any useful temperature very difficult.

If long term storage of heat was not at the present time such an intractable problem solar heating of buildings using active systems would, in this basic analysis, become a comparatively simple procedure – heat would be collected and stored in the summer and used during the winter. The essential problem however is storage of heat for a long period of time without incurring an unacceptably high loss together with a decrease in temperature which can in itself render the remaining stored energy almost worthless. These matters are currently being investigated at BRE as part of a programme of energy-oriented research but for the moment it must be made perfectly clear that these systems are still in the realm of research and cannot at present prove cost-effective in UK housing. Since BRE has received many enquiries on the subject of solar space heating using flat plate collectors it would be appropriate to explain briefly the basic fallacies inherent in many of the schemes that are put forward; housing will be used as an example, but the principles hold true for other building types.

In winter houses need to be maintained at comfortable temperatures during those hours when they are occupied, and during the remaining hours need to be kept at a moderate temperature so that excessive condensation does not occur.

For convenience it will be assumed that the house is to be kept at 20°C and this is in fact a reasonable living temperature for an energy-conscious household. The first observation is that heat cannot be supplied to the house unless the heating appliance (or 'source' of heat) is at a temperature exceeding 20°C. For practical reasons connected with heat transfer rates the source temperature should in fact be above 30°C or else there may be problems; essentially the heat must be persuaded to go into the house and it is only the existence of a reasonable temperature gradient (here taken as 10°C) that can facilitate this.

It is instructive to review the operation of central heating systems of the warm-air and wet-radiator types since it is sometimes suggested that solar 'preheating' of these systems can be readily accomplished.

Schematic diagrams of a warm-air and a wet-radiator system are shown in Figure 17; the temperatures depicted are typical of those found in domestic space heating systems and it may be seen that in the warm-air system the lowest temperature in the circuit is in fact room temperature whilst for the wet-radiator system it is about 60°C – the return temperature to the boiler.

In the latter case it is clear that no preheating of the water circuit can be achieved using a heat source which is at a temperature of less than 60°C, and since this is an impossibly high goal for flat plate collectors operating in wintertime in the UK it is evident that this type of system is impracticable.

In the case of the warm-air system it would be possible in theory to install a preheat coil in the air intake for the heater but this could lead to a slight decrease in the efficiency of the heater because the secondary temperatures on the exchanger would be increased. With electric systems no change in efficiency would of course occur.

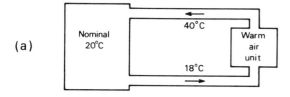

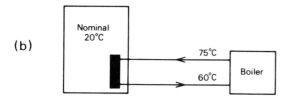

Figure 17 Typical temperatures in domestic space heating systems when the nominal room temperature is 20°C: (a) Warm-air system, (b) Wet-radiator system

The other alternative, which could not decrease the performance of the heater, would be to inject solar energy into the output air stream and here the temperature is typically 40°C which imposes upon the solar system the requirement that its heat must be delivered at a temperature exceeding 40°C – a possible but onerous task in wintertime and one that cannot but lead to very low collection efficiencies.

A better solution is however to accept that solar pre-heating of existing space heating systems is unlikely to be practicable and to consider instead installing a separate distribution system for using the solar energy.

Immediately this introduces the prospect of significantly increased capital costs and since the heating system most suited to working from low-temperature sources is forced-air a bulky unit or units may be required. In new housing use of floor coils or other extended-surface emitters may be considered. In systems already employing warm-air heating or extended-surface emitters it may be possible to use the existing distribution units as sinks for solar energy independently of the auxiliary heater; this would result in lower return temperatures to the solar system and is a concept that is being evaluated in the Milton Keynes solar house[30]. It would appear that this concept might be useful even with conventional wet-radiator systems when they are running under low part-load conditions (typically, in spring and autumn). If the time constant of the heating system were far smaller than that of the load space then after a period of high temperature operation the radiators would cool down relatively quickly and low temperature solar heat could then be injected into this circuit until such time as the temperature of the load space fell to the minimum acceptable level. The boiler would then be refired but only after the solar store had been taken out of circuit. The necessity for a fairly sophisticated control system is one of the more obvious disadvantages of this scheme but in buildings where appreciable demand for space heating occurs in spring and autumn there may be potential for development.

It should be realised however that the useful heat supplied over a year is likely to be small, and the viability of such

systems may be expected to be very poor unless the collectors are employed in other circuits in summertime.

It has also been suggested however that a fraction of the autumn and spring space heating load, small as it is in a well designed well insulated house, could be carried by solar collector systems which had as their principal duty the preheating of domestic hot water. The essential idea here is that in spring and autumn the solar systems (comprising about 5 m² of panel per house and therefore of quite a usual size) could be used with perhaps a floor-coil space heating system to provide background warmth. If the systems are designed according to the usual rules (see Section 4) it may be assumed that 5 m² of collector is associated with about 200–250 litres of water storage and that the hot water demand per day is of the same order. If maximum utilisation is to be made of the solar collectors they should be left switched to water heating duties until the solar store attains a temperature of (say) 30°C at which time it would be possible to switch them to supplying space heat via the floor coils. The crucial question then is for what proportion of the autumn and spring for which there is a genuine space heating requirement will the solar collectors be able to contribute to this requirement.

Days in spring and autumn can be very varied in nature, at one extreme cold and wet and at the other warm and sunny, and obviously during the latter, when the solar system will be most able to supply some heat there is likely to be no real demand for it. This itself does not encourage enthusiasm, but some calculations based on average data are instructive. Assuming a supply water temperature of 10°C for these months the energy required to heat (say) 170 litres of water to 30°C is 3·9 kWh. The insolation on 5 m² of panel during an average early spring or late autumn day is about 50 MJ or 13·8 kWh. Assuming an optimistic collection efficiency at these relatively low temperatures of 60 per cent the energy supplied would be 8·3 kWh per day of which 3·9 kWh would be required for water heating. The surplus, 4·4 kWh per day (on this 'average' day), would be available for space heating. Making the probably optimistic assumption that in a year the system could be fully used on 60 days the energy supplied is 264 kWh which, if supplied by an efficient gas boiler would be worth about £2.50. Since the necessary diverter valves and electronic control unit or thermostats would cost about £40 and the floor coils, even for one room, a minimum of £20, the return on investment will be poor.

It has not been the intention in this section to discourage innovation or experimentation in solar space heating system technology but rather, to point out that very simple calculations may often show that a proposed system does not stand any chance of real success.

In conclusion therefore, integration of solar systems with existing space heating circuits may rarely be practicable and it is not at present possible to foresee solar space heating systems approaching cost-effectiveness in the UK. It should be noted that this situation might be little changed by a breakthrough in heat storage technology since this would increase the competitiveness of other high-

capital-cost low-running-cost energy supply systems:
a continuing appraisal of these options is however justified
in view of their possible long-term potential.

2.4.4 Industrial and commercial systems

It is convenient to consider that what are here termed
industrial and commercial systems may be divided into
two distinct types. This somewhat arbitrary division is not
universal in its application, but serves to separate systems
which are little more than upscaled versions of domestic
preheaters from those that are fundamentally different.

The first classification contains systems which supply hot
water for hand washing or other ablutionary purposes.
Typical examples would be washbasins in offices and
schools, and the much heavier usages that occur in
hospitals. These systems, before solar preheating is considered, are all alike in that there is no internal recycling
of heat; Figure 18 shows this situation in diagrammatic
form and indicates the point at which injection of solar
heat may be considered.

If storage is incorporated at the solar stage then the
system is conceptually identical to the domestic hot water
preheaters described previously, but different engineering
design approaches are necessary, not only because of the
physical size of the equipment but also because the load
patterns may be either more or less favourable than in
domestic systems.

The second classification of industrial and commercial
systems comprise those in which there is already some
internal recycling of heat and these systems are usually
less amenable to solar heating than are systems of the first
type because the lowest temperature in the circuit may be
considerably higher than the supply water temperature.
This distinction is of fundamental importance. Systems
initially of the first type do, through incorporation of heat
reclaim equipment, become of the second type.

Figure 19 shows generalised layouts of systems of the
second type such as may be found in many industrial
processes and also in laundries, swimming pool halls and
other premises, where heat recovery is already accomplished using either heat exchangers or heat pumps.

This book does not consider in detail the methods of
analysis that may be used to determine the optimum
arrangement of heat recovery and/or solar heating that
will be applicable to any specific process but some general

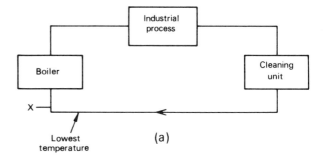

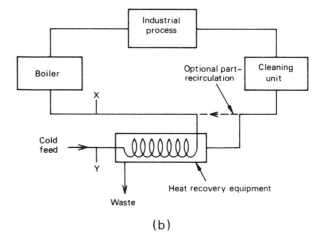

Figure 19 Simplified layouts of industrial water heating systems
in which some degree of recirculation and/or heat recovery is
already incorporated. Solar heat may be injected at either
X or Y: in the latter case the benefit from the heat recovery
equipment will be reduced

guidelines are given below; it should be noted at the out-
set that only in a few processes is it considered likely that
use of solar panels will feature in the most beneficial
option. For simplicity, processes using water will be
considered, but the thermodynamic arguments hold
true for other systems.

Considering systems of the first type, there are several
factors which singularly or collectively may enable the
system to achieve a better thermal performance than a
typical domestic preheater. If the load pattern is more
steady in time and if the final water temperature required
is lower than in a house, then a system may be installed
in the knowledge that if it is properly designed and used
all year round the energy output per square metre of solar
collector may exceed the oft-quoted figures for
domestic installations of between 200 and 500 kWh/m²
year (see Section 6).

An ideal application would therefore appear to be in
hospitals where, in geriatric wards for example, there is
a very large usage of hot water which is delivered (for
safety reasons) at a temperature not exceeding about
40°C. The usage of water may be quasi-continuous
throughout the daylight hours with a reduced usage at
night and this militates against the need for a large
amount of preheat storage to be incorporated, thus saving
on both capital costs and space. The reason for this
improvement over the domestic sized equivalent system is
that in the latter water must often be stored for 6 or even
12 hours before use, and sufficient storage must therefore

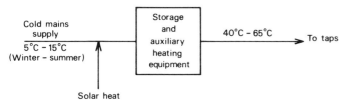

Figure 18 Simplified layout of a water heating system fed with supply
water and not fitted with any type of heat reclaim equipment. Solar heat
may be injected as shown with (usually) little effect on the efficiency
of the auxiliary heater

be incorporated to enable the solar collectors to work at moderate temperatures all day. Alternatively if there is a good probability that any volume of water will not spend longer than a couple of hours in the preheat storage vessel then the vessel may be sized so that a reasonable temperature rise is given to this water in this time and the normal design rule for domestic systems of 50–100 l/m² (see Section 4.2) becomes perhaps 10 l/m². In the limiting case of course, no preheat storage at all need be incorporated and the system then becomes a simple inline heater, which is in fact conceptually similar to a swimming pool installation because the inlet temperature in each case can be both low and substantially constant.

For any given situation where a large solar system is to be installed it may be considered essential that computer simulation studies be performed in order to determine the appropriate size of both the collector array and the preheat storage facility. Two most necessary pieces of input data are a knowledge of the likely load pattern and the system temperatures and if these cannot be accurately estimated the solar system will have to be installed in the knowledge that its design may be far from optimum.

In some cases however the likely heat output may be estimated without the use of sophisticated computer programmes. For example, a (somewhat hypothetical) system installed as an inline heater and sized only to provide the first few degrees of heating for previously unheated supply water could be expected to work at high efficiency when the system was operating, and at zero efficiency when the plant was shut down. If the collectors were unglazed, efficiencies in excess of 100 per cent (based on the received insolation) could be realised because for much of the operating periods the local air temperature might be higher than the average collector temperature. As a first approximation therefore, the efficiency during any one hour could be taken as either 100 per cent or 0 per cent, and the only data required would be the average hourly insolation values for the particular site. In practice, these will rarely be known to an accuracy better than that obtainable by extrapolation of nearby meteorological station records, and further sophistication in the computation becomes somewhat academic.

The design errors that may occur in large systems will affect most adversely those using collectors having high U values. If (for example) very sophisticated collectors, incorporating a vacuum and infra-red-reflectors for heat loss suppression were used, then a design error might have relatively little effect because the collectors could function well even if the average temperatures exceeded by 20°C or 30°C those assumed in the design.

If poorly insulated collectors were used however the effect of such an error could be catastrophic – the system might hardly work at all.

Bearing in mind the fact that even in the most favourable circumstances (see Section 2.4.1) the output of a solar panel is unlikely to exceed 600 kWh/m² year in the UK the upper credible figure for glazed panels in large systems where higher temperatures than in outdoor pools are required may be taken to be between 550 and

650 kWh/m² year – an efficiency of between 55 and 65 per cent. These efficiencies are however unlikely to be achieved in practice; the figures are given only so that rough calculations of the likely *maximum* benefit from a proposed system may easily be performed before a decision whether to proceed with further design studies is taken.

A question that is often asked is what is the best option to employ in reducing the energy consumption of a given industrial process. In many cases the answer will be some form of heat recovery because not only can proven hardware of known performance be used but a reduction in the capital cost of the initial boiler plant can also result. An example will make this clear.

If a given process requires a power input of 100 kW then the simplest method of providing this heat is to install a boiler or other appliance that has a rated output of 100 kW or more at the specified temperature. If heat recovery may be applied to the end product and, for example, if a 30 per cent reclaim is possible then the boiler need only be sized to deliver 70 kW – which may in itself save some capital.

If solar preheating is considered instead of heat reclaim then the size of the boiler cannot be reduced because there will be many periods in a year when the solar contribution will be zero.

In summary, it is considered that the potential for solar energy utilisation in the UK in the industrial and commercial sector is extremely limited especially in view of the fact that as the energy efficiency of processes improves with the introduction of more heat reclaim equipment (for which there seems to be a relatively large potential market) there will be fewer and fewer points at which low temperature solar heat can be injected: many type one processes will become type two and the potential for solar collectors will diminish accordingly. These conclusions are supported by the fact that the least valuable form of energy is low temperature heat and since UK industry at present discards immense quantities of this, and also discards much higher temperature ($>100°C$) waste heat the prospects for expensive systems whose average output can only be heat below 100°C must be minute. A more fundamental limitation to the potential usefulness of solar energy in industry is however the fact that many industrial processes are very energy intensive and the power requirement per unit area of the site may be very many times the average intensity of solar radiation: even if the whole site were covered with collectors the percentage contribution to the demand could still be small. The prospects in the UK for large scale use of solar cells which produce high grade (electrical) energy have already been reviewed[31], and were found to be minimal.

A recent conference[32] considered the use of solar energy in industry but much of the proceedings were devoted to systems that would seem unlikely to be viable in the UK climate. It is instructive however to note from the paper by Spongberg that only 2·6 per cent of USA process heat requirements occur at temperatures below 100°C. The corresponding figure for the UK is unlikely to be markedly different and this reinforces the conclusions derived above.

The overall conclusions from the above discussion would appear to be that UK industry should continue to investigate its use of energy and the methods by which in future it may be both reduced and internally recycled, and it would seem that indigenous solar energy will never be able to supply more than an insignificant fraction of the present industrial requirement.

3 Component parts of solar systems

3.1 The solar collector

If satisfactory life and performance are to be obtained from solar collector units the following points need to be considered.

3.1.1 The collector plate

The collector plate should be manufactured from suitable materials. Usually metals are used because they are robust, relatively easily fabricated, and can possess high thermal conductivities[33]. There are four principal ways in which solar collector plates may degrade. The fluid passages may corrode if the fluid and metal are incompatible, the plate may corrode where it is joined to the fluid passages if dissimilar metals are used, the black or other absorbing surface may flake off or otherwise deteriorate under exposure to thermal cycling, humidity, and radiation, and the joints in the fluid passages, and the fluid passages themselves, may distort or fracture through being subject to high temperatures or pressures.

Collector plates should be designed to withstand the most severe conditions that could possibly be met during installation and service. Important considerations here are that the stresses induced by repeated thermal cycling should be allowed for in the design and that the plates should be capable of withstanding the high temperatures (up to 200°C) that could be generated if the collector assemblies were exposed to intense solar irradiance whilst drained of transfer fluid. Such conditions may be met during installation and during service if (say) the pump failed or the system was drained in midsummer for some reason.

All of these eventualities may be guarded against by employing suitable design criteria and fabrication methods, and by ensuring that the plates are subsequently used only in accordance with manufacturer's recommendations.

Of the materials in common use for the fluid passages in solar collector plates copper will be one of the most trouble-free; copper is used extensively for both hot and cold water supply systems and a solar collector circuit will almost inevitably contain copper somewhere along its length. Copper is a relatively noble metal, high in the electro-chemical series, and as such may accelerate the corrosion of less noble metals present in the same system. Other metals, if installed correctly and with due regard for their inherently more reactive nature may also be expected to function satisfactorily in a solar collector circuit.

Mild steel and stainless steel are both attractive materials for the collector plate but stainless steel in particular suffers from poor thermal conductivity; the tube spacing of the collector must therefore be reduced or the plate thickness increased if a satisfactory level of performance is to be maintained. The relationships between thermal conductivity and tube spacing, and their effect on collector efficiency are fully covered by Duffie and Beckman[34].

Aluminium alloys are potentially excellent materials for solar collector plates since they are cheaper than copper, have a low density, possess good thermal conductivity and can readily be roll-bonded or otherwise fabricated into suitable units. Unfortunately they suffer from what has proved to be a serious disadvantage in that they can corrode rapidly in the presence of even a few parts per million of either copper or chloride ions. Other contaminants can also cause problems. Pitting corrosion is the most common mode of failure and is characterised both by its relative unpredictability and by the fact that, once started, a corrosion pit may rapidly progress through the wall of the fluid channel whilst the surrounding material remains unattacked. Cast aluminium radiators have been used in central heating systems both in Europe and the UK for many years but often in association with steel rather than copper pipework. Experience of the reliability of these radiators should not directly be related to roll-bonded constructions where the metal thickness is typically only about 0·6 mm; in addition, roll-bonded plates can incorporate areas where the metal is stressed and this may give rise to an enhanced risk of corrosion.

The use of aluminium collector plates for solar panels has recently been reviewed[35]. As for other metals, various inhibitors are available which when mixed with water form solutions that are less corrosive to the aluminium than is plain water but unless the inhibitors are kept at the correct strength and ingress of aggressive ions such as chloride is prevented corrosion is still likely to occur. The various types of inhibitors in common use are reviewed in Section 3.6.1.

Good design of metal collector plates for use in domestic water heating and similar applications will include consideration of the following requirements.

1   All joints in the collector fluid passages should be high-temperature-soldered, brazed or welded. Use of soft solder may be acceptable for single glazed moderate performance collectors but as yet there appears to be a lack of reliable experimental evidence.

2   Due attention should be given to the bimetallic expansion effects that may occur when (say) a matrix of copper tube is bonded to sheet steel or aluminium.

3 Provision should be made for a good and lasting thermal bond between the fluid passages and the plate. Some designs that have been sold may not retain their initial performance for any length of time because corrosion between plate and fluid passages when these are constructed from dissimilar metals may form an insulating oxide or other compound layer. Other designs use only weak spring clips or similar devices to press the components into mutual thermal contact and degradation of this bond is to be anticipated, especially as corrosion of the clips can in some cases be expected. In collectors where the fluid passages are soldered to the absorber plate it is recommended that high-melting-point solder be used, especially if either a selective surface or double glazing is incorporated.

4 Provision for thermal expansion of the collector plate relative to its enclosing box is a rather obvious requirement but some panels that have been tested at BRE are of such a design that the fluid passages become stressed when heated because they are located against supports that are in turn fixed to an unyielding outer casing. Basic good engineering design should ensure that faults of this type are not carried through to production models.

5 The fluid passages should be arranged so as to facilitate draining of the fluid whenever required. This characteristic is not a feature of collector plate designs which are based on a single length of tubing wound into a planar spiral. Whilst these units may be thermally efficient they may exhibit maintenance problems; for example, if it were required to drain an inflammable heat transfer oil from the system for the purpose of resoldering some pipe joints.

Collector plates, unless manufactured from a self-coloured material such as black plastic are usually finished on their top (exposed) surface with either a matt black paint or a selective surface. In either case longevity is a prime requirement. The adhesion of black paint finishes is often determined by the surface treatment given to the plate prior to application of the top coat and an etch primer is usually recommended for copper, zinc and aluminium. BRE Digests 70 and 71 (references 36 and 37) give recommendations on paints for exterior use and are applicable to the protection of collector casings and support frameworks, but the high temperatures attainable by absorber plate surfaces present additional difficulties and expert guidance should be sought. One brand of black paint (Nextel)* is worthy of note since it has been used, apparently with success, for some time both in the UK and overseas and consists of a suspension of neoprene granules which produces a velvety finish having good absorptance for solar radiation. Recently developed high durability finishes such as PVF2 may be used increasingly in future, but at present PVF2 requires a stoving temperature of about 210°C: this may preclude its use on collector plates incorporating soft-soldered joints.

* Trademark, 3M Company.

Selective surfaces are usually based on a layer of semi-conducting oxide and can be used to give a metal collector plate a superior thermal performance. A high proportion of the incident solar radiation can be absorbed whilst the underlying metal can give an emissivity in the infra-red region beyond 3 microns (3×10^{-6}m) considerably below the 0·9 that is typical for a matt black finish. The effect on thermal performance is greater at higher temperatures and may be detrimental at low temperatures such as those found typically in solar panels used for heating swimming pools. The properties of selective surfaces have been discussed by Duffie and Beckman[38], and Meinel and Meinel[39].

One of the first selective surfaces to be used in the UK was nickel black, a standard feature of an imported Israeli collector. More recently British manufacturers have developed a copper oxide process following on Australian work[40] and several have experimented with black chrome surfaces, used for many years as a decorative finish on steelwork. Black chrome is generally considered to have the highest durability of all the commonly used selective surfaces but recent work on multi-dip copper oxide based finishes apparently also shows encouraging results[41]. Selective surfaces that may be applied by painting have also been developed but it should be understood that most if not all processes require either use of chemicals under precisely controlled conditions or electro-chemical apparatus or both. Often the required chemicals are dangerous and experimentation by unqualified personnel cannot be advised.

If selective surfaces that cannot be guaranteed to retain their low emissivity for long periods of time are used then they should, if possible, be of a type that can be expected to degrade to a good matt black specification; selective surfaces that are expected to degrade to a state characterised by low absorptivity and high emissivity should not be used unless a warning is given to the purchaser that the collector plate surface will need either retreating or overpainting with matt black after a few months or years.

The durability of all collector plate surfaces in the relatively humid and polluted UK climate may be less good than that realised in other countries: moisture penetration, especially through thin semiconductor layers, may be expected to accelerate degradation of the underlying substrate. Porous surfaces on copper, aluminium or steel may prove to be particularly troublesome, but enhanced durability may be expected if a nickel coating is used beneath the semiconductor film; this is already standard practice on some collectors finished with black chrome. An interesting development in the UK is the recent introduction of a stick-on selective surface; the material is available in roll form backed by a pressure-sensitive adhesive. It is claimed that the foil can successfully be applied to aluminium, steel and copper, and that it may be removed from the collector plate after many years of service if replacement is necessary.

It is generally thought that once developed on a commercial scale, application of a selective surface is likely to be no more expensive than using a good matt black paint and it is probable that selectively-coated collector plates will be used increasingly in the UK unless their superior initial performance is marred either by greater overheating problems in summertime or by a short effective life. As noted above, use of selective surfaces for low temperature applications may be disadvantageous because little use is made of the low emissivity and the lower absorbtivity (when compared to a good matt black surface) may prove to be the critical parameter. Care should be taken when handling selectively coated collector plates since even when unglazed they can reach high temperatures in strong sunlight. Some selective surfaces may be affected by contamination and it would be advisable if prior to final installation they were to be kept free of dust, fingerprints, soldering flux and other foreign substances. Packing in clear plastic film has been tried but on at least one occasion plates were exposed to the sun before the plastic had been removed and melting of the latter occurred.

There would appear to be a need for monitoring of the decrease in performance of selective surfaces installed in industrial areas of the UK, since a significant amount of chemical pollution may be expected to reach the surfaces even when they are covered with glazing: this follows from the requirement that collector boxes should be ventilated (see Section 3.1.2). Section 3.1.13 considers the use of selective surfaces in high performance collectors.

Correct design of the fluid passages in solar collector plates is important if a uniform flow rate per unit area is to be achieved. In some designs these considerations are not relevant because the fluid passage consists of a single channel which winds its way back and forth across the surface of the plate; in these units the heat transfer fluid has little choice but to follow its designated path: air-lock problems are however not unknown. Most trouble occurs with 'header and riser' designs and the following cautionary notes are relevant not only to the design of individual plates but also to the interconnection of a large number of plates (of whatever design) to form an array of solar collectors; some work on the latter topic has already been published[42].

In order to obtain optimum collection efficiency a fairly uniform collector plate temperature must be maintained and this may be accomplished by ensuring an equal flow rate in all the risers, assuming these to be equally spaced. The emphasis given below to header and riser designs reflects only their popularity at the present time: it must not be inferred that other designs may be less prone to problems. Indeed, in many alternative systems both velocities and changes in velocity are higher and this alone should be sufficient to augur caution.

It is important to realise that there are several distinct effects which operate together to produce the distribution of flow that is experimentally observed in any collector system: these are

1 Thermosyphon pressures, which arise because fluids change their density as they are heated.

2 The Bernoulli or Venturi effect, which arises whenever the effective diameter of the pipework changes for any

given flow: this effect can occur at pipework junctions and is used to advantage in some flow measurement devices.

3 The pressure losses produced by virtue of the fact that real fluids are viscous: this is often the predominant effect, especially if balancing valves are fitted to the circuits.

4 Pressures due to gravity: these need to be considered only in open circuits.

Thermosyphon pressures provide the sole motive power in solar systems that do not use a pump, but occur in all installations except those in which all the collectors and pipework are horizontal.

The order of magnitude of this effect is often such that it does not have a significant influence on the flow pattern. It was shown in Section 2.2.2 that the pressure head developed in a 3 metre high installation would be about 7.5 mm of water ($75 \ N/m^2$) at a temperature of about $25°C$ and with a $10°C$ temperature difference. In a typical pumped system both the temperature difference and the vertical distance* may be considerably less and so the thermosyphon head available may reduce to less than $10 \ N/m^2$, which is insignificant in many applications. Exceptions occur where both the header and riser tubes of a collector are of large cross-section (these designs are of course most commonly found in thermosyphon systems) and in large arrays where too many collectors have been connected in parallel; it is shown in Appendix II that very small pressure differences may then exist across some of the risers and under these circumstances thermo-syphon pressure can produce a significant corrective influence.

The Bernoulli effect arises because the principle of conservation of energy may be applied to any mass of fluid moving in a pipe.

In a simplified analysis the equations may be reduced to
$$au^2 + p = b$$
where a and b are constants, u = velocity and p = pressure.

It is clear that if the velocity of any mass of fluid is increased (for example, if the pipe size changed from 28 mm to 15 mm) then the pressure within it would be decreased. These pressure changes are often insignificant but they can become noticeable in much the same situations as can thermosyphon pressures and also where large changes in velocity occur; the detailed design of pipe joints must however be considered in computing the likely numerical values.

Four different ways of joining risers to a header tube may be considered as depicted in Figure 20. The first design is 'neutral' in that it might be expected to behave in a predictable fashion and this might be thought to be the case for the second design also, but this is not necessarily so. The third and last designs appear to be asking for trouble in the sense that whilst it is intuitively obvious

---

* The relevant distance here is the vertical height of the collector alone, not the height of the complete system.

28

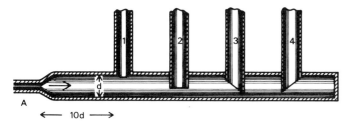

Figure 20 Four methods of joining riser tubes to headers. In all cases the feed pipe 'A' should be at least 10d away from the first riser

that more fluid will be pushed up the riser in the third design than the last it is not at all obvious how this may be quantified. Indeed, it is possible that the magnitude of the effects introduced by such designs changes with flow rate, especially if the collector plate is operating in the transition region between laminar and turbulent flow.

It would be pertinent to note that the Venturi (Bernoulli) effects which can cause problems in solar collector design are actually used to good advantage in specialised fittings that increase the flow in the gravity circulation water heating primaries of some central heating installations. A typical design of unit is shown in Figure 21.

Given that these methods of construction can introduce large departures from the idealised behaviour of a collector plate it is not surprising that more than one research team in the UK has found that in some commercially available designs the flow in one or two risers is actually reversed, and that in others it is near zero. This confusion has unfortunately led to advice being published in respect of collector interconnection that is likely to be incorrect for most installations[43].

No attempt is made here to produce a panacea for these ills but it might be helpful if some basic principles were outlined.

1 Equal flows in all risers may be achieved if the pressure drop across the risers is considerably greater than that along the headers. This implies either that the risers must be long compared with the headers or that the headers must be of considerably larger diameter than the risers or both.

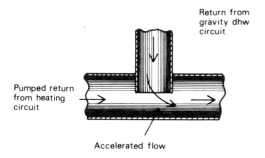

Figure 21 Typical design of a fitting used for boosting the flow in a gravity circulation primary circuit. These fittings are also used in single-pipe heating systems. Not to scale

2 Satisfactory methods of testing a panel design that do not require expensive equipment are either to make an *exact* replica in a clear plastic and to use dye tracer techniques or to subject a prototype to thermal performance tests in which the flow in each riser is deduced from very accurate measurements of the temperature rise along its length: this in itself is not an easy experiment because of the difficulty of accurately measuring very small differences in surface temperatures but may be preferred to methods that seek to introduce flow meters or other transducers or probes into the fluid stream, since these could affect the flow patterns and, consequently, the flow rates. Use of differential manometers installed along lengths of risers that were removed from any end effects could however be acceptable if carried out by suitably experienced personnel. The easiest method of test however is probably to hire a sensitive infra-red imager and to examine the collector under operating conditions but without the glass cover in place; selective surfaces should be well overpainted with matt black prior to testing.

3 Tests should be conducted at both the flow rate and angle of inclination that are to be used when the collectors go into service; use either of different flow rates or fluids could conceivably alter the flow pattern.

The paper by Dunkel and Davey[42] should be consulted for a mathematical discussion of flow distribution in large absorber arrays, but for the less technical reader the following greatly simplified explanation may assist with an understanding of some of the basic principles that are involved.

The flow rate in the individual risers of a header and riser design of collector plate may be calculated from a knowledge of both the pipe lengths and sizes and the total flow rate. The calculations are involved and if performed manually very time consuming but it is possible to derive precise answers. (See Appendix II.) Implicit in idealised calculations is the assumption that there are no pressures created by virtue of the local geometry of the junctions between headers and risers; the only pressure changes considered are those resulting from the movement of a viscous fluid in the pipes. Additional assumptions are often built into the mathematical models, especially with regard to whether laminar or turbulent flow equations are used.

Consider a collector plate as shown in Figure 22a in which the flow and return are taken from the same side. Assume that the plate behaves ideally and that the flows are represented by the arrows (one arrow for each unit of flow). The highest pressure is clearly at the inlet (point A) and the lowest at the outlet (point J). Since pressure drop in a pipe is determined (approximately) by the square of the fluid velocity under turbulent flow conditions the loss in pressure in the lower header will be progressively less per unit length of header as each riser takes away its share of the flow.

Conversely, the pressure drop per unit length in the upper header becomes progressively greater towards the

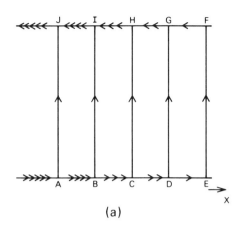

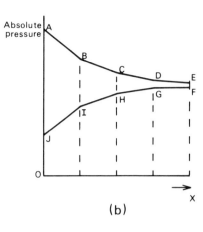

Figure 22 (a) Idealised flow pattern in a header and riser collector plate in which the flow and return are taken from the same side of the plate. (b) The pressure diagram that would result from the idealised flow pattern shown in (a)

(a)   (b)

outlet as more and more fluid is added to the stream. An approximate pressure diagram for each of the headers may now be drawn and is shown in Figure 22b.

Since the flow rate in any riser is determined by the pressure difference across it (given by the ordinate distance between the 2 lines on the graph) it is at once obvious that a collector plate used in this way is only likely to work ideally (with equal flow in each riser) if the diameter of the risers increases from left to right.

Clearly, this is not very satisfactory if standard size tubes are to be used but roll-bonded plates can easily accommodate progressive changes in both header and riser size; changing the headers is the usual solution adopted.

An improvement may however be realised by taking the flow and return from opposite corners of the plate, as is shown in Figure 23a. Again the assumption is made that the plate behaves ideally (equal flow in each riser) and the pressure diagram is then as shown in Figure 23b.

The result is clear enough – assuming that all the risers are identical there will be a greater flow in those at either end of the plate.

If these curves are smoothed out then the result is qualitatively the same as that given by Dunkel and Davey, and it should not be doubted that if large systems are installed with little regard for these effects then a most unsatisfactory performance can result. The importance of correct plate interconnection in large solar systems is well recognised overseas: see, for example reference 44. In general, series-parallel connection is the preferred solution and was adopted by the author for use in the solar system at Tunbridge Wells School[6].

The reasons why this arrangement can be generally recommended are that it can offer good flow distribution whilst requiring only moderate pumping power. The alternatives of all-series or all-parallel connection can suffer from, respectively, a high pumping power requirement, and uneven flow distribution.

Another disadvantage is sometimes claimed for series connection – that since the collectors run hotter the system will be less efficient. This is incorrect, and a little thought will show that, assuming perfect flow distribution, there will be no difference in thermal performance provided that the total area and the total flow rate are the same in each case. Arguments relating to second-order effects can be advanced to show that either design may be slightly more efficient, and one of the most convincing of these is that the series-connected system will benefit from the higher fluid velocities; if a change from laminar to turbulent flow occurs then a measurable improvement in performance may result.

As already noted, there are several distinct methods of coping with flow distribution problems. The first approach (adopted by manufacturers of some swimming pool panels) is to make the diameter of the headers enormous compared to that of the risers. The pressure loss across the headers is then so low that the pressure diagrams are almost flat lines and since the risers have appreciable flow resistance the lines for the top and bottom headers are well separated and the percentage difference in flow across the panel becomes acceptably small. This 'brute-force' method is satisfactory for swimming pool panels where the thermal capacity of the headers is not a great disadvantage, but is not to be recommended for panels intended for domestic hot water applications.

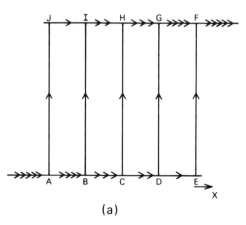

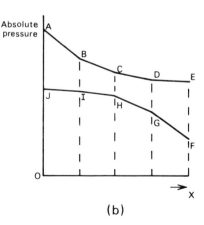

Figure 23 (a) Idealised flow pattern in a header and riser collector plate in which the flow and return are taken from diagonally opposite corners of the plate. (b) The pressure diagram that would result from the idealised flow pattern show in (a)

(a)   (b)

An alternative design approach is to use mathematical analysis together with experimentation to determine acceptable sizes for risers and headers; manufacturers could then be in a position to advise their customers on the interconnection methods that should be used with their products. In this method of design a balance has to be struck between riser size, header size, tube costs, and other variables and the exact techniques are complex: a less elegant solution is often advocated, and entails introducing flow restrictors (such as balancing valves) into each section of a large system.

Yet another solution is sometimes adopted and consists of increasing the total flow rate by a factor of 5 or even 10 above that advocated in this book (0·014–0·03 l/m²s for domestic hot water systems and 0·04 l/m²s for swimming pools).

In a simplified analysis (see Appendix II) the ratio between the flows remains constant, and the temperature gradients along the fluid passages will all reduce to lower levels but in practice application of this crude solution may or may not be thermally beneficial – flow patterns may change abruptly at critical velocities and Venturi effects may become more important. There are however several disbenefits to accrue – the pumping power that becomes necessary can increase to inordinately high levels and erosion of fittings and pipes can occur because of the high fluid velocities.

It may be stated categorically that if the flow distribution in a collector array is incorrect then either the collector plate or system design is poor, or the plates have been interconnected wrongly, or part of the system is air-locked. Increasing the total flow rate may or may not remove the symptoms, but it cannot usually cure the disease; mild cases of air-locking are the exception here.

Finally, it is noted yet again that the definitive test remains one of building a prototype system and determining by experiment whether it performs correctly.

3.1.2 Condensation in solar collectors

Condensation within the collector assembly is likely to prove more of a problem in the UK than in other countries where solar collectors have been used extensively and where levels of relative humidity are lower. There are very good reasons why condensation should not be allowed to form in solar collectors in any substantial quantity. All types of insulation material that are subject to water and/or water vapour absorption lose a substantial part of their insulating ability when damp, and insulation materials of this type are usually employed in solar collectors because they are substantially cheaper than the genuinely water repellent alternatives. Wet insulation material will of course dry out if heated for a sufficient length of time and if no compaction has occurred no permanent damage may result; however, drying out wet insulation may militate against effective operation of the solar system, probably for several days or even weeks. Condensation dripping off the underside of a cover glass on to the collector plate may produce degradation of the

plate surface and will certainly decrease the thermal performance of the unit – a heat pipe effect in which liquid evaporates from the plate, condenses on the cover glass and drops back to the plate may occur in collectors at shallow angles; such effects are useful for solar powered distillation but not for flat plate collectors.

Double glazed collectors have an increased chance of suffering from condensation if not properly designed; the use of hermetically sealed double glazing units (as used in many double glazing systems for windows and doors) may seem an attractive solution since the interglass space is filled with dry gas and sealed from the atmosphere. Unfortunately experience both in the UK and overseas suggests that differential thermal expansion can cause cracking of one or both panes. The risk of thermal breakage can be completely overcome by use of toughened glass, but at a considerable extra cost. In any case, the air gap in most of these units is below the optimum[45] and an alternative design is to use two mechanically independent pieces of glass; this introduces the problem of ensuring that condensation does not occur in the interglass space. It would at this point be pertinent to consider the two basic methods by which condensation, which occurs because moist air contacts a surface whose temperature is below the dewpoint of the air, may be eliminated in solar collectors, double glazing, and similar structures[46, 47]. The surface at risk may either be sealed from moist air (as in hermetically sealed double glazing units) or sufficient ventilation adjacent to the surface with dry air (usually colder air with a lower humidity) may be provided.

One of the worst mistakes that can be made in designing a solar collector (or a double glazing system) is to allow *some but insufficient* ventilation into the unit. Under these circumstances warm moist air will under some conditions be present in the unit, and if the temperature falls condensation will occur before the air that is reaching its dewpoint is replaced by drier outdoor air. Not all currently available collectors on the UK market avoid this fault and, consequently, condensation becomes a problem. The most usual design error is to seal the cover glass to the outer casing completely, whilst allowing a very small amount of air infiltration where the pipes pass into the unit, and also through joins in the outer casing.

Either the whole collector unit should be truly hermetically sealed (with a guarantee that it will remain so) or adequate provision for ventilation should be provided. The former option is not easily realised in practice and it would probably be expensive to manufacture a collector that could maintain the necessary degree of integrity over its design life (say 20 years). The latter option may therefore be preferred and adequate ventilation, following double glazing practice, should be provided at the bottom edge of the collector (but see Section 5).

Provision of excess air leakage at both top and bottom of collector units (again a feature of a few designs) whilst preventing condensation may lead to a chimney effect with hot air being driven out of the collector, to the detriment of its thermal performance.

A quite different approach is to incorporate a small bag of reversible desiccant (usually silica gel) in the collector box. The function of this material is clearly not to absorb all the water vapour entering the collector over its lifetime (the amounts used are far too small) but it may provide a small 'damping' effect absorbing water until such time as the collector next becomes very hot when the water may be driven off, and, it is to be hoped, removed from the unit completely. It seems implausible that the small quantity of desiccant used can perform this function over a few wet months in the UK climate, and one is led to speculate that this desiccant merely serves to keep the units free from condensation for the short time between manufacture and installation. In any case, reversible desiccants can lose their effectiveness with time, especially if overheated, and designs of collectors relying on their continued effectiveness may be considered unsatisfactory.

In conclusion, the only satisfactory design solution is probably to allow adequate ventilation at the base of all units, or to provide a small amount of leakage at both the bottom and the top, sufficient for the purpose but not so as to seriously degrade the thermal performance.

Probably the best way of achieving the optimum is to progressively reduce the air leakage on prototype models until condensation problems start to become apparent. The fact that some double glazing systems for windows still suffer from condensation after many years of development might not appear to bode well for the solar industry, but the problems in solar collectors are less severe than those of double glazed window systems and so manufacturers should, it may be hoped, be able to produce satisfactory designs.

3.1.3 Outgassing of materials in solar collectors

Collectors should not incorporate materials which outgas to any significant extent. Among the likely problems would appear to be the breakdown of unsuitable types of black paint used on collector plates and the sublimation of resinous substances from softwoods; excessive quantities could coat the inside surface of the cover glass with a semi-opaque layer thus reducing the transmission of solar radiation. Similar difficulties have been experienced under stagnation conditions with collectors that incorporate unsuitable types of glazing strips.

3.1.4 The transparent cover

Nearly all flat plate collectors designed for preheating domestic hot water or similar applications, and some 'semi-concentrating' designs, use a clear glass or translucent plastic cover whose principal functions are to help to prevent heat loss and to protect the collector plate and insulation from the weather. Traditionally, glass has been in the forefront of the materials used for this purpose but its supremacy is now being seriously challenged. The characteristics of clear float glass are well known; it is

almost completely transparent to solar radiation, 98 per cent of which is incident at wavelengths between 0.3 and 3.0 microns*. At longer wavelengths, above 3 microns, glass becomes opaque and this characteristic makes it almost ideally suited for use in solar collectors[48, 49]. Reflections from clear glass at normal incidence are typically 4 per cent from each interface (about 8 per cent per sheet) and absorption can account for another 5 to 10 per cent resulting in a transmission of about 85 per cent; the reflection is a result of an impedance mismatch between glass and air and the absorption is due mainly to iron impurities. At other than normal incidence a greater amount of reflection will occur with correspondingly less of the incident radiation being transmitted. This effect is not as severe as might be imagined because the transmission curve is fairly flat out to incidence angles of about 55°, after which however it drops rapidly[48]. It is possible to coat glass with a precisely controlled layer of a material having a refractive index between those of the glass and of air and this process, commonly used on camera lenses and other optical instruments can be quite effective over a small spectral range (usually the visible). The drawback is that it is relatively expensive and produces what is really only a small change in the overall transmittance taken over the spectral range of solar radiation; in a solar collector application where surface dirt and exposure to the weather are inescapable such coatings are probably not worth further consideration.

Other types of coatings that can be applied to glass are potentially much more useful and involve (typically) the deposition of a precisely controlled layer of doped tin oxide or indium oxide on one or both surfaces of the glass[50,51]. This layer acts as an infra-red reflector and whilst (ideally) it has little effect on the passage of solar radiation through the glass it reflects the long wave (thermal) radiation emitted from the collector plate. The efficiency of the collector is thus markedly enhanced at high temperatures where radiation loss, especially if a matt black collector surface is used, can be the predominant loss mechanism. Of the two compounds noted above indium oxide is the better having virtually no transmission bands in the infra-red but it is more difficult to apply. One of the first widely publicised uses of indium oxide coated glass occurred in the Philips low energy experimental house at Aachen[52] and the process, if widely developed, offers the prospect not only of more efficient flat plate and concentrating collectors but of double glazed window units having U values as low as 1.8 W/m² °C. (A typical untreated double glazed window has a U value of about 3.2 W/m² °C and radiation losses are typically 50 per cent of the total.) The improvement in a solar collector's U value will be more pronounced because of the higher average temperature differences.

It should be noted that neither patterned nor anti-reflection (picture) glass can be expected significantly to improve the performance of a flat plate collector; patterned glass may improve the appearance at the expense of the thermal performance. Antireflection picture

---

* 1 micron = 10⁻⁶ m.

glass does not prevent reflection of light but merely reduces specular reflection whilst increasing the diffuse component; the amount of energy reflected remains substantially the same.

The disadvantages of glass for solar collectors are that it is quite a dense material, easily broken and having cut edges that are exceedingly sharp. Except for the experienced builder, handling sheets of glass on a roof is not to be advised. The characteristics of glass are more fully covered elsewhere, and tables are also available for determining the necessary thickness for any given application[49, 53]. Although thicknesses less than those stipulated can be handled and installed satisfactorily this practice cannot be recommended since failure owing to hail, snow loads or wind will probably result in even greater expense, together with the very real risk of severe injury.

There are many types of transparent or translucent plastics on the market some of which may be considered suitable for use as the cover material in solar collectors. The most commonly known of those available in sheet form are PVC, acrylics and polycarbonate. BRE Digest 69[54] contains information on their characteristics but for solar collector applications two of the most important properties are their maximum working temperature and their resistance to u-v induced degradation. The latter has long been a problem with clear plastics but u-v stabilized types are now available and there is no reason to suppose that the better of these will not last in excess of 10 years without marked deterioration. Other properties that should be considered are the increased susceptibility to abrasion of plastics over glass, the probable decreased transmission of solar radiation, and the poorer collector performance at high temperatures that may result from the far-infra-red transmission bands exhibited by many clear plastics[48]. If however these materials are used with selectively coated collector plates their partial transparency beyond 3 microns is not a great disadvantage because at moderate operating temperatures convection and conduction are the predominant loss mechanisms. The lower thermal conductivity of plastics will not contribute to an increased collector performance because the U value of the cover is determined principally by its boundary layers of air and by its optical properties. One material that perhaps deserves special mention is poly-vinyl fluoride produced under the trade name of Tedlar*. This material, usually used as films only a small fraction of a millimetre in thickness has proved to be durable, and has been incorporated into several collector designs. There is however some question as to its ability to withstand high stagnation temperatures, and cases of embrittlement have been reported from the USA.

The use of some composite materials usually based on glass fibre is also possible but there is little experience of their long term performance in this application. One potentially promising product uses a GRP base protected with an outer skin of Tedlar. Recently, improved types of clear PVC sheet have been produced in the UK and

* DuPont trademark.

some of these may be considered for use in solar collector applications: the high temperatures attainable under stagnation conditions may however be a problem. The final choice between glass or plastics must rest with the designer or purchaser and in some circumstances a particular property of a plastic (for example poly-carbonate's extreme resistance to breakage when hit by flying objects) may prove the deciding factor. On balance however, glass is such a proven material for outdoor long term use that it may continue to dominate the market for some time to come; it is also cheaper than many of the high quality plastic alternatives but this may be offset by increased handling problems.

3.1.5 Sealing the cover to its supports

Sealing of the glass or other transparent cover to the collector casing is an area where some concern may be expressed as to the likely durability of some currently produced units. There are two essential requirements. Firstly, and probably of greatest importance, the glass (if glass is used) should be positively prevented from detaching itself from the collector unit either under the action of gravity or as a result of the considerable suction forces that can be generated in high winds. In a few collector designs the glass is simply bedded into mastic in a channel and there are no mechanical fixings – only the viscosity of the mastic prevents the glass being sucked out of the collector under wind loads.

It is not satisfactory for ordinary float glass to be retained by clips located at a few points around its circumference because under high suction loads the glass will become heavily stressed at these points. Plastic cover materials may be more likely to 'spring out' of the collector if inadequately retained and guidance regarding the necessary overlap of beading is available[49].

Temperature gradients in the glass (or other cover material) near to its edges should be minimised because of the risk of thermal stress cracking; examples of good and bad practice are shown in Figure 24. Experience in the UK to date indicates that glass in single glazed collectors is seldom broken by thermal stresses but the opposite is true for double glazed units, and as already noted in Section 3.1.2 hermetically-sealed double glazing intended for use in windows should not be used in solar collectors. If two mechanically independent sheets of glass are used then the design should preclude as far as possible the build-up of thermal stresses, especially in the inner pane. Alternatively, toughened glass may be used. In Figure 24a the cover glasses are shown bedded into heat-resisting thermally-insulating strips and the edges can now reach a temperature similar to that of the bulk of the glass. The essential requirement is clearly that the effective thermal conductivity of the strip or other device be much less than that of glass itself. In the poor design the glass is simply laid in an aluminium channel and since this is cooled by ambient air thermal stress may be produced (see Figure 24b).

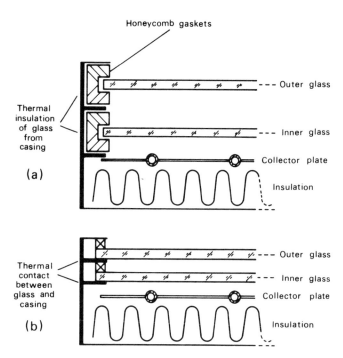

Honeycomb gaskets

Thermal
insulation
of glass
from
casing

(a)

--- Outer glass

--- Inner glass

Collector plate

Insulation

Thermal
contact
between
glass and
casing

(b)

--- Outer glass

--- Inner glass

Collector plate

Insulation

Figure 24 Avoidance of thermal stress in the cover glasses of flat plate collectors: (a) A good design, in which the edges of the glass are thermally insulated from the collector casing, (b) A poor design, in which there is good thermal contact between the edges of the glass and the collector casing

The outer pane of a double glazed collector will only be as subject to breakage as the glass in single glazed units since it will attain much the same temperatures, but care should still be taken to design all the edge supports so as to minimize thermal gradients.

If a plastic is used as the cover material then depending on its properties many of the precautions outlined above may be unnecessary, but the thermal expansion of some plastics is considerable[54] and the design should ensure that this can occur freely; many plastics become brittle at low temperature and any mechanical restraint applied under these conditions may result in cracking.

3.1.6 Thermal insulation material

Thermal insulation material for use in a solar collector must, as well as having a long expected life, be suitable for occasional exposure to temperatures as high as 160°C (200°C in a double glazed or selectively coated collector).

The most commonly used material, and one of the cheapest, is glass fibre of the type used extensively for loft insulation. Mineral wool is equally suitable for solar collectors, but in either case the material should be secured so as to preclude significant movement if the collector is subsequently installed at a steep angle.

Expanded polystyrene should not be used because it starts to lose its strength at about 80°C[55] and begins to melt at temperatures slightly in excess of this; the exact upper working limit depends on the grade of material (of which there are several) but none are here considered suitable especially if the collector is of above average

performance. Polystyrene may, however, be used as the rear-most section of a correctly designed multilayer construction, subject to its being used only in situations where its inflammability does not constitute a fire risk. Many organic chemicals have a softening action on expanded polystyrene and for this reason contact with heat transfer oils, solvents, and oil-based paints should be avoided.

There are many types of foams that could be used as thermal insulation in solar collectors but the principal cause for concern, as with polystyrene, may be their maximum working temperature. BRE Digest 93[55] contains details of several types of foams a few of which could either be spray applied to solar collector plates or injected into a casing. The suitability of any given material for use at high temperatures should be carefully checked with the manufacturer.

If solar collectors are to be incorporated into a roof structure (as opposed to being laid on top of it) then the Building Regulations (see Appendix I) may dictate the mandatory fire resistance of the insulating material. Since fire resistant foams are more expensive than either mineral wool or phenolic-resin-bonded glass fibre it seems unlikely that they will be used extensively in this application.

The optimum thickness of insulation will depend upon the average collector working temperature but for units used in domestic hot water preheat systems there would seem to be little point in exceeding 75–125 mm of glass fibre or equivalent since the rear losses are then only a small fraction of the total loss from the unit. Section 4.1 should be consulted for a more detailed discussion of this topic.

3.1.7 The outer casing of solar collectors

The outer casing of a solar collector should provide mechanical rigidity so that the glass or other cover may be securely retained and should be sufficiently strong so that the fixings to (say) the roof of a building are not likely seriously to weaken within the lifetime of the unit.

Amongst the unsatisfactory designs are those where the load from the fixing bolts is taken only on a small area of thin GRP; with time this might be expected to weaken, thus impairing the integrity of the fixings. Particular attention is called to this design fault because the material surrounding a drilled hole may be susceptible to moisture penetration, with consequent loss of strength in exactly the area where stength is most required[54].

Other designs rely on a few small rivets for structural strength and where the rivets and the sheets are of dissimilar metals long term corrosion and weakening of the whole casing assembly may be anticipated. A similar problem occurs in those designs using steel self-tapping screws to secure aluminium angle frameworks to GRP casings. Corrosion of the screws might not seriously impair the safety of the collector for some years but use of unprotected steel fixings cannot be regarded as acceptable. The minimum protection for iron and steel should be hot dip galvanising: in many situations stainless steel may be preferred, but should not be used in contact with aluminium in marine conditions. The useful life of galvanising, even if carried out to BS 729[56], can be as low as 4–5 years in polluted atmospheres; regular painting may be necessary thereafter.

These criticisms of existing practice might be regarded as trivial but it must be realised that failure of this part of a collector could lead to serious damage or injury and it is to be hoped that designers will in future pay more attention to the requirements of basic mechanical integrity.

Among the newer materials to find use in solar collectors is GRC (glass reinforced cement), a composite of ordinary Portland cement strengthened with alkali resistant glass fibres. The material was developed jointly by Pilkingtons and BRE and details of its expected long term properties may be found in BRE publications[57].

degradation. Other black polyolefines such as high density polyethylene (HDPE) may also be suitable but all types should satisfy the requisite British Standard for being catalyst free and antioxidant stabilised. If well designed units are manufactured from a suitable grade of material they may be expected to have an adequate life, probably in excess of 5–10 years. The advantages of black polyolefine collectors over metal designs are clearly their self-colouration and freedom from corrosion problems. They cannot however tolerate excessive temperatures[54] and should never be glazed. The life of these collectors may be determined by cumulative stress cracking: build-up of the latter can be slowed by ensuring complete freedom for thermal movement whilst limiting any possible movement due to wind. Flapping of the collectors against their supports, especially at low temperatures, may prove detrimental. Designs based on copper pipes and aluminium sheet may be expected to degrade with time as outlined in Section 3.1.1: poor thermal bonding has a severe effect on the performance of unglazed collectors[34].

3.1.8 Collectors for swimming pools

Solar collectors used for heating swimming pools during the summer months need be only simple unglazed units. This fact is often stated but some confusion as to the actual reasoning still occasionally arises and so the following explanation is given.

The principal thermal function of the glass or other transparent cover in a solar collector is to reduce heat losses from the plate surface; such losses can occur whenever the surface is at a higher temperature than either the surrounding air or the effective long wave radiation temperature of the sky.

A disadvantage of any type of cover is that it will absorb some of the incident solar radiation, thus preventing the latter reaching the plate and being converted into potentially useful heat. A swimming pool collector will operate for a significant period of the year with water temperatures not far removed from air temperatures and the driving force for heat loss (the temperature excess over ambient) is therefore small and it is not worth providing an expensive glass or plastic cover to help prevent heat loss when such loss is not in any case occurring at any significant average rate. In an installation where the pool is heated only to low temperatures a cover on the collectors may actually result in a decrease in the quantity of heat obtained because the initial loss of short wave (solar) radiation is not fully compensated for by the slight decrease in the heat loss.

The most usual designs of collector plates for swimming pool application use either black polypropylene, or copper waterways thermally linked to aluminium sheets. Alternatively trickle collectors (see Section 3.1.10) may be employed. The principal requirements for swimming pool collectors are that they should be durable, reasonably cheap and have waterways that are compatible with chlorinated water. Good grades of black polypropylene have all of these qualities and are also resistant to u-v

3.1.9 Freeze-safe collectors

In areas where the supply water is of low temporary hardness there may be considerable advantages in using direct systems, and if these are to be kept in operation year-round then either the collectors must be freeze-safe (that is, they will not be damaged by having water freeze in them) or they must be otherwise protected.

Freeze-safe collector designs are not difficult to envisage but it would perhaps be helpful if the basic reason why freezing is usually associated with burst pipes were explained, since from a proper understanding of this comes the realisation that collector systems are probably not as susceptible to frost damage as at first it might appear. Pipes can be burst under the action of frost only when immense pressures are produced – greater than 16 MN/m² (2320 psi) for 15 mm copper tube to BS 2871[58]. If, for example, a section of pipe freezes solid then if the other end of that pipe is terminated by a leak tight tap the remaining water is constrained in a nominally fixed volume – it cannot escape. If freezing conditions persist the stress may increase until the pipe bursts*. The stress may of course be relieved in other ways – a poorly soldered capillary joint or a type A compression fitting may simply slide apart and in these cases subsequent repair is usually straightforward (but it should be remembered that any pipe which has been highly stressed may be permanently weakened as a result). It is therefore clear that the two necessary conditions for rupture are:
1 Initial confinement of a volume of water
2 Subsequent freezing of that same volume of water
It is not therefore obvious that damage will necessarily occur when solar collectors freeze; this will depend very much on the design of the collector waterways and also

---

* The volume expansion of water upon freezing is large – about 9·1 per cent.

on whether the connecting pipework is well insulated. Some plastic collectors may be inherently freeze-safe because the waterways may be able to expand sufficiently to accommodate the ice, but at these temperatures the impact strength of the plastic may be decreased and its brittleness much increased. The collectors must therefore be adequately restrained against wind induced movement and should not be knocked or moved under freezing conditions.

Collectors having tubes of circular cross-section are more prone to rupture than other designs because, assuming a fixed circumference, no distortion of a circle can result in an increase in cross-sectional area. Even with these types of collectors rupture upon freezing is far from certain, especially if the pipe runs to the store are short and well insulated because in this case the collector is likely to freeze first and may be able to eject a small amount of water to the rest of the system. Unfortunately these conclusions are not general; with high water capacity collectors their time-constant is such that the connecting pipework may freeze before the collector, which is undesirable since the water remaining in the collector is thereby trapped.

Upon thawing, and assuming no rupture has occurred, a partial vacuum may be generated in those parts of the collector to thaw first but this is unlikely to result in any damage. A novel method of protecting pipes from frost damage has recently been described[59] and a similar idea has been advocated for application to solar collectors[60]. The basic concept here is that if suitable compressible strips are installed in pipework then their deformation under freezing conditions may prevent the generation of excessive pressures.

It must be emphasised that it is not the intention to advocate immediate installation of these types of systems but, rather, to point out the possibilities and to encourage manufacturers and others to experiment with different designs so that guaranteed freeze-safe systems are produced which could subsequently form an important part of the future UK market: these simple systems, especially those based on gravity circulation, may be cheaper to install and maintain than systems using antifreezes or oils as heat transfer fluids. Another – and rather obvious – type of freeze-safe system could employ a non-aqueous heat transfer fluid that solidified at low temperature without any associated change in density. Some care is necessary here however because damage could occur upon thawing if the density increased upon freezing. It is recommended that prototype systems be shown to withstand at least 30 full freeze-thaw cycles before the design is pronounced satisfactory.

3.1.10 Trickle collectors

So called 'trickle' collectors are, as their name implies, collectors in which the water or other heat transfer fluid is allowed to trickle down the collector plate under the action of gravity.

The thermal performance of these types of collectors will, if the heat transfer fluid is water, be worse than that of a good conventional design because of the constant evaporation and condensation that will occur – that this effect can lead to large heat losses has already been discussed in Section 3.1.2. However, designs based on this principle can have lower capital costs than more conventional collector plates and so if sufficient area is available they could find application especially in systems where lower grade heat is acceptable.

Since the application of these collectors in the UK is likely to be limited this section will only deal briefly with some of the problems that can arise.

Unless the heat transfer fluid is toxic or at least unappetising to life forms of various orders then growths both on the plate and in the fluid may be expected as a result of exposure to plentiful sunlight. Algal growths, especially on the underside of the glass, where they are protected from poisons in the heat transfer fluid may give trouble after a few years. Experience in greenhouses suggests that the problem may not be too serious, but provision for cleaning the glass should be considered at the design stage. A difficulty sometimes encountered is blockage of the holes in the sparge pipes by either debris or hard water deposits: for some installations both filtering and use of an indirect circuit may prove necessary if long term reliability is to be assured.

Another obvious problem is that of excess moisture getting into the roof space, to the detriment of the timber or steel members. If the collector plate is allowed to become too hot before the pump is switched on, there may be a sudden vaporization when the trickle starts, sufficient to drive steam out of the collector and into the roof. This water vapour is unlikely to be harmful in itself but if condensation subsequently occurs damage is likely to result. An effective vapour barrier must therefore be provided between the collector assembly and the roof structure.

There is considerable experience of these types of roofs in the USA, where they have been an integral part of 'Thomason' solar houses for many years and the interested reader is referred to the literature[61, 62].

In the UK various materials have been used for the collector plate including corrugated asbestos and corrugated aluminium sheet. The former will not give a very good performance simply because of its poor thermal conductivity and the latter is potentially prone to corrosion problems: it has been suggested to the author on several occasions that corrugated aluminium sheet could form the basis of cheap trickle collectors for swimming pools, but where chlorination is employed the most notable feature of the design may be its short life. Special (but expensive) vinyl based paints or other durable finishes such as PVF2 might be used to prevent corrosion but especial care would be necessary during installation to ensure that the surface coating was not damaged in any way.

Some promising variations on usual trickle collector designs are worth noting. As a solution to the basic problem either of spreading the water out over the entire surface area or providing a reasonably conducting plate in the case of a channel design, it has been suggested either that the surface tension of the water be reduced by additives (this will help to spread the water out as it flows over the surface), or that the surface be made 'furry' or absorbent, which will have the same effect. A thermal performance superior to that attainable by a good conventional collector plate cannot however be expected. 'Black liquid' collectors are often based on trickle designs but the concept has also been applied to conventional flat plate collectors[63].

3.1.11 Air collectors

The term 'air collectors' is used to describe what are essentially flat plate collectors which use air as a heat transfer fluid. The plates in such designs are rarely simple plane surfaces because of the basic need to achieve as much thermal contact with the air stream as possible, but in their optical properties they may usually be treated as 'flat plate collectors'.

The use of these devices in the UK is likely to be limited because their only real advantages are possible cheapness combined with suitability for use with rock bed storage units[64]. Their basic problem is one of poor heat transfer and this arises essentially because gases are usually much less efficient as heat transfer fluids than are liquids. Different constructional techniques are needed from those employed for liquid collectors because good air-tightness at all points should be assured. Fitting air collectors to existing buildings may be difficult because of the size of ducting required; the essential problem here is the low volumetric specific heat of air.

A related problem is that high-powered fans have to be used to blow the necessary volumes of air around the circuits and since electricity has a high energy overhead[65] the primary energy savings from air collectors can be small and this should be reflected in any economic assessment.

In summary, it is considered that the most suitable applications for air collectors in the UK may be for those systems which by their nature already use air as a working fluid; their incorporation into domestic water heating or swimming pool systems would seem to be illogical.

3.1.12 Collectors combined with storage

In various overseas countries cheap solar collectors have been used extensively, and some of the design concepts have been imported into the UK. These units take many forms but the essential feature is that the storage and collector functions are combined into one; the simplest designs comprise a roof mounted cistern covered by a

clear plastic sheet – the cistern is filled with cold water in the morning and in tropical countries is usually warm enough for a shower in the evening[66]. It seems unlikely that any of these designs will find widespread application in the UK, both because of the relatively poor performance that may be expected and, perhaps more importantly, because some are so heavy when filled with water that their installation could result in overstressing of some types of UK roofs: this is further considered in Section 5.4.

Aesthetic problems have been encountered overseas where use has been made of systems that incorporate water storage above roof level[67].

3.1.13 High performance collectors

Several different types of solar collectors have already been described, and comprise those designs that have remained substantially unchanged for 20 or more years. Amongst the more advanced types that may some day find application in the UK are the following: the first group comprise collectors having a performance beyond which it is difficult to progress without some fundamental design change. It may be noted that the result of combining a selective absorber plate with an infra-red-reflecting cover glass would be disappointing because both these coatings only suppress radiation loss: this case is therefore not considered below*.

Selectively coated and/or double glazed flat plate collectors

The performance of selectively coated collector plates when incorporated into otherwise standard designs is well described elsewhere[34] and it is often thought that the performance of a double glazed matt black collector is about the same as that of a single glazed unit in which the collector plate is selectively coated. (For a discussion of selective surfaces see Section 3.1.1 and references 39 and 68). This used to be true but recent developments appear to have overcome what was one of the principal drawbacks of selective surfaces – their substantially lower absorption for short wave radiation when compared to a good matt black paint.

It would be premature to state that these improved selective surfaces are yet fully tested for use in the relatively humid UK climate. If they do prove satisfactory then single glazed selective surface collectors are likely to exhibit a superior performance in all system types when compared with that of double glazed collectors which suffer from a lower value of τ – the fraction of the incident solar radiation that reaches the collector plate. The essential reason is that their performance curve could be better than that of double glazed units at all values of

---

* This is not to say that the two should not be combined, only that the gain in performance from including both will be much less than that to accrue from adding either one alone. Many sophisticated collectors do in fact incorporate both a selective absorber and an infra-red-reflecting cover glass.

$\Delta T/I$. This is in contrast to the difference between a single glazed matt black collector and a double glazed matt black collector whose performance curves intersect; in these cases the optimum collector for use in any given installation depends upon the system characteristics.

The reason for plotting efficiency curves as shown in Figure 25 may be deduced from a simple energy balance on a collector *plate*. The maximum efficiency of heat collection occurs when the plate is losing no heat to its surroundings, and is determined by the fraction of the incident radiation I that both passes through the cover glass (if any) and is subsequently absorbed by the plate. This fraction is denoted η_{max} or η_0. At elevated plate temperatures the rate of heat loss from the plate will be given by $U\Delta T$:

U is the overall U value of the collector assembly and ΔT the temperature difference between the plate and its surroundings. Under steady state conditions

$$\text{Power In} = \text{Power Out}$$
therefore $$\eta_0 I = \eta I + U \Delta T$$
whence $$(\eta) = \eta_0 - U(\Delta T)/(I)$$

It should be clear from Figure 25 that at a $\Delta T/I$ value of X_1 collector A will exhibit a better performance whilst at X_2 collector B will be superior. Computer analysis to determine the amount of time that a system spends at each $\Delta T/I$ value may be considered necessary to determine which collector would deliver the most heat in any given system. However, collector B will be inferior to C at all temperatures and in all systems. In practice the analysis is complicated by U values that increase with temperature giving rise to a family of curves for each collector.

Vacuum-insulated flat plate collectors

The essential problem of flat plate collectors for very many years has been not their ability to convert solar radiation into heat (80 per cent conversion is readily attainable) but their inability to retain that heat at elevated temperatures. In short, their U value is too high; selectively coated absorbers can only partly solve the problem because they only suppress radiation loss.

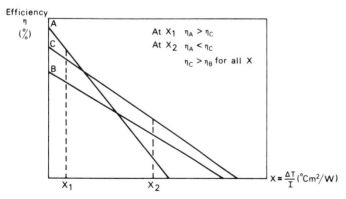

Figure 25 Linearised performance curves of three collectors A, B and C. Where: A = Single glazed, matt black absorber, B = Double glazed, matt black absorber, C = Single glazed, high absorption low emission selectively coated absorber

Most of the heat loss from even a selectively coated and double glazed collector still occurs through the cover glasses; the rear and side losses which occur only by conduction through insulation material may relatively easily be minimised.

Significant developments have taken place in the last 5 years both in Europe and the USA and prototype collectors having very low U values have been produced by Philips[52], Owens-Illinois[69] and Corning[70]. The developments are two-fold; firstly, methods of coating glass with infra-red-reflecting layers of semiconductors such as doped indium oxide and tin oxide have been further developed and secondly, methods for incorporating a high vacuum in both flat plate and tube collectors have been investigated. Such experiments are not new[71] but the 'energy crisis' of the early 1970s gave an increased impetus to the development of these ideas and prompted re-evaluation of their possible applications. It is too early to predict whether these concepts can be incorporated into collector designs that might be economically viable for use in the UK but the prospects may be reasonable for those types where a moderately increased performance is obtained by means which are amenable to low cost mass production.

A promising design at the present time appears to be the Philips unit in which high performance and low weight are obtained by using a number of evacuated and coated glass tubes (similar to fluorescent light tubes) in combination with an ordinary metal absorber plate.

Aspiring DIY enthusiasts may however be cautioned that a moderate vacuum will only suppress convection losses[72]; a pressure of less than about 1 mm of mercury (130 N/m^2) must be attained before any reduction in the conductivity of air becomes noticeable and prototype high vacuum collectors run at between 10^{-4} and 10^{-6} mmHg. A moderate vacuum will have little effect on the performance of a flat plate collector unless radiation loss is suppressed by some type of selective coating.

Honeycomb collectors

The alternative to a partial vacuum for suppressing convection heat loss between the absorber plate and cover glass of a flat plate collector is a honeycomb of either reflective or transparent foil which acts by dividing the air space into compartments each one of which is below the critical size for the onset of bulk convection[73]; most designs also achieve a measure of re-radiation loss suppression. It is possible for collectors of this type to attain high temperatures and this imposes limitations on the types of materials that can be considered as potentially suitable for the cell walls.

The other essential requirements are that the cell walls should be thin, poorly conducting, and specularly reflective; materials which exhibit substantial absorption of solar radiation can lead to reduced collector performance, particularly for incidence angles in excess of about 30°.

Usually honeycombs are only used with selective surface collector plates and these units can easily reach temperatures suitable for powering absorption air conditioners for a useful fraction of a day. Practical units with non-ideal honeycomb materials have a narrower 'acceptance angle' than do unmodified flat plate collectors and to obtain the best performance must be tracked to follow the sun; there is however no requirement for precision.

Low-ratio concentrating collectors

These types of collectors may find some application in the UK because they are still able to use a portion of the diffuse solar radiation. There is an elegant relationship between the concentration ratio of a collector for direct beam radiation and the maximum fraction of isotropically distributed radiation that it can collect when compared with a flat plate absorber of equal aperture. If the former is c the latter is $1/c$ and is realised by the 'ideal' design of Winston[74, 75]. These types of collectors, and others having broadly similar characteristics, may be considered for applications where low temperature heat is of no use but where high temperature heat is required.

An ideal application (ignoring the economics of these possibly expensive devices) would seem to be in combination with absorption cooling equipment where demand for cooling coincides (approximately) with periods of high intensity direct radiation; because of this correspondence little storage capacity need be incorporated. Another low-ratio concentrating design that appears promising for application in favourable climates makes use of so-called linear Fresnel lenses[76, 77].

The number of days in a year that the equipment could be used in the UK is of course limited, but there may be significant export potential.

High-ratio concentrating collectors

Since high power concentrating collectors cannot utilise diffuse radiation their potential for application in the UK would seem to be small, especially when their possible higher overall costs per unit of subtended area are considered. Tracking systems are often necessary with high-ratio concentrating collectors and while the potential for energy collection per square metre of subtended area can be thereby much increased the actual heat output from a system may be only slightly increased: the essential reason is that the greatest increase in potential collection occurs during the midsummer months when, for many applications, even ordinary flat plate collectors can supply nearly the full demand. Care should therefore be exercised in translating claimed collector performance levels into probable system outputs. The interested reader is referred to Meinel and Meinel[77] for a more complete discussion of concentrating collectors.

In summary, whilst advanced collector designs may have a part to play in the use of solar energy in the UK it would be over-optimistic to suppose that they will be able significantly to enhance the overall prospects. In low temperature systems, such as swimming pools, there can be little improvement over present equipment (which can deliver over 60 per cent of the summer insolation as useful heat), whilst in medium and high temperature applications doubling the collector's performance (equated perhaps to a halving of its U value) may not result in a doubling of useful output because of the negative feedback effects that occur in systems where the collector's temperature rises significantly as it delivers more energy. Clearly, if the efficiency of collection of the system was 50 per cent then no improvement could be expected to double the output! However, as already noted in Section 2.4.4, the efficiency of low U value collectors is less sensitive to temperature changes than is that of ordinary flat plate collectors, and if the price of the former fall sufficiently perhaps as a result of extensive overseas sales, high performance units may form a significant fraction of the total UK sales for domestic water heating and similar applications. A disadvantage of all high performance collectors is, of course, the ease with which they may overheat in midsummer; this problem is particularly acute in countries such as the UK which has a high ratio of summer to winter sunshine, since the summer peak levels are well above the average level. The cost of adequately protecting the system against excessive temperatures may outweigh the advantages of the increased annual efficiency.

3.1.14 Collectors using phase-change heat transfer

There have been several attempts both in the UK and overseas to use either self-contained heat pipes or freon circuits in flat plate solar collectors but there is no reliable evidence to indicate that any significant improvement in thermal performance has been achieved.

The usual reason for experimentation with these systems is an attempt to escape from the corrosion and freezing problems that can prove troublesome when using water as a heat transfer fluid. However, in view of the long term reliability and servicing problems that may result from the use of twin-phase heat transfer it seems unlikely that any significant overall advantages will be realised for flat plate collectors operating in the 0–100°C region.

3.2 Pipework

As a result of the widespread and successful use of copper tube in water service systems in the UK the properties of this material are so well known that no extensive repetition is necessary here. In summary, copper tube of suitable grades is easy to bend, solder and install and it has proved to be resistant to attack by most of the chemicals normally found in supply waters. Reputable manufacturers supply copper tube to BS 2871[58]; imported or home produced tube which does not meet this specification should be used with caution because even though it may appear identical to tube that meets the specification the possible lack of thorough cleaning, especially of the carbon film that can be present after annealing, can lead to severe corrosion. In many water systems copper is very slowly taken into solution and whilst this usually causes no problems in domestic situations it may result in corrosion in mixed-metal solar circuits. Inhibitors are available to suppress this solubility (see Section 3.6.1).

Copper has also found widespread application in motor vehicle radiators and because of this may be used with considerable confidence in indirect systems using ethylene glycol based antifreeze solutions; further details are given in Section 3.6.1. The Copper Development Association publishes leaflets detailing the properties of copper tube, and these should be consulted if specialised information is required.

Other materials that may be considered for domestic use are stainless steel and certain plastics. Stainless steel tubes may be used with a considerable degree of confidence in water supply systems and a British Standard for this material has been published[78].

BRE Digest 83[79] summarises the properties of stainless steel tube and details the precautions that should be taken when producing soldered joints.

Many types of plastic tubes have long been proposed for hot water applications but have not yet been proved totally satisfactory at high temperatures; if these materials are used in solar collector circuits it should be acknowledged that they may introduce an element of uncertainty not present with either copper or stainless steel. Of the two latter materials copper is the easier to bend and solder and for these reasons may be recommended for do-it-yourself enthusiasts. Some types of plastic pipe may however be suitable for use in swimming pool and similar systems where generation of high fluid temperatures is precluded by the use of unglazed collectors.

In cases where dissimilar metals must be joined, for example, copper tube to collector plates constructed from galvanised steel or aluminium, there can be a substantial risk of rapid bimetallic or galvanic corrosion and direct metallic connection of these metals should be avoided. The risk, in the case of galvanised steel and copper tube, may be reduced by making the join with a gunmetal fitting but for aluminium and copper the wisest course of action is to use an insulating coupling such as a length of silicone rubber coolant hose.

Flexible joints need to be introduced into solar collector circuits to accommodate thermal expansion, to take up manufacturing tolerances where header and riser plates are to be joined in parallel, and as already noted, to help prevent corrosion. Where flexible coupling is necessary silicone rubber coolant hose may be recommended in preference to any organic rubber hose, despite its high capital cost (between £2 and £5 per metre). Silicone rubber is resistant to most if not all of the chemicals

likely to be found in aqueous heat transfer fluids and may have a life in excess of 10 or 15 years. Its suitability for use with any given fluid, especially oils, should be checked with the manufacturer. Silicone hose is virtually unaffected by outdoor exposure, can tolerate temperatures in excess of 150°C, and has good long term sealing properties when clamped to clean smooth tubes.

3.3 Storage vessels

There are two basic types of storage vessels that find use in domestic hot water preheating systems; larger installations in industrial or commercial premises may incorporate different types of hardware but since these projects are usually carried out under the supervision of an engineer who is conversant with water storage technology this book deals only with domestic systems.

The terms 'tanks' and 'cisterns' are often used synonymously but this is incorrect; a tank is a vessel that stores water or other liquid under greater than atmospheric pressure whilst a cistern is a vessel that stores water or other liquid under atmospheric pressure only, and for this reason may have an open top.

3.3.1 Cisterns

Traditionally, domestic cisterns in the UK were constructed from galvanised steel, which was painted with bitumen in soft water areas in order to prevent corrosion. More recently however plastics have almost completely taken over this market and use of plastic cisterns will be assumed. If old galvanised units are considered for continued service as part of a solar heating system then two points should be noted. Galvanised cisterns should not be directly connected to copper pipework nor should they have copper heat exchanger coils installed in them; additionally, the maximum working temperature should not exceed 65°C since above this limit the protection normally afforded by the zinc can in certain circumstances be negated, and rapid corrosion can result.

It cannot generally be recommended that any attempt be made to give old galvanised cisterns a new lease of life as part of a solar heating system.

Plastic cisterns are normally used in houses both for storing cold water and as the expansion vessel for a central heating system. In solar systems plastic cisterns may, with certain reservations, be used both for storing warm water and as the expansion vessel of a solar primary circuit.

Many types of plastic cisterns are currently produced in the UK; amongst the most popular materials are glass reinforced polyester (GRP), polypropylene, and polythene. All of these have good resistance to a wide range of chemicals but the suitability for use of any particular product with a specific chemical should be checked with the manufacturer since there are many grades of these basic materials. Polythene cisterns are flexible and may be folded up so as to pass through the small loft trapdoors that are a feature of too many UK houses but their maximum working temperature is low and they should not be used as storage vessels for solar heated water. GRP cisterns may have similar temperature limits (depending very much on the type of resin used in their construction) but polypropylene cisterns are usually suitable for hot water and so may be used with some confidence; they are also likely to be suitable for use with antifreeze solutions.

The basic installation rules that apply to all plastic cisterns are that they should be located on a firm level base which extends under the full area of the cistern – and that the pipework should be connected using only the correct types of washers. Additionally, it is important to ensure that stress is not transferred to the cistern from any of the connecting pipework. Failure to observe these rules may result in both leakage and irreparable damage to the cistern. Since cisterns are often installed in loft spaces proper support must be provided – simply laying a piece of plywood anywhere on the ceiling joists is un-likely to be satisfactory in view of the weight of the cistern when full – a 225 litre (50 gallon) cistern full of water weighs 225 kg (500 lb) and can easily cause structural damage. Installing the cistern on a piece of 20 or 25 mm plywood which itself is located on the ceiling joists above a loadbearing internal wall will usually be satisfactory but special provision will have to be made in houses having no loadbearing internal walls. The essential requirements here are that the load should be spread between several trusses and taken at those points most able to bear such forces[80].

Additional precautions, in addition to ensuring that usual good practice is followed with respect to the positioning of valves and overflow (warning) pipes, are to ensure that where a float valve is used with hot water it is suitable for this duty, and that where the solar system is a draindown type the cistern(s) are of sufficient capacity relative to the capacity of the solar collectors, so as to ensure that undue lifting force is not applied to the float assembly when draining occurs.

Any cistern used in a loft space should be fitted with a suitable cover designed so that water condensing on the underside of the cover is returned to the cistern and can-not drip externally; this is particularly important where hot water is to be stored. The cover should be close fitting, and the whole cistern (excepting the underside) together with all the connecting pipework should be well insulated.

3.3.2 Cylinders

The most common forms of hot water storage vessels in UK houses are copper cylinders and since these usually give long and troublefree service if properly installed they can be recommended for the storage of solar heated water. In a few areas the supply water may be so aggressive that stainless steel has to be used, but this is rare and a

reputable plumber will be able to advise on any local difficulties. It is a mistake however to regard use of stainless steel as a panacea for corrosion problems.

Copper cylinders are very expensive in terms of cost per litre of storage when compared with plastic cisterns but can in many situations be more convenient, and can give a better thermal performance because of the greater ease with which stratification may be produced*.

Good quality copper cylinders will meet either BS699[81] or BS1566[82] and these should always be used in preference to any cheaper alternatives. Cylinders are available in several 'grades', the difference being the thickness of the copper sheet and, consequently, the safe working pres-sure. Indirect cylinders of a size suitable for domestic use are supplied with a heat exchanger coil wound from 28 mm copper tube and may be used in all indirect types of solar circuits, subject to the local water undertaking's approval of the heat transfer fluid. Indirect cylinders to BS1566 having corrugated annular heat exchangers have a higher ratio of minimum heat exchange surface to stored water volume than do the coil type but cannot be used with high pressure primary circuits; the increased heat exchanger area is necessary to compensate for lower fluid velocities, but that of both coil and annular types may be insufficient to ensure efficient operation of solar circuits. Some UK manufacturers now offer cylinders with a greater heat exchanger area than required by BS1566 and their use may be recommended especially in areas where the supply water has a high temporary hardness.

In overseas countries indirect cylinders having their heat exchangers wound externally have apparently been used in order to overcome objections to the use of toxic heat transfer fluids. It is possible that these designs may be introduced into the UK if continued use of toxic anti-freezes and inhibitors is considered essential for some types of indirect circuits. The thermal efficiency of external heat exchangers will depend strongly on the integrity of the joint between the coil and the wall of the cylinder. Similar strictures as noted above for the installation of cisterns apply equally to cylinders; they should be located on a structurally sound base and should be well insulated (see Section 2.3.7). Single feed cylinders are not suitable for use in solar circuits.

3.4 Pumps and valves

3.4.1 Pumps

Several types of pumps have been used in domestic solar heating systems in the UK but it is probable that the most reliable of these will be the units originally designed for high temperature operation in central heating circuits. Lower powered pumps of the type usually employed to

---

* Unfortunately the very high thermal conductivity of copper may be significant in subsequently destroying any stratification; if conduction alone is considered the heat flow down the cylinder walls will be typically five times that through the water, but neither term is important for diurnal storage systems.

operate garden fountains have been used by some companies who installed Type 3 systems (see Section 2.2.2) but these cannot be expected to exhibit a long working life if they are used at temperatures in excess of their design limits. Central heating pumps are correctly described as centrifugal accelerators, and their construction renders them tolerant of a wide range of operating conditions; this is in contrast to other pump designs where the unit must be closely matched to its intended duty. Some pumps must be installed with their motor axis horizontal: manufacturers' instructions should be followed. Three different materials are commonly used to construct the bodies of centrifugal accelerators: cast iron, bronze and stainless steel. The cheapest and most commonly used is the cast iron type, and this is suitable for many heat transfer fluids but not for supply water; cast iron bodied pumps must not be used in open systems. Both bronze and stainless steel are more resistant to corrosion than cast iron and either type may safely be used with most supply waters.

Most pumps intended for central heating duty have input ratings of between 60 and 130 W and are too large for a small solar system having short pipe runs. Recently, at least one major manufacturer has indicated the imminent introduction of low wattage pumps specially designed for small solar circuits; these should be used if they develop sufficient power for the system in question. Design rules for sizing pumps are given in Section 4.3. In view of the fact that pumps may need occasional repair or replacement it is considered good practice to fit isolating valves; removal may then be accomplished without draining the system. Many pumps are now sold complete with connectors having integral ball valves and this simplifies installation. In some cases however the rubber sealing rings and gaskets in both pumps and couplings may prove unsuitable for use with oils, and alternatives must be specified.

There are two aspects of pumped circulation solar systems which are both important and often misunderstood; these are considered below. Venturi effects and thermosyphon pressures have been assumed negligible.

Pumpover (Pumping over)

Pumpover can occur in vented indirect circuits and usually arises either from bad layout or incorrect pump or pipe sizing. A simple illustration of how the phenomenon may occur is given in Figure 26.

The fluid leaving the pump outlet at A clearly has a choice of two return paths, it may either flow round the closed loop A B C D E or go by way of the cistern. The latter will occur whenever the pressure head developed by fluid flowing in B C D exceeds the head necessary to force fluid to the top of the vent pipe (point G). In the limiting case, (if for example a valve at C was closed) the fluid would have the choice of remaining stationary or of pumping over but even in this extreme case could be prevented from doing so if the vertical distance F G was sufficient to produce a stall condition in the pump

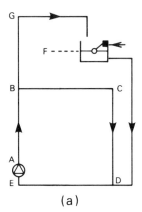 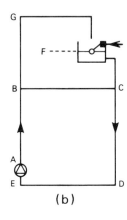

Figure 26 Conditions for the occurrence of pumpover: (a) Pumpover occurs, (b) Pumpover does not occur

(for typical pumps F G would have to be between about 2 and 8 metres). Pumpover may easily be prevented by good system design and in the example given it might be thought that the risk could be lessened by transferring the feed from D to C as in Figure 26b.

In this case pumpover would certainly be less likely to occur but, as will be seen, parts of the system are then more likely to run under a negative pressure condition.

Negative pressure

The term 'negative pressure' is commonly used to describe a situation in which a section of circuit is under less than atmospheric pressure when the pump is running. Pressures must of course always be positive relative to a perfect vacuum but if zero is defined as atmospheric pressure then clearly a vacuum is at -1 bar (-10^5 N/m²). The term 'negative pressure' is synonymous with 'sub-atmospheric pressure'. Negative pressure may be described as an insidious disease of plumbing circuits; it is common, seldom recognised, and can have serious consequences for the system lifetime because of the corrosion that can be induced.

In the circuit shown in Figure 27a the greatest reduction in pressure caused by pumping is clearly at the pump

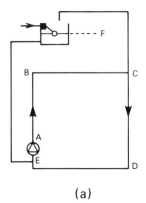 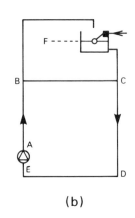

Figure 27 Conditions for the occurrence of negative pressure: (a) Negative pressure cannot occur unless pumpover occurs, (b) Negative pressure may occur if CDE contains high resistance elements

inlet (point E) and if this is kept under a pressure greater than atmospheric by having the feed connected to it then no part of the circuit can ever be at a pressure less than atmospheric assuming that pumpover does not occur. However, if the circuit shown in Figure 27b is constructed then the section C D E may at some point be at a pressure less than atmospheric and if any slight leak exists then the fluid will become oxygenated as a result of air being sucked in.

The design condition is clearly that the suction head developed at any point in the length of pipe C D E must be less than the static pressure head at that point calculated from level F; (when these two pressures are exactly equal and opposite the absolute pressure will equal atmospheric, and the gauge pressure will be zero). In some solar installations in the UK this condition may not be satisfied; most trouble may occur in Type 5 systems (see Section 2.2.2).

If for some reason the flow through the pump must be limited by closing off a valve this should always be done on the pressure (outlet) side since restricting the inlet can cause a high negative pressure in the pump and cavitation damage may occur. Flow limitation using valves is however not generally to be recommended.

The fundamental design rules that should be followed to prevent pumpover and negative pressure conditions in simple domestic systems are that:

1 the feed from the cistern should be taken to a point close to the inlet of the pump. If some separation is desired (for example, in Type 5c systems) then that part of the circuit joining the feed and the pump inlet should have a low flow resistance.
2 the vent pipe must rise sufficiently far above the free water surface to prevent pumpover.

An equivalent design rule for central heating systems, the importance of which is illustrated below, is that where the available height above the top of the circuit is limited the pump should be situated in the flow from the boiler and not in the more usual position in the return to the boiler. The essential point to appreciate here is that in the latter case the vent pipe is on the pressure side of the pump whilst in the former it is on the suction side. Detailed analysis of the absolute pressures in vented plumbing

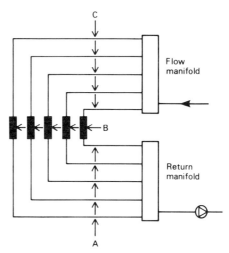

Figure 29 Location of areas of negative pressure in the author's central heating system. The balance points (see text) move from A through B to C as radiator valves are progressively closed. The sections of circuit between the return manifold and the balance points run under a negative pressure. In the circuits that are closed off a high negative pressure extends from the return manifold to the radiator valve. Pressures due to gravity are ignored

circuits may be reduced to consideration of the boundary conditions under which the system is constrained to operate; in practice these conditions are provided by the reference pressures at the locations where either vent or feed pipes join the main circuit, but it must be remembered that the fluid level in vent pipes can vary over wide limits.

In order to illustrate the above analysis the author used the central heating system in his own flat which had been installed as shown in Figure 28. It is apparent that pumpover is unlikely to occur because the vent and feed pipes are taken from points of almost equal pressure (essentially from the flow and return of the boiler). It is evident that if all the radiator valves were turned fully on, the flow resistance of all the parallel circuits might be sufficiently low to prevent the generation of negative pressure in the radiators; this situation is realised in practice as was proved by opening each radiator air vent in turn and observing that water escaped under pressure.

However, if the three largest microbore circuits were turned off the total flow rate decreased and the suction head developed increased; if the air vents on the remaining radiators were now opened no water escaped but there was no evidence of suction – the pressure at these air vents was now close to atmospheric. Closing off one more radiator circuit decreased the pressure in the rest of the radiators to below atmospheric and air could be drawn in at the air vents on the radiators that were still operative. These effects are as predicted and still occurred after the pump flow control had been reduced from maximum to its median position.

Figure 29 shows how the balance point (where the absolute pressure in the circuit equals atmospheric) moves round the circuit as radiator valves are progressively closed.

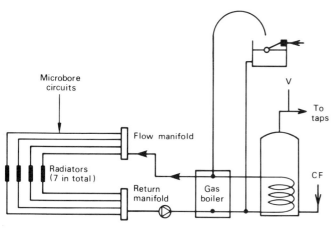

Figure 28 Layout of the author's central heating system

The effects of incorrect system design, whether in a solar or central heating circuit are sometimes minimal, as in the case described above so long as all the radiator valves are kept fully open. However, potentially damaging effects could easily occur if thermostatic radiator valves were fitted to the same circuit since many of these might be expected to be closed for much of the operating periods. Such problems have been observed in practice[83]. Systems using automatic air vents of either the float operated or self-sealing type* (the latter are often fitted to radiators in place of a key operated vent) can suffer as a result of large quantities of air being admitted to the circuit.

It seems to be true that whilst most plumbers have heard of pumpover and know how to prevent it (by placing the vent and feed pipe connections close together as described above) some do not seem to be conversant with negative pressure and this may be one of the reasons why iron and steel components in some central heating systems in the UK have relatively short lives.

The view is sometimes expressed that if a mixed-metal central heating or solar system is dosed with corrosion inhibitors and is observed not to exhibit pumpover then it can be assured of a long and trouble free life. Unfortunately, nothing could be further from the truth!

Details of central heating system design have been published by HVCA[84] and BSI[85], but the fact that some systems are not installed in accordance with these guidelines should serve as a warning to purchasers of solar systems many types of which are very sensitive to being installed incorrectly; simple and proven tests that can be applied to check their efficiency of operation are not yet available (but see Section 2.2.1).

3.4.2 Manually-operated valves

Many types of valves may be used in solar collector systems, and brief descriptions of the most common are given below; the suitability of any particular valve for use with any fluid should however always be checked with the manufacturer or supplier. Pressure-relief valves are discussed in Section 3.5.

Stopcocks

These valves, commonly used at the principal cut off point in domestic water systems, are characterised by their ability to achieve a leakfree seal against high pressures even after many years of service. The underlying reason for this is that the seal is made by a washer of compressible material which can be screwed down hard on to a metal seating; slight imperfections in either of the mating surfaces, for example caused by erosion or scale formation, can therefore be accommodated. Stopcocks

have a moderate to high flow resistance and should never be used as part of a thermosyphon circuit; their use in solar collector systems will probably be confined to the filling point in sealed primary circuits and for this specific application a non-return type may be specified if the circuit is to be filled directly from the mains supply. Many types of stopcocks are only suitable for use with cold water and especial care must be exercised if they are specified for use with heat transfer oils or other fluids that may attack the internal rubber components. BS 1010[86] covers the types of stopcocks commonly used in housing.

Draincocks

Draincocks should be fitted at all the low points of any system so that the complete system may be drained if required; it is important that the drain points are installed in such a position that subsequent addition of a hose is possible. Standard types of draincocks perform well and share with stopcocks the characteristic of being able to close securely against high pressure. Some types do however tend to leak when discharging and a more suitable alternative in some applications may be a small ball valve.

Gate and globe valves

There are many different designs of gate and globe valves and some of the more popular types are covered by BS 5154[87]. Gate valves are generally characterised by a low flow resistance and in complicated circuits where many valves have to be used they may be recommended.

Many of these valves rely upon perfect fitting metal to metal seats to achieve a seal and must be treated accordingly; some types are particularly sensitive to foreign particles being trapped between the seating faces and should only therefore be used in very clean circuits. As a general rule parallel-slide gate valves and globe valves with renewable disc seatings are the least susceptible to permanent damage. Many of these valves are suitable for steam water or oil applications and may be used with confidence in most solar collector circuits.

It is not generally recommended that valves are used to regulate flow resistance in a circuit and this applies especially to those valves where the metal mating surfaces might be eroded by fluid travelling at a high velocity if the valve were used in a half-open position; as a general rule both gate and globe valves should only be used in the fully-open or fully-closed positions.

Ball valves

There are a variety of ball valves available in sizes from 12 mm upwards and some types are very suitable for use in situations where space is limited since they can be

---

* Frequently referred to as hygroscopic air vents.

44

operated either by a screwdriver or Allen key. Depending upon their construction ball valves may incorporate rubber O-ring seals and/or PTFE or other plastic seats and it is very important to ensure that these are of a type that is suitable for the fluid to be used; different sealing materials are commonly used for hot water, cold water or oil and some are only suitable for their specific intended duty. Many of these valves are however only produced in hot-pressed brass which can be subject to dezincification when used with some supply waters[15]. Some types can be used for flow regulation and are not adversely affected by small amounts of suspended solids since there is a wiping action on the ball faces as they rotate.

Non-return (check) valves

There are many different designs of check valves but broadly they can be classified into direct weight operated types and swing types. Designs are available for use in both horizontal and vertical pipes but in the latter case the valve must of course be installed in a pipe where the normal direction of fluid flow is vertically upwards.

Since a significant pressure drop is developed across check valves they should not be used in solar powered gravity (thermosyphon) circuits.

Automatic air vents (air-release valves)

Most automatic air vents intended for use in domestic plumbing systems operate on the principle of a float which is denser than air but less dense than the fluid that is contained in the circuit. This latter qualification is important since some valves intended for duty on water circuits may not operate so satisfactorily with low density oils. Unfortunately some of the valves currently produced have a tendency to stick in the closed position and can only be revived by a sharp tap; since these valves will often be situated in inaccessible and infrequently visited loft spaces some improvement in their design would appear desirable.

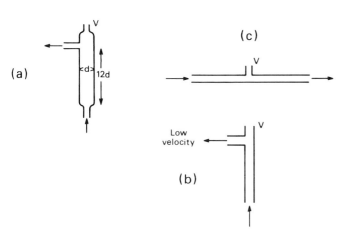

Figure 30 Design of venting points for use with automatic air-release valves: (a) Preferred design, (b) Acceptable design with low fluid velocity, (c) Poor design.

Much of the trouble sometimes encountered with automatic air vents is due to inadequate design of the pipework in the neighbourhood of the valve. As a general rule the fluid velocity in this area should be low so that any bubbles of gas have a chance of escaping; if fluid velocities are too high then both intuition and experiment lead to the conclusion that the bubbles will simply be dragged past the valve and it is only when the pump stops operating that the small amount of gas that may be contained in the length of pipe directly beneath the valve is permitted to rise and escape.

Examples of good and bad practice are shown in Figure 30.

3.4.3 Electrically operated valves

Electrically operated valves that would be suitable for use on domestic or other small solar heating systems can be classified into two types – solenoid operated and motorised.

Solenoid operated valves are generally characterised by high head loss and rapid switching, which can lead to water hammer* being produced. In addition, power must, with most types, be supplied continually if the valve is to be kept open. The main virtues of solenoid valves are their ability to open and close rapidly and repeatedly and to close very securely against high pressures; for many applications servo-operated types are available which utilise the fluid pressure to assist with opening and closing of the main valve port. These are not characteristics that are often required in solar circuits and it seems unlikely that solenoid valves will be used extensively in these applications.

Motorised valves, as their name suggests, are operated by an electric motor. There are many types of small motorised valves and it is important that their respective characteristics are fully appreciated since outwardly similar models may not both be suited to any given application. Some types of motorised valves are likely to seize if used with water of high temporary hardness and in a part of the system where deposition occurs; the risk of failure is greater the less the valves are used. The following discussion relates only to non-modulating valves used as diverters.

The critical design feature of a so called lift-and-lay 3-port valve is that if is is used as a diverter (where the valve has one inlet and 2 possible outlets) water hammer may be produced if the valve is energized when the fluid is circulating, because of the very rapid closure that can take place as the valve plug nears one of its seatings. This type of 3-port valve should usually only be used as a mixer (where the valve has 2 inlets and one outlet), and may be used as a diverter if it is switched only when the

---

* In this section the term 'water-hammer' is used to describe the high pressure pulsations that can occur when a liquid flowing in a pipe is brought suddenly to a stop by the rapid closure of a valve; since the phenomenon most frequently occurs in water systems the origin of the name needs no further explanation.

fluid velocity is at or near zero; the latter conditions can rarely be guaranteed and it is preferable to use one of the rotary shoe types of design which are far less prone to producing water hammer.

There are two distinct types of motors used to operate these valves; either the motor is energised all the time that the valve is required to remain in one of its positions and subsequently returns under spring action: or the valve is electrically driven throughout its operating periods.

In the latter design, an internal switch cuts off the motor current when the valve reaches one of its extreme positions and the motor is subsequently energised via a second feed wire. The latter type of control requires a changeover switch whilst the former requires only a simple on–off switch and ideally should be used only in circuits where the motor will be kept energised for short periods.

The alternative solution, which may be preferable if high flow resistance must not be introduced into the circuits, is to use two 2-port valves for each diverter application. The 2-port valves could in theory use either type of motor (spring-return or driven in both directions) but in practice the latter are almost universally used and are very suitable for complex solar systems where valves may spend long periods in either open or closed positions. If this system is used then upon changeover being initiated one valve closes as the other opens and the limit switches in each motor cut off the electrical supply as each valve reaches its new position. When 2-port valves are used in this way it is often important that the motors are not wired in parallel (that is, that no attempt be made to use only one changeover switch to control both valves): the reason for this lies in the internal circuitry of the motors. A satisfactory solution is to use separate changeover contacts for each valve with the poles wired in parallel to the mains supply. The electrical consumption of most small motorised valves is about 4–6 W and may usually be neglected in energy balance calculations.

Many 2 and 3-port valves are limited both by an absolute pressure and a differential pressure; the former is the maximum pressure that any part of the valve may be subjected to and the latter is the maximum pressure difference that the valve will be able to close against. Some trade literature states that valves are not suitable for use on mains water supplies but this usually relates to the excessive differential pressure that may be encountered and not to any corrosion that could occur – many valves can in fact be used on oxygenated and chlorinated water but this should always be checked with the manufacturers' technical advice department. A few 2 and 3-port valves are suitable for oil but they can be more expensive than those intended for water service; no attempt should be made to use the latter types with oil-based heat transfer fluids.

Whilst no small 3-port valves are available with very low flow resistances several types of 2-port valves have a low resistance and may be used in solar gravity circulation systems; in this application valves should preferably

have a k_v value of at least 15 (15 m³/h to produce a 1 bar pressure drop; such a valve would have a flow resistance equal to about 4 m of 28 mm copper tube or 1·2 m of 22 mm tube).

3.5 Sealed system equipment

The use of sealed system equipment is illustrated in Section 2: the underlying advantages of sealed systems are that corrosion rates can be reduced and system flexibility (as regards the relative positioning of components) can be much increased. Sealed system equipment for a small solar installation will typically comprise an expansion vessel, automatic air vents, one or more pressure-relief valves, a filling point, and a pressure gauge.

The basic operation of all of the equipment is easy to understand; the expansion vessel provides for expansion of the working fluid in the primary circuit by means of a diaphragm acting on a cushion of air or nitrogen. The pressure-relief (safety) valve is a very necessary device especially in circuits where the working fluid could reach its boiling point, and one or more automatic air vents replace the open vent pipe.

One of the most important design criteria for any solar system is that all the hardware should be suitable for use with the chosen heat transfer fluid and this is particularly important with sealed system equipment because of the number of rubber components that are used. Nitrile and viton rubbers are generally compatible with mineral oils.

Since sealed systems operate at relatively high pressures it is important to ensure that every component is suitable for use at the maximum pressure that it could experience in service. With the pump inoperative this pressure is determined by the safety valve setting and, for components located below the safety valve, the additional static head so imposed. When the pump is operating some parts of the circuit may experience an additional pressure, the limiting value of which is the stall head of the pump (typically 2–8 m of water or about 0·2–0·8 bar).

The expansion vessel should be sized according to the volume of primary fluid, having due regard to its likely maximum operating temperature and its volume expansion coefficient. The expansion vessel may be placed at any point in the circuit provided that the system is charged to a sufficiently high static pressure, but should preferably be located near to the inlet of the pump; ease of subsequent maintenance should however be considered. The fluid connection on the expansion vessel should be installed uppermost so that air cannot be trapped and a short deadleg from this to the main circuit will ensure that the diaphragm is not subjected to very high fluid temperatures, thus prolonging its life. It is an advantage if the pressure test point on the expansion vessel is left accessible, and the necessary initial gas pressure will be determined by the position of the expansion vessel relative to the top of the system; for domestic situations where the overall height of the system does not exceed 5 m an initial gas pressure of 0·5 bar is usually adequate. Excessive initial gas pressure must *not* be used because under working conditions there may then be no reserve liquid capacity in the expansion vessel.

The volume of heat transfer fluid that should initially be installed should preferably be such that there is a minimum gauge pressure of 30 kN/m² (0·3 bar) at the top of the system. This should ensure that negative pressures (see Section 3.4.1) are not produced with the pump running; the risk is greatest if the expansion vessel is placed near the outlet of the pump. This minimum pressure must be maintained with the system at its coolest so an allowance should be made for the system temperature at time of installation and a slightly higher pressure than required is no disadvantage especially if it may be expected that air will vent from the circuit when it first becomes hot.

The positioning of the safety valve and pressure gauge (often combined into a single unit) is not critical in a small solar system because of the low rates of increase of temperature that could be expected at high operating temperatures; this contrasts with situations in which sealed systems are used with fossil fuel boilers capable of delivering tens of kilowatts at high temperatures. The safety valve must however be installed on a pipe which is connected to the solar panels without any intervening check or isolating valve.

The outlet from the safety valve should be taken either to waste or to a suitably sized container but, preferably, should have an atmospheric break to ensure that any blockage in the discharge pipe does not render the system dangerous. It will often be convenient to site the safety valve in the loft and to take the outlet to waste alongside the existing warning pipes. It should be noted that even if the maximum stagnation temperature attainable by the collectors is below the nominal boiling point of the transfer fluid a safety valve must still be installed, both to prevent excessive pressures during filling of the system and to preclude the risk of an explosion during a fire*. Since any discharge will usually consist of hot fluid containing oil or glycol the overflow pipe should, preferably, not terminate above a footpath or patio area. Additionally, oil filled systems must not discharge onto a felted garage roof or similar structure since damage to the membrane could occur.

The pressure gauge should be fitted in an easily viewed position in the airing cupboard or other frequently used space and the householder instructed to the effect that if the pressure falls below a clearly marked level the system should be inspected both for leaks and for faults that would cause boiling. If the pressure fluctuates over an unduly wide range reaching the safety valve setting on hot sunny days this indicates either that the expansion vessel is too small, or that its gas pressure is low (or far too high), or that the diaphragm has failed.

* Explosions are usually associated with gas-filled rather than liquid-filled systems (hence hydraulic testing of gas cylinders), but sudden release of super-heated liquid can be just as dangerous.

Automatic air vents should be fitted at the high points of the system especially if the heat transfer fluid contains dissolved gases; if oils are used then manual venting of the system during commissioning may be adequate if its design ensures that no pockets of air can be trapped. In all cases the pump should be stopped and started a few times to drive any air to the top of the system where it should collect under the air vents and be expelled; it is a mistake to run the pump continually during this initial venting since large pockets of air may simply be dragged at high speed straight past the air vents (see Section 3.4.2). For large systems a 'centrifugal' air separator should give good results but is an unnecessary expense on a small domestic system.

It should be noted that some installers use a manifold to which all the sealed system equipment with the exception of the air vents is connected. These manifolds are often valved to facilitate maintenance and the possibility therefore exists that a valve may inadvertently be closed thus depriving the solar circuit of both its expansion vessel and safety valve. Under these conditions high pressure could be generated in a very short time and due care should be taken if these types of manifolds are used. In large systems, each collector array that is capable of being isolated from the main circuit should preferably have its own safety valve.

In order to accommodate very small leaks in sealed circuits automatic top-up equipment is available and consists of a non-return valve fitted below a 1 or 2 litre reservoir of fluid. Under normal operating conditions the pressure in the circuit exceeds that in the reservoir (which is open to atmosphere) and the valve remains shut. If a leak results in the circuit pressure falling to nearly atmospheric the valve should open to admit additional fluid. In all cases the reservoir must be fitted above the topmost point of the circuit and a distance of about 3 metres would be necessary if the minimum pressure of 0·3 bar referred to above was to be maintained. Since sealed systems are often used in situations where headroom is limited it is clear that this distance may not be available, but if the automatic top-up equipment is connected to the circuit near to the inlet of the pump (with the reservoir at high level) a satisfactory pressure will be maintained unless the non-return valve sticks. The only universally satisfactory solution to these problems is of course to find and cure the leak. In view of these difficulties it is advisable to use capillary-soldered or cone joints wherever possible.

Sealed circuits may conveniently be pressurised using an adapted 2 or 3 litre garden sprayer of the type designed for insecticides and this forms a suitable low-cost solution for the DIY enthusiast. The author has successfully used this type of equipment on several solar systems and whilst no long term problems should occur with water, oils or undiluted glycol antifreezes may produce softening or cracking in some of the plastic components and since the resulting explosion could be dangerous these fluids should only be installed using equipment that has been approved by the fluid manufacturer. In many systems it will be acceptable to install most of the fluid charge via a filling

47

point at high level; the amount of fluid that must subsequently be introduced under pressure is therefore kept to a minimum.

A possible disadvantage of air pressure operated equipment is however that the fluid is aerated before being introduced into the circuit but this should not cause any lasting difficulty.

A review of sealed system equipment for large installations has recently been published[88].

3.6 Heat transfer fluids

The fluids considered in this section comprise those that are often used in solar collector circuits where the system is designed to operate in the temperature range $-20\,°C$ to $+200\,°C$. The use of heat transfer fluids in domestic situations is treated in some detail because it is in this area that concern may be expressed regarding some current practice.

Liquid-phase heat transfer fluids may be divided into two groups – aqueous and non-aqueous. The aqueous fluids normally contain over 50 per cent of water as a base and the additives are either antifreezes and/or corrosion inhibitors. The useful working range of these fluids is usually up to about $100\,°C$ but in a sealed pressurised circuit $130\,°C$ may be practicable.

The principal problems associated with aqueous fluids are the corrosion of metals and the eventual decomposition of antifreezes and corrosion inhibitors. The two problems are related since some decomposition products can promote corrosion.

Corrosion in systems using aqueous fluids is always a possibility because of the aggressive nature of water: this may be enhanced when dissolved mineral salts are present, but the degree of corrosion experienced may depend as much on the design of the system as on the composition of the fluid.

Non-aqueous heat transfer fluids are usually based on a mineral or silicone oil and can have a working temperature range well in excess of that required for a solar water heating system in the UK. The principal disadvantages of many of these fluids are their inferior thermal properties when compared to those of water, and their higher viscosity and cost.

3.6.1 Aqueous fluids and corrosion inhibitors

One of the more common heat transfer fluids used to date in solar systems in the UK has been a 20–30 per cent solution of ethanediol (ethylene glycol). The properties of ethanediol are well known from experience in motor vehicle cooling systems where it has been used for many years. Addition of other chemicals, often at 1 per cent or lower concentration, is necessary and these act not only as corrosion inhibitors but also help retard breakdown of the ethanediol.

Ideally, maintenance might be restricted to an annual check of the pH, the freezing point and the inhibitor strength of the solution and renewing when necessary but since this is likely to be outside the scope of most householders the alternative is to flush the system and renew the fluid every 2 years. This course of action may be recommended until such time as reliable data on the effective life of inhibitors when used in these systems becomes available. In the absence of specific guidance from the system supplier the wisest procedure would be to use distilled water for both flushing and for making up the new working fluid, but with an all-copper system this may be an unnecessary expense.

It must be emphasised that ethanediol and also some of the corrosion inhibitors that are used have toxic properties and this may preclude their application in domestic solar systems having only a single-wall heat exchanger. There are however certain other options, and many companies now use propanediol (propylene glycol) as the basic antifreeze constituent. Proprietary fluids based on propanediol have been approved by the National Water Council for use in domestic solar systems, but there is as yet little knowledge of their expected useful life under these conditions and the same maintenance recommendations as outlined above for ethanediol should apply. It is however emphasised that future work may show that longer periods can safely elapse between fluid changes and the interval of 2 years quoted above should not be taken as other than interim advice.

Amongst the less commonly considered additives for water are glycerol and potassium carbonate, both of which can serve as freezing point depressants. Any system that uses these additives must be able to resist any corrosive properties that the fluid may exhibit.

In general, corrosion in systems using aqueous fluids is encouraged by the following factors:
1. the presence of dissolved oxygen
2. the presence of chloride ions (which may be introduced from flux residues or from supply water)
3. the presence of more than one metal in the circuit
4. the presence of crevices or 'dead-ends' in the system in which free circulation of the fluid cannot occur.

All of these factors are interrelated; in general, removal of any dissolved oxygen from the system may be expected to reduce the tendency of metals to corrode. A notable example from the field of housing is the lack of appreciable corrosion in well designed and properly installed wet central heating systems: some initial corrosion does occur but, due to the dissolved oxygen reacting with the steel radiators, the rate of corrosion then falls to a very low and acceptable level. This continuing corrosion produces magnetite (black iron oxide) which is normally adherent to the steel surface, and which usually causes no trouble.

It is perhaps worth noting, as an illustration of the importance of good basic system design, that the consensus of expert opinion is that well designed and properly installed wet central heating systems that use steel radiators will not benefit from the addition of corrosion inhibitors. Unfortunately, the same may not be true of solar systems in which the same combination of metals is used since it may also be necessary to provide high concentrations of antifreeze additives.

The corrosion behaviour of aluminium and aluminium alloys (hereafter termed simply 'aluminium') is very much dependent on the composition of the material, water composition and pH, cleanliness of the system and, particularly, the presence of copper in the system and dissolved in the water (as copper ions). With the best combination of circumstances aluminium may have good corrosion resistance; for example, in a clean system using pure water (distilled or deionised) with no copper present. Where these conditions are not met it will be necessary to use inhibitors. Direct metallic contact between these two metals is not essential for troubles to occur since small traces of copper dissolved from one part of the system may deposit on the aluminium and cause galvanic (bimetallic) corrosion. These galvanic processes are encouraged by the presence of dissolved oxygen but should be of less importance in well de-aerated sealed systems.

In the case of stainless steel the presence of some dissolved oxygen is usually advisable to maintain the integrity of the oxide film on the metal surface, this film being responsible for the 'stainless' condition. Nevertheless, under clean conditions, stainless steel should not corrode at the lowest levels of oxygen content that are likely to be achieved in sealed solar circuits.

All metals are likely to be prone to some degree of corrosion in crevice regions particularly in the presence of water containing dissolved oxygen. (This same phenomenon can give trouble in respect of fixing solar collectors to roofs and is further considered in Section 5.4). System design should therefore aim to minimise the number of such areas, especially within collector plate waterways.

Despite good basic system design it may still be necessary to use corrosion inhibitors. This is particularly the case when antifreezes are used since their chemical decomposition over a period of time may lead to the production of acidic conditions within the system.

Many chemicals can be used as corrosion inhibitors but their effectiveness is by no means universal since their inhibitive properties are usually specific towards particular metals and alloys. Also, their effectiveness may be decreased by particular conditions such as the concentration of dissolved oxygen and the presence of other chemicals in the same system. In many cases it is necessary to use a combination of two or more inhibitors.

A summary of the more commonly used inhibitors and their properties is given below although it must be emphasised that the conditions obtaining in any particular system may influence these properties. In general all of these comments apply equally to water and to ethanediol or propanediol solutions.

Sodium benzoate

Sodium benzoate is a good inhibitor for mild steel and for soldered joints, is reasonably effective for aluminium, perhaps less so for copper, and ineffective for cast iron. Thus, circulating pumps with cast iron bodies or impellers might still corrode in benzoate-inhibited systems.

Sodium nitrite

Sodium nitrite is an effective inhibitor for mild steel and cast iron, less effective for copper and aluminium and corrosive towards soldered joints. Doubts have been expressed about its use in de-aerated fluids because of the possibility of chemical reduction to ammonia which could then lead to corrosion of copper and brass.

Benzotriazole

Benzotriazole is an excellent inhibitor for copper but of limited effectiveness for other metals. It is often used in conjunction with other inhibitors (see below), and here its function is usually one of preventing activity by copper in mixed metal systems.

Sodium tetraborate (borax)

Borax is a good inhibitor for steel and has some inhibitive properties for other metals. It is not usually recommended for use with aluminium, but is contained in antifreeze to BS 3152[89] which is sometimes advocated for car engines containing aluminium alloys.

Sodium mercaptobenzothiazole

This compound is a good inhibitor for copper but less effective for other metals. It does however have limited solubility at ambient temperatures and its concentration can fall rapidly in systems containing a large area of copper.

It is used in antifreeze to BS 3150[90] but for most purposes has been superseded by benzotriazole.

Triethanolammonium phosphate

This compound is a good inhibitor for aluminium but can cause corrosion of copper and so lead to loss of effectiveness with aluminium. It is not however very effective with cast iron and steel but is used in antifreeze to BS 3150 which was formulated for all-alloy engines.

Sodium benzoate and sodium nitrite

This is a widely used mixture being the basis of several proprietary products sold for central heating systems, and is used in BS 3151 antifreeze[91].

The combination of benzoate and nitrite, usually used in the proportions 10:1 and to a total concentration of about 1 per cent (10,000 ppm benzoate and 1000 ppm nitrite) overcomes some of the deficiencies of the separate constituents but some concern about its behaviour in de-aerated systems remains. Its performance in systems containing copper could probably be improved by the addition of benzotriazole at a concentration of between 100 and 200 ppm. In many systems the nitrite may be gradually used up, and maintenance of an adequate concentration can be important if severe local attack of iron or steel is to be prevented.

Sodium tetraborate and sodium nitrite

This is a cheaper alternative to a mixture of benzoate and nitrite but can be nonprotective to soft solders.

The problem of nitrite decomposition under de-aerated conditions may still prove troublesome and, as with benzoate-nitrite, the concentration of nitrite should be maintained if iron and steel components are to remain fully protected. The mixture is used at concentrations between 0·3 and 1·0 per cent with a borate:nitrite ratio of 10:1. For systems containing copper, benzotriazole may be added at a concentration of 100–200 ppm (0·01–0·02 per cent).

Dichlorophen

A biocide is often used in water systems to prevent the growth of unwanted bacteria – which in severe cases can produce residues capable of blocking filters and impairing the performance of heat exchangers. The most commonly used biocide is the sodium salt of dichlorophen at a concentration of between 50 and 100 ppm. Maintenance of an adequate but not excessive concentration of biocide can be an important factor in determining the useful life of an inhibitor system. This is particularly the case with mixtures based on benzoate-nitrite.

Other inhibitors

In addition to the above, various undisclosed inhibitor formulations are on the market. The effectiveness of these will vary according to both the product and the conditions of use and the manufacturers should be consulted for data on the performance to be expected in any given situation.

In all cases the local water undertaking should be consulted before corrosion inhibitors or any other chemicals are added to any part of a domestic water system.

Do-it-yourself chemists may be advised that many of the chemicals used as corrosion inhibitors are poisonous (especially in high concentrations) and due care should be taken; note should also be taken of the fact that twice the concentration may not produce twice the degree of corrosion inhibition, and the recommended levels should not be exceeded.

3.6.2 Non-aqueous fluids

There are comparatively few non-aqueous fluids currently used in solar systems but the range available will probably increase if solar energy becomes more popular in the UK.

Mineral-oil-based fluids

Low viscosity mineral-oil-based fluids have been produced specifically to try to overcome the problems of using aqueous fluids with aluminium components; they can also be considered as an alternative to aqueous fluids in other solar systems and are claimed to have a long working life if used in a sealed pressurised circuit. It is important that no water is allowed to contaminate the circuit at any time or the inertness of the oil may be affected and corrosion can result; systems destined for use with oil should therefore never be flushed out with water at any stage of their construction or during any maintenance work. If by mistake a substantial quantity of water were introduced it could not easily be removed but a viable (if rather hazardous) method might be to rinse the system with methylated spirit and then to cryopump the alcohol vapour and remaining water using liquid nitrogen. Alternatively, the rinse could be omitted and vacuum and cryopumping employed for many hours; these techniques are all specialised and should not be attempted by unqualified personnel. In any case, the system would have to be constructed from components that could tolerate being held under vacuum. Attempting to dry the system using compressed air is unlikely to achieve the required degree of cleanliness. In view of the difficulty of removing unwanted water it would be sensible if explicit instructions regarding flushing and fluid charging were to be securely attached to systems designed for use with heat transfer oils.

The term 'low viscosity' when applied to these mineral oils should be taken in context – the viscosity is certainly much lower than that of more familiar types of oils (used as lubricants in car engines for example) but is still greater than that of water (see Appendix II) and as a consequence the pumping power required will exceed that necessary in a similar system using an aqueous fluid. This disadvantage is heightened by the lower specific heat of these oils as compared to that of water – which means that a greater volume flow rate is required; the specific heat is usually about 2·7 kJ/kg °C or 2·2 kJ/l °C compared to 4·2 kJ/l °C for water.

Since mineral oils are not miscible with water the risk from contamination of the potable water supply resulting from a leak in the heat exchanger might be considered to be reduced, but if contamination did occur this immiscibility could be a major handicap if it was necessary to clean out the secondary system. It is likely that the whole system from the cistern to the taps would have to be flushed through with hot detergent in order to ensure that all traces of the oil were removed. A further cautionary note is that many of the rubber seals and washers used in 'off-the-shelf' plumbing components may be attacked by heat transfer oils.

Since mineral oils are inflammable their use in systems having any free surface (such as that in a cistern) cannot be advocated and a sealed circuit having the minimum fluid content is to be preferred. Suitable precautions should be taken when using a naked flame to repair or extend any part of a system that has contained an inflammable oil; flushing with nitrogen gas during the soldering operations should provide a degree of safety. Future interpretations of Building Regulations and other legislation may elucidate the circumstances in which these oils may or may not be used in buildings.

Silicone heat transfer oils

Silicone heat transfer oils are available for use in solar systems and will probably exhibit an almost indefinite life. Their principal disadvantages are, as for mineral oils, high viscosity and low specific heat; the viscosity problem is however usually more serious and is not ameliorated by a specific heat of typically 1·6 kJ/l °C. The high capital cost of these fluids may not be considered a disadvantage in view of their expected working life and since they are relatively non-toxic they may safely be used in many types of collector plates and systems, and might be considered for use with plates that were thinner than those that could be employed if a potentially more corrosive heat transfer fluid were to be used. The use of silicone fluid in solar systems has recently been described[92].

3.7 Electronic control systems

3.7.1. General

Several basically different types of devices may be used to control pumped circulation solar systems; these range in complexity from simple thermostats to electronic systems having multiple control functions.

A solar system consisting of an array of collectors and a storage vessel may be controlled by a thermostat on the collectors, by a time switch, by a circuit responsive to solar radiation intensity, or by a differential thermometer which measures the difference in temperature between the collectors and the store.

All of these devices have been used to control solar systems but a consideration of their likely behaviour indicates that only a differential thermometer is likely to be suitable for solar systems characterised by operation over a wide temperature range.

For swimming pool systems where the thermal inertia is so great that very little variation of the store temperature occurs over a day a thermostat which is fixed in the outlet from the collectors and adjusted perhaps weekly to a setting a few degrees above the pool temperature may be reasonably satisfactory. Similarly, a simple device where the control function is derived from a photovoltaic cell may work adequately on a pool system because there will be a reasonable correlation between the solar intensity and the ability of the collectors to supply heat to the pool; this follows from the fact that the pool temperature remains substantially constant. A time switch might also perform satisfactorily in these systems.

However in a system where the store temperature can vary over a wide range during the course of a day there will only be a weak correlation between the ability of the collectors to supply heat and either the solar intensity or the collector temperature and only a differential type of control system can be considered suitable: this is especially true in a climate such as is experienced in the UK where there is little constancy in the insolation pattern from day to day. In a climate where the insolation pattern was known to be substantially stable over (say) a 6 week period then a simpler control system could be set so as to give a reasonable system output if the usage pattern was also known.

There can however be no doubt that use of a differential controller will lead to the greatest collection of solar heat in any system since its function closely matches the logic of switching on the pump whenever there is heat available for transfer to storage, but the criteria for setting the temperature differences at which the device switches depend upon the type of solar system that is to be controlled.

In a typical solar system for heating an outdoor pool only during the summer months the collectors will be of the unglazed and uninsulated type, and will operate on a direct circuit (that is, without a heat exchanger). Since the collectors have a high U value it is important that they are run as cool as possible and since no heat exchanger is incorporated in the system there is no reason why a fairly low temperature differential of (say) 0·3°C should not be employed. With a flow rate of about 0·04 l/m²s (see Section 2.4.1) the rate of energy collection from a 20 m² system will be 1·0 kW which is sufficiently high to justify running a small pump – which may consume a fraction between 0·1 and 0·2 of this power*.

---

* In some pool systems excessive flow rates have been specified and over-large pumps installed. Designers should remember that pumping power increases as the cube of the flow rate (approximately) and that collecting free solar energy can become expensive: this is valid even if all the pump energy is transferred to the pool.

With a smaller solar system it may be considered wise to increase the switch-on differential since the energy supplied to the pump should be kept to a small fraction of the collected energy and pumping power does not scale linearly with system size; this conclusion is not immediately obvious since there is in fact a net gain of energy whenever the solar power transferred to store is greater than the power required for the pump but there are two reasons why control systems should not be finely tuned in an attempt to reach this 'ideal' state. Firstly, it is unlikely to be economic to run a pump unless there is a several-fold net power gain since some allowance must be made for the wear of the pump.

Secondly it must be remembered that electric pumps in solar systems almost invariably use on-peak mains power. In a national context it does not make sense to run a pump in a solar circuit unless the solar power transferred to storage is at least twice the power required to run the pump; however in a system where the auxiliary fuel is electricity the ratio is of course unity, except for the fact that the pump will be worn out to no purpose.

In a system employing an indirect solar circuit some consideration must be given to the fact that a larger control differential may be advisable. The reasoning is straightforward but calculation of exact values requires a knowledge of the characteristics of both the heat exchanger and solar panel, and is complex. At one extreme, if the heat exchanger in the store were very efficient and the solar panel had a high U value then the same control differential as for a direct system would be appropriate. However, if the heat exchanger were poor and the panels had a low U value then it would make sense to increase the temperature differential of the control system so as to wait until a difference of perhaps 5°C could be produced across the heat exchanger which would then be capable of transferring heat at the required rate.

The reasoning here can best be appreciated by realising that under transient start-up conditions it is the rate of heat loss from the heat exchanger and not the rate of heat gain to the collectors which should properly be compared to the pumping power. With low heat capacity collectors there may in fact be little difference in the pump-run hours if the switch-on differential is set to 0·5 or 5°C since the collectors will heat up quickly but with high heat capacity collectors tens of minutes may elapse before their output temperature reaches a sufficiently high value to justify pumping – and it is only with this high temperature available at the heat exchanger that the input to storage will more than match the pumping power. The optimum switch-off differential will depend upon the location of the store sensor, and will be higher if it is located in thermal contact with the store than if it is located in the outlet from the heat exchanger.

In some types of solar systems the position of the temperature sensor on the collector plate is important, and incorrect positioning can lead to a waste of pumping energy. These problems are often overcome in more sophisticated controllers which have a time delay circuit incorporated so that after the pump switches off it will not switch on again for a few minutes. It should be noted that the logic here is different from that of a system where the pump has a minimum on-period; this latter type of logic should in general not be used because it can lead to pumping during periods of zero gain, especially if the minimum on-time was set to be larger than the transit time of fluid through the collector plates. If however a controller without a time delay were used with a collector having very large header tubes and a relatively low heat capacity plate (for example, some panels intended for heating pools have this design) then the sensor on the collector should be affixed to or into the header tube and not on to the plate; the latter location could lead to switch-on whilst the top header was still cool and switch-off could occur before the small quantity of warmed water that was in the plate had reached the store. This is only one example of how pump hunting can occur, and system design and sensor position are important in preventing undue occurrence of this phenomenon.

The most generally correct position for the collector plate sensor in a simple control system is that it should be affixed to (or preferably inside) the top header of the plate in such a position that switch-on only occurs when the fluid in the header (and by implication, that in the riser tubes) has reached a useful temperature. Since the fluid in the risers will probably reach this temperature a short time before that in the top header some small delay in switch-on is inevitable but probably unimportant. Switch-off will occur only when the last of the water at a useful temperature has left the collector plate and it must be accepted that the usually small amount of warmed water left in the pipe connecting the top header to the storage vessel must be allowed to cool.

Controller designs incorporating a time delay to overcome this problem could in theory show a slightly increased system performance but in practice the risk of not having the delay matched to the transit time of the fluid in the relevant pipe militates against such a scheme. In any case, this slight reduction from the theoretically realisable heat transfer that occurs after each switch-off will often be partly compensated for by a slightly increased transfer immediately following the next switch-on if this occurs soon afterwards. The unavoidable time constant of the collector sensor will however alleviate this problem to some extent, but either excessive thermal inertia or inappropriate positioning of the sensor can give rise to an overshoot condition.

The correct position for the store sensor is often the subject of some debate when stratified stores are considered; the position on largely unstratified stores such as swimming pools is of course unimportant so long as the sensor sees a representative store temperature and not, for example, the outlet from the filtration system or collector array.

With a typical domestic water heating system using either an indirect or a direct circuit there exists the possibility of stratification occurring during the warm-up period of the solar store; stratification in any store can of course result from partial draw-off of the contents and one of the possible consequences of this is outlined in Section 2.2.1. There are clearly four distinct areas in which a sensor could be placed on such a store: at the top, or at the top, middle, or bottom of the heat exchanger. In addition, feasible positions exist in the upper and lower connections to the heat exchanger (see Figure 31). Locating the sensor at the top of the cylinder is clearly non-optimal since the collectors may remain inoperative for long periods when they could usefully be heating the lower section. The lowest temperature in the solar system when the pump is operating will almost always be in the water surrounding the bottom of the heat exchanger at D. This position for the sensor thus gives the possibility of running the pump for the longest possible time, and perhaps of collecting the most heat. It should be noted however that maximising the input of heat to the solar store is not necessarily analogous with maximising the heat supplied if the former leads to destratification. If a situation arises where considerable stratification exists between the top and bottom of the heat exchanger this position of the sensor could lead to destruction of the stratification. Whilst more heat might have been added to the solar store during this process the usable heat for that day could be decreased, which may not be desirable since there is no guarantee that the system will be used the next day: energy quality (ie, temperature) is often more important than the quantity of energy. Similar reservations may be expressed concerning position E.

Alternatively the sensor may be positioned at the level of the top of the heat exchanger (position B) when less destratification of the lower half of the store will occur, but at the expense of a probable reduction in total heat collection. In the absence of any definitive data concerning the best position for the store sensor in such a system it is recommended that it be placed near the centre line of the coil, at C in Figure 31. This position may ensure that none of the undesirable effects detailed above occurs to any predominant extent, and it would also seem to be an appropriate location for a direct system. Location F should not be used because it can lead to lock-on of the controller.

In all cases it is important to ensure good thermal contact between the sensor and the solar system in order that the measured temperatures do not reflect changes in ambient temperature; amongst the more satisfactory designs are those in which the sensor is clamped in a metal block which is itself soldered to either the collector plate or storage vessel. Insertion in a deep pocket filled with heat transfer grease should also give good results. The connecting wires to the sensors should be of very small cross-section so that they do not constitute a thermal leakage path to or from the surroundings.

The above discussion has concentrated on controls for systems in which the collectors do not drain when the pump stops. For draindown systems the logic remains much the same except that there are some additional possible situations which may give rise to hunting. For example, if a high fluid capacity collector plate is used in a draindown system the pump may be switched on when the empty plate achieves a temperature perhaps 2°C greater than the reference store temperature. The resulting inrush of fluid to the collector plate could cool it down to perhaps 0·5°C above store temperature with the result that the pump switches off again (assuming that the switch-off differential is greater than 0·5°C). A 'yo-yo' effect is thus generated with fluid repeatedly just managing to complete the circuit before being drained again as a result of its cooling effect on the collector plate sensor. These effects are unlikely to be troublesome but observant owners of domestic drain-down systems should not be surprised if they occasionally occur. A serious case of this malady may occur with swimming pool systems that are operated on a draindown basis since the water capacity of some of these panels is large and simple controllers set to switch off at (say) 0·3°C may have a switch-on differential of only 0·6°C. In draindown systems the panel sensor should be both small and affixed to the collector plate: insertion into a header tube may not give good results especially with sensors having a large thermal mass.

Pump hunting problems can be overcome to some extent if controllers having independently variable switch-on and switch-off differentials are used; for high water capacity collectors operating in a draindown swimming pool circuit a high switch-on differential of perhaps 5°C could be combined with a switch-off value as low as 0·2 or 0·3°C. For a small indirect domestic water heating system the same switch-on differential of 5°C could be combined with a switch-off differential of no less than (say) 1°C.

It is however sometimes argued that a high switch-on differential can lead to a substantial loss of collected energy, but this may easily be disproved in the ideal case of a collector having no thermal capacity.

If the store temperature is T°C and the switch-on differential (T_{so}) is 5°C then if the collector plate reaches a stagnation temperature of only $(T+4\cdot9)$°C the pump will not be activated. The power balance on the collector plate under these conditions may be written (see Section 3.1.13):

$$\eta_0 I = \eta I + U(T_c - T_a) \quad (W/m^2)$$

therefore $\quad \eta_0 I = 0 + U(T + 4\cdot9 - T_a)$

where T_a is the ambient temperature.

The extracted energy in this case is of course zero. If the pump were to be activated and T_c reduced to T (the lowest conceivable value) then:

$$\eta_0 I = \eta I + U(T - T_a)$$

therefore $\quad \eta I = 4\cdot9\ U.$

The power extractable from the collector is therefore 19·6 W/m² if its U value is 4 W/m² °C.

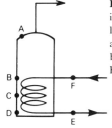

Figure 31 Possible locations for the store sensor in domestic water heating systems. Preferred location is shown as C; B, D and E may be acceptable, A is non-optimal, and F should not be used. Store stratification and counterflow heat exchange are assumed

In practice T_c may drop only to about $(T+1)°C$ giving a value of $\eta I = 15\cdot6$ W/m², which is insufficient to justify running a pump in a typical domestic water heating system and only marginally sufficient for a 40 m² swimming pool installation.

If however I was at a sufficiently high level that the stagnation temperature of the collector was 20°C above the store temperature then the possible output would become 76 W/m² if the average plate temperature fell to $(T+1)°C$.

A simple criterion for switch-on based on a 4 m² system and a 60 W circulating pump is therefore that $(T_{so} \times U)$ should be greater than 30 W/m².

In practice however a value of 50 W/m² might be more appropriate in view of the previous arguments concerning pump wear. A surprising conclusion therefore, is that a high performance collector having a U value of 2 should be allowed to heat up 25°C above the store temperature before it was switched on. The correctness of this conclusion is however obvious if the reasoning is extended to a 'perfect' collector having a U value of zero; in practice however the tendency that this perfect collector might have to melt or explode decrees that a differential somewhat less than infinity should be chosen.

The switch-on differential must also be related to the flow rate because there is little point in activating the pump unless the flow can be maintained*: with a flow rate of water of 0·016 l/m²s, a retained power of at least 20 W/m² is necessary if the switch-off differential is set to to 0·3°C (this assumes that the store sensor is located in such a position that the temperature difference recorded is very close to that across the collector panels).

Unfortunately, some real collectors have such high thermal capacity that these arguments, if applied in practice, could lead to a much reduced energy output from the system.

The next stage in the argument however is to realise that under transient conditions the rate of increase of the collector temperature with time provides information concerning what the stagnation temperature is likely to become if the same weather conditions persist for long enough.

This offers the possibility that an advanced controller could be programmed to respond to both temperature and rate of change of temperature, and that it could be matched to any given type of collector. Another method of predicting the stagnation temperature is to incorporate into the collector a thin piece of metal having the same surface finish as the collector plate and to which a second 'collector plate sensor' is fitted. This second sensor (which would have to be of low thermal mass) would then relay information concerning the expected stagnation temperature of the main collector plate under the prevailing conditions. Alternatively, controllers operating variable-

speed pumps may be further developed: this would appear to be an attractive option, especially if pump efficiencies can be maintained at low speeds.

It is the author's opinion that although relatively crude control systems operating fixed-speed pumps may offer much the same overall thermal performance as more sophisticated variable speed controllers there is probably room for significant improvement in control system technology as applied to solar systems in the UK. It seems unlikely that more sophisticated controllers will be able to offer a cost-effective improvement in performance but for a system that is itself not cost-effective this should not deter development; the optimum solar system is one in which each component is equally non-cost-effective. Improvements in control technology may however prove to be truly worthwhile in large systems because of the greater total gains from a given percentage increase in thermal performance. It may however be advised that sophistication in electronics should not be allowed to take precedence over the logically deduced requirements of a control system as derived from a consideration of the thermal properties of the solar circuit.

These statements do however need qualifying in the light of what seems likely to be the rapid deployment of microprocessor chips: it may be anticipated that control systems having a high degree of intelligence in comparison with those presently available could in future be produced very cheaply. A possible constraint on their usefulness could be the cost of the extra sensors that might be required rather than that of the electronic circuits: another constraint, which mirrors a difficulty of much temperature measurement technology, is that the accuracy of a system is usually determined not by its electronics but by both the calibration of the sensor units, and the care with which they are installed.

Given that the subject of control system logic is often more difficult than at first is apparent it is understandable that complex controllers have already been produced in an attempt to ameliorate some of the deficiencies of simple equipment. The logic that has been used to design some of these controllers does however leave a little to be desired, in that the basic necessity of matching the response of the controller to the response of the panel appears to have been neglected. The principal requirement remains that of ensuring that the pump is only operated when a useful amount of heat can be added to the stored water. It is shown in Section 2.2.1 that a simple differential controller can fail to perform this function under some conditions and a second differential measurement, with transducers fixed across the heat exchanger, may be necessary to ensure that switch-off occurs as soon as the power input to the store falls below a preset level: this method of controlling switch-off may be expected to operate satisfactorily even if the characteristics of the heat exchanger change with time, perhaps owing to scaling.

Prevention of hunting, especially with draindown panels for swimming pools, seems to have caused a considerable amount of trouble but this application is suited to a controller based on the concept of the switch-on differen-

---

* Unless of course the collector has a high fluid capacity and is not used in a draindown system.

tial being related to the U value of the collector: since a drained collector plate usually has low thermal capacity a small sensor in good thermal contact with the plate may be used to control both switch-on and switch-off. However, because of the high flow rates used in some pool systems (often in excess of the 0·04 l/m²s advocated in this book) the switch-on differential may be determined by the flow rate and the switch-off differential rather than by the U value. For example, if a flow rate of 0·08 l/m²s were to be combined with a switch-off differential of only 0·2°C then a retained power of at least 67 W/m² would be required for continuous operation: this is in contrast to the figure of 15·6 W/m² which was derived above, and which might justify running the pump on purely net-power-gain criteria. With an assumed U value of 10 W/m² °C the correct switch-on differential is not 1·56°C but 6·8°C*, unless of course a variable speed pump is used: it should be noted that at high temperature differences the effective U value of an unglazed panel may be double the figure used above.

In conclusion, it is recommended that until more data from accurately monitored test systems becomes available simple controllers for domestic hot water systems should switch on at a differential of between 3·5 and 7°C and off at a differential of between 0·5 and 2·5°C: the higher values would apply to indirect systems having poor heat exchangers.

For swimming pool circuits pump hunting will be reduced both by a moderate flow rate and by a switch-on differential of about 4 or 5°C: pumping may, in a direct circuit, be justified down to 0·3°C or even lower if the system can be guaranteed to switch off before the true differential goes negative. When using these very small switch-off differentials care should be taken to ensure that the pool reference temperature is not lower than that of the water leaving the pool on its way to the collectors. Positioning the pool sensor close to this exit pipe is advised. Experience may show however that a simpler control system such as a time switch or a thermostat is adequate: installations in which the collector area is a large fraction of the pool area may exhibit significant negative feedback (see Section 4.2) and any 'deficiency' in the control system might thereby be rendered unimportant. The possible waste of expensive pump energy when using simple control systems should however also be considered.

3.7.2 Principles of circuit design

The safety requirements of electrical supply equipment for use in buildings are covered by comprehensive IEE regulations[93] and nothing in this section may be taken to override or supersede any of these regulations. It must however be realised that widespread use of solar systems is a phenomenon comparatively new to the UK, and that their special characteristics and requirements were not considered when the IEE regulations were drafted. It is

therefore considered worthwhile to outline some of the more basic requirements of solar system controllers both as regards the types of transducers that may be used and in respect of basic safety-orientated design.

Devices using solar cells can easily be designed to be electrically safe since the cells need not be affixed to any part of the plumbing system. Thermostats of the type used in electric immersion heaters should be used with a suitable sheath unless they are designed for direct immersion; the usual function of switch-off as temperature increases may be inverted using a changeover relay – the electric circuitry is trivial but care should be taken to use a suitable insulated or earthed metal box for the relay.

Thermostats sold for tropical fish tanks could be used in low cost DIY controllers for outdoor pools, but some types cannot tolerate temperatures in excess of about 35°C. Many types of thermostats may only prove suitable for use where the collector plates remain full of water when the pump stops. However, in view of the small cost of a differential controller in relation to the total cost of a large solar system it could be recommended that neither time switches nor thermostats be used. Nevertheless, these systems are attractive because of their simplicity. Only outline details of electronic circuits for differential temperature controllers are given below since once the basic requirements are understood many satisfactory circuits may be developed. The principal operating components of an electronic differential controller are the two transducers which sense the collector and store temperature and translate these into an electrically measurable quantity.

There are many types of transducers that vary one or more of their electrical properties with change of temperature and amongst the most commonly used are diodes, platinum or nickel resistance thermometers, thermistors and thermocouples. The principal properties that are required of devices to be used in solar systems are that they should be stable with time, reasonably rugged, and capable of withstanding the extremes of temperature that may be experienced in service. In order to aid both initial setting up of the equipment and subsequent repairs the sensors should be available to closely specified tolerances so that individual matching of pairs or delicate adjustment of offset controls on site are rendered unnecessary.

All of the transducers listed above are available with these properties with the possible exception of diodes whose maximum service temperature may not be sufficiently high. However, once the relative costs of the different types are assessed it appears that thermocouples made from copper-constantan are likely to be one of the more suitable choices since these can be made by any competent small workshop and their use requires only a little specialised knowledge. It must however be realised that to use thermocouples for detecting temperature differences as low as 0·2°C (where the net emf available is approximately 8 microvolts) is not a subject that may be dismissed as trivial, since spurious emfs of this order may easily be introduced into the circuits by insufficiently good workmanship or use of inappropriate materials.

---

* (6·7+0·1)°C where 0·1°C is half the switch-off differential.

Many authorities advocate welding as being the only satisfactory method of making thermocouple junctions and for some materials this is undoubtedly correct. From experience however the author believes that copper-constantan thermocouples may be manufactured quite successfully by soft-soldering provided several basic rules are rigidly adhered to, the most important of which are that small lengths of the wires should be tightly twisted together before soldering, that the minimum of freshly-melted resin-cored solder be used and that all the residual flux should be cleaned off the completed junction with a dry cleaning solvent. Thermocouple pairs for differential temperature measurement are most conveniently made using only one length of constantan; lengths of thermo-couple quality copper wire are then soldered to each end of the constantan and may (preferably) be taken straight to the input of the electronic circuitry or if necessary may be joined to ordinary PVC covered copper wire – these joins must also be made to the standards noted above. The success of these methods in achieving matched multiple thermocouples may be judged from the author's published work on this subject[94]. A disadvantage of these systems for domestic use is however that the electronic circuits need to be of high quality if their thermal drift is not to prove troublesome: the options are that either multiple (series-connected) thermocouples be used so as to increase the basic signal or that the amplifier circuits be designed to reduce thermal drift to a suitably low level.

For other types of transducers it is only necessary to ensure good clean joints in all the electrical circuits, and spurious emfs are less important because the voltages that are used in typical bridge networks are usually consider-ably above the single-digit microvolt range: these are both desirable characteristics, especially for systems that are to be installed by inexperienced personnel.

Transducers intended for immersion in liquids should be encapsulated so as to provide electrical isolation: potting in epoxy resin within stainless steel or copper sheaths should prove satisfactory. Surface mounted thermocouples should be electrically isolated from pipework and not (as was the case in one installation inspected by the author) fixed to a copper pipe with a generous amount of plumber's solder.

Any transducers fixed inside a glazed collector should preferably be connected using heat resistant cable: whilst PVC covered wire will not tolerate high temperatures PTFE insulation is likely to be suitable for use inside most if not all flat plate collectors. With all circuits it is good practice not to run the transducer leads in close proximity to mains wiring, immersion heaters, pumps or other devices that contain magnetic components and/or are subject to repeated cycling.

Since any wire can act as an aerial for radio or television signals circuits must be designed so as to ensure that these cannot produce spurious effects if long transducer leads are used; inadvertent rectification of strong radio or TV signals even if only accomplished very inefficiently by some part of a bridge or amplifier circuit might lead to microvolt level dc voltages being produced, which in turn might produce serious errors of measurement.

It is recommended that the control box be located in a position readily accessible to the householder and where it may be inspected for correct operation during certain well defined types of weather. For example, if 2 long-life neon or LED lamps are provided (one to signal that the controller is in receipt of mains power and the other to signal when power is being applied to the pump) it should be possible to ascertain that in very dull cold weather and at night only one light glows whereas in hot sunny weather the pump could be expected to be running especially if hot water had recently been drawn off in any great quantity. Such qualitative checks when coupled with checks of preheat water temperature (see Section 2.2.1) can go a long way towards ascertaining that a solar system is functioning without any very major faults. Con-trary to some current practice, it is recommended that controllers are not located in either kitchens or bathrooms for reasons of high humidity and risk of internal conden-sation leading to electrical cross connection. The risk of long term degradation of components should also be considered.

The design of solar collector control systems should be such that they are electrically safe, and some basic principles may be outlined. A control system that operates from mains power (240V ac) must be insulated so as to preclude passage of this high voltage through to the transducers and their cables which will normally run at a very low voltage (typically less than 5V). This provision is of fundamental importance since it may often be im-practicable to ensure that all the transducers and their cables are constructed and installed in such a manner as to be safe in the event of their becoming live; the preferred solution would appear to be that the control box itself should be inherently safe: these concepts are already recognised for equipment such as car battery chargers and children's train sets where the low voltage output circuits are exposed.

The generalised scheme outlined in Figure 32 is valid for most if not all electronic differential controllers and shows that mains voltage can be introduced into the low voltage area either via the transformer that supplies the logic circuitry or via the relay or triac that switches mains power to the pump or motorised valve. Since no one barrier or protective device can be considered safe unless of very high quality some duplication and/or redundancy must be incorporated, and there are many ways in which this may be achieved.

The transformer that supplies the logic circuitry will typically be rated at about 1·2–1·5 VA (about 1·5 watts) and this amount of power should be more than sufficient to operate both the logic circuitry and the relay coil or triac. A typical 12 V relay capable of switching a reactive 300 VA load will require between 0·1 and 1 W to drive its coil; a small triac will require almost zero power, but many circuits used to control triacs consume several watts of power since the gate drive is derived from a potential divider across the 240V supply.

The first line of defence in many systems may therefore be a fuse of very low rating, typically 50 mA, and if the low voltage supply is smoothed by a large capacitor the

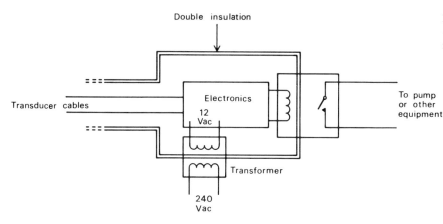

Figure 32 Basic design of a differential temperature controller showing the mains voltage circuits isolated from the low voltage electronics and transducer cables

fuse should be an 'antisurge' type which will permit the high switch-on currents. If under test a quick-blow 50 mA fuse proves satisfactory then this should be used in preference. The transformer itself should either be of split-bobbin construction or incorporate an interwinding screen (which should be earthed). Alternatively, a double-insulated transformer may be used but in all cases it should comply with BS 3535[95]; since double insulation is often considered safer than a system that relies on good earthing the former may be recommended.

The other component in a typical system that is supplied with mains power is the relay or triac. Isolation of a poor design of relay may be accomplished electrically but it is preferable to rely on good mechanical design: units in which the frame is live may be considered unsuitable for domestic use, but many alternative and satisfactory models are available. The danger here is partly that the fuse in this circuit must be capable of handling the power of the device to be controlled, and is typically rated at 5 A. The potential thus exists for a single fault in the relay insulation to connect a 5 A 240V ac supply into the low voltage circuits, which could, depending upon the detailed design of the electronics, feed this voltage into the transducer cables. Earthing one point of the transducer circuits is not an attractive solution because most designs require these to be as noise-free as possible. The same problem occurs in circuits where a triac is used to control

the pump or valve since the triac's main terminals must have access to mains voltage and the gate may be connected to the low voltage circuitry. It is the author's opinion that optical isolation devices may prove to be of benefit in these systems, and Figure 33 gives a suitable schematic circuit.

An even better option however would be to use an optically coupled solid-state relay, and although these are expensive at the present time (about £8 each in small quantities) it seems likely that their price (in real terms) may fall significantly in future years.

The view has been expressed in some reports dealing with solar system design that a metal box for the control system is necessary to guard against dangers from insulation breakdown, but this is incorrect; the most serious danger arises from possible leakage of mains voltage into low voltage cables and an earthed box can offer no protection. Similarly, there is little point in trying to rely on a metal case for screening either radio or TV signals (or mains pick-up) unless the transducer cables are screened and earthed, and the circuits properly designed.

Other incorrect advice that has been published in the UK includes the recommendation that to save energy a controller powered from an old car battery is preferable to one powered from the mains supply. The concept would be sound in an ideal world where both energy

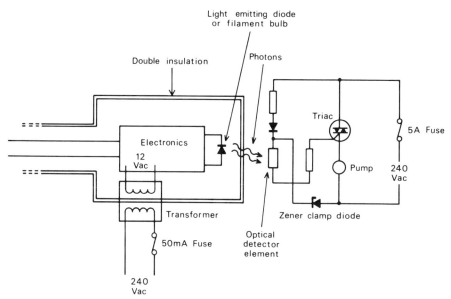

Figure 33 Suggested safe design of a differential temperature controller. The transformer is double-insulated and the triac gate drive optically isolated from the low voltage electronics

conversion and storage were accomplished without loss, but in practice the energy losses that will occur in both the battery charger and in the battery itself will exceed those of an efficient mains powered unit, and purchasing a relatively loss-free new battery cannot be justified. For either a battery or mains-powered controller the decision to use a relay or triac must rest with the circuit designer but a few of the basic properties of each type of device should be appreciated.

One of the most common modes of failure in relays is points-burn caused by excessive arcing; this problem is much more acute when inductive dc loads have to be switched and should present no problem with low current ac loads. Modern relays have a mechanical life often exceeding 10^6 operations – corresponding to over 50 operations daily for 50 years. Relay coils can produce a large voltage spike when switched off and protection of the drive electronics is often essential; a reverse-connected fast-switching silicon diode is commonly used with dc-powered relays. Relays are very easily checked for correct operation.

Triacs are semiconductor devices and must therefore only be used well within their design limits if reliable operation is to be assured. One of the problems with using triacs to control pumps is the high starting and stall currents of the latter; high current triacs are expensive and require higher gate-drive power than smaller devices, which with some circuits necessitates a higher quiescent power loss in the controller.

It must be appreciated that if a triac is triggered by a dc signal then this must be of sufficient power to trigger the triac in both its I and III modes; use of too low power will result in triggering only in the more sensitive I mode and whilst this is often acceptable in lamp dimming circuits and similar applications it must not be allowed to occur in circuits intended for pump control. A relaxation of this rule may be permissible if the pump is suitable for variable speed operation.

It is considered worthwhile to detail a couple of the design faults that are a feature of some current types of differential temperature controllers. A potentially danger-ous design error occurs where a single row of barrier strip terminals is used to connect all the necessary wires to the electronic circuitry; incorrect connection of one of the 10 wires usually necessary could lead to mains voltage being fed into the wires leading to the temperature sensors. If the wires were originally connected correctly the mains leads from the supply and to the pump are often caused to be physically close to or touching the sensor leads. It would be good practice if in future de-signs all the mains connections were situated at one end of the box and all the low voltage connections at the other. Separate outlets for the two sets of wires should of course be provided, and at no point on the internal printed-circuit boards should mains power be run in close-proximity to the low voltage circuitry. These improve-ments may also be expected to reduce the amount of mains hum fed into the electronic circuits.

A potentially troublesome but not dangerous fault that has been incorporated into some control box designs is the use of cheap miniature preset potentiometers for trimming the circuit characteristics so as to set the switch-ing differentials. This adjustment is normally carried out at the factory and the average consumer or installer will have no means of checking whether the control box is working correctly. It has been found that some of these potentiometers are sensitive to vibration and that the switching differential could be varied simply by subjecting the box to the type of rough treatment that it might reasonably have been expected to withstand as a com-ponent destined for use by the building industry. The problem was first noticed when 2 control boxes were being 'matched' prior to installation on test rigs at BRE and a cure was effected by replacing the presets by high quality multi-turn trimmers at a cost of £1 per unit. As a further precaution all the fixed resistors were replaced by high stability types. Attention is drawn to the fact that a control box incorporating good quality reliable com-ponents will cost in production probably less than £3 more than a similar unit built to the lowest price specifica-tion. In view of the difficulty of checking control systems after they have left the factory and with regard to the importance of the settings being maintained for the life of the unit, it is recommended that only high quality, high stability components should be used. A conference paper outlining use of control systems in the UK is available[96].

4 Sizing of components: design rules

4.1 General

In this section some of the basic design rules useful for sizing various components of solar systems are illustrated, but one overriding principle needs to be recognised relating to the economic effectiveness of solar systems in most applications.

It is normal engineering practice to attempt to design a system so that each component is 'balanced' in its value to that system when compared with any other component. For example, if the energy consumption of a building was to be reduced, it might be possible to attain the required reduction by employing several different techniques to varying degrees; one option might be to use cavity fill insulation and double glazing whilst another option might be to install a much more efficient and well controlled heating system. A third option might be to use cavity wall insulation in combination with an improved (but perhaps not well controlled) heating system. Any one of these options might achieve the required reduction of (say) 50 per cent in the fuel bills for the building and in a simple analysis the winning design would be the one that achieved this required result for the least cost. More complex analysis would have to take into account the fact that taking up one option now (perhaps to install the moderately good heating system) might preclude installing the very efficient heating system at a later date – perhaps because the 2 sets of hardware were incompatible and subsequent change would involve considerable expense for relatively little additional benefit. If, there-fore, projected fuel price rises were such that applying all the conservation techniques might be feasible in time, then it might make sense to apply now only those options which would not preclude application of other options in the future. In the example used above the existing inefficient heating system would not be removed unless the second option was chosen.

These analyses all have one common factor – the worth of an option is assessed and compared against alternative options or other criteria. In designing solar systems the same principles can apply but the criteria for success or failure should be changed so as to scale with the inherent non-viability of the basic system. An example will make this clear. A standard engineering problem is to decide how much thermal insulation to put on a storage vessel or pipework system that contains fluid at either above or below ambient temperature. Using the chosen method of calculation (of which there are several – see Section 6.4) and assuming figures for fuel price rises, investment rates, inflation etc the optimum thickness may be determined[97]. If, however, the storage vessel or pipework system were part of a solar installation the optimum thickness would

be expected to be greater because the insulation would be saving energy that had been obtained from a system having a very high capital cost per unit of average power delivered.

This result may be derived another way; if a solar system were being designed to supply a certain amount of heat this might be achieved either by using x m² of collector and not insulating any of the pipework or storage vessels, or by using only y m² of collector (y < x) together with some thermal insulation. The thickness of insulation that would be 'economic' in this example would be calculated on the basis of its displacing (x − y) square metres of solar panel, whereas had the same system been heated by natural gas the optimum thickness of insulation would be only a fraction of this figure. Strictly, this argument is valid only if the cost of the solar panels is a sizeable fraction of the total system cost: this is often realised in practice. A more rigorous analysis would take into account the possibility of changing the quantity of storage in the insulated system, but since the cost of storage is rarely directly proportional to its volume each case would have to be assessed individually if exact answers were required. It should however be noted that insulating small diameter pipes can lead to an *increased* heat loss[97].

An interesting question arises when a solar system and an auxiliary energy supply system are combined, for example in the heating of domestic hot water. It is stated in Section 2.3.7 that the insulation on a preheat (solar) cylinder should only be about half that on the auxiliary cylinder because of the lower average temperatures. The paradox arises because whilst it is possible to physically combine the 'solar' and 'auxiliary' systems it is not possible to reconcile their economics without applying scaling factors; further consideration of this topic is some-what academic, but it should be noted that practical considerations may dictate the insulation thickness on the auxiliary cylinder if it is situated in an airing cupboard.

4.2 Solar collectors and storage vessels

For an average household in the UK the current optimum size of solar collector is probably zero; this follows from Section 6.4. Given however that a household wishes to install a solar collector system, its size will be determined not only by the expected water usage, but by other factors such as how much money the household wishes to spend and how much importance is attached to the prospect of having a large system installed at once rather than perhaps adding to a small system if fuel prices rose sharply sometime in the future. Practical considerations will usually render this latter option infeasible – principally because collector design (if not technology) is changing rapidly as manufacturers seek more efficient or cheaper production methods.

Once the decision to install a solar system is taken then the householder is committed to a heavy expenditure for labour costs and profits together with the purchase of those items of a system whose price is largely insensitive to the final system size. It may be surmised from Section 6.2 that this initial commitment is of the order of £100–£400 in the UK at 1978 prices. Brinkworth has suggested that economics are likely to favour smaller rather than larger systems principally because of the decrease in the energy supplied per square metre that occurs as more collectors are added to a given system[98]. This effect is illustrated in Figure 34. Previous BRE publications[1, 3] have quoted between 4 and 6 m² as being reasonable areas for a household using about 170 litres of hot water per day, which was found to be the average consumption in large flats[99]. It should be noted that whilst the IHVE Guide[100] gives between 70 and 140 l/person.day as the maximum hot water requirement these figures may be regarded as high for normal design purposes and in fact are metric conversions of data first incorporated in the Guide over 20 years ago. A recent BRE paper[101] following on work done by BSRIA has shown that 45 l/person.day at 55°C is a reasonable design rule for hot water systems in the UK. This is in line with the rules of thumb used in Australia where a figure of 45 l/person.day is used for designing solar systems[102]. Data from the Milton Keynes solar house has however indicated a hot water usage of 170 l/day at 60°C for a family of two adults and one child[103].

If delivery temperatures are reduced from the norm of 55–65°C then an increase in the expected average usage to perhaps 55 l/person.day might be anticipated. However, encouragement of excessive usage aimed merely at increasing the solar contribution cannot be justified.

The true optimum area is determined in part by two effects; small systems may suffer because of the high fraction of both the initial commitment and the subsequent maintenance costs that are associated with each square metre of collector and large systems will deliver less energy per square metre because of the higher temperatures that will be achieved. If the costs of all the hardware together with auxiliary energy costs were exactly quantifiable, and if the ratio between hardware and fuel costs was such that cost-effectiveness would be achieved, it might be possible to derive a unique optimum area of collector for any given situation but since there are at present such wide divergences in most of the parameters, the only conclusion can be that for an average household any area between 3 and 6 m² should not be too unsuitable. Designing a system to suit the house size rather than the current occupancy might however be considered logical. Many solar systems sold in the UK to date have incorporated less than 3 m² of collector, and some of these have been purchased for more than £800. However, it is shown in Section 6.2 that it should be possible for the installed cost of a good 4 m² system to be reduced to about £450 at 1978 prices; it should be noted that it is the net and not the gross area of collector that is the relevant parameter in these calculations.

Work in the UK to date published both by the Solar Energy Unit at Cardiff University and by BRE has confirmed that solar systems for preheating domestic hot water in single-family dwellings are remarkably insensitive in that they may be expected to deliver much the same amount of energy annually when used under a fairly wide range of operating conditions[104]. This 'negative feedback' effect arises principally because these systems operate over a wide temperature range*, and is emphasised in systems which manage to supply all the energy requirement for domestic hot water during the best summer periods; this follows because the better systems are effectively out of action for longer periods of time. It should be noted that the system outputs quoted by Courtney[104] appear, in the light of other recent work[13], to be optimistic. However, later computer work performed under the auspices of BSI, and which also modelled a stratified store, substantially corrects this anomaly[105]. The bias in favour of westerly orientations given by Courtney is however to be disregarded.

One of the principal parameters in the design of a solar water heating system is the ratio of the preheat storage volume to the area of collector. For domestic water heating systems work in the UK to date may be summarised by stating that the optimum value of storage per unit area has been found to lie anywhere between about 35 and 120 l/m². Since storage is expensive and often difficult to incorporate into existing dwellings a figure of 40–50 l/m² is often used as a design rule and this seems unlikely to be significantly modified by future work. It should be noted that a purely technical optimum derived without reference to economics can be found for this particular parameter because although larger stores can accumulate more heat they do so at lower temperatures and it is the product of the volume drawn off and the temperature that determines the energy saving. Once economics is introduced into the calculations the optimum reduces towards 35 l/m² but, as noted above, care should be exercised in applying standard cost-effectiveness tests to component parts of solar systems. A practical disadvantage of systems having a low ratio of preheat storage to collector area is that they are more prone to overheating in the summer especially if high performance collectors are used at shallow angles. This problem is particularly acute in the UK climate where the ratio between summer peak and average insolation levels is high.

For larger systems used for swimming pools or industrial applications different design criteria apply which will not be covered in detail here. It is worth noting however that since a swimming pool system is characterised by collectors which usually work at high efficiencies (but see Section

---

* Strictly, it is the fraction of the collectors' performance curve that is traversed that determines the degree of negative feedback.

2.4), a moderate change in the size of the collector array can result in an acceptably small percentage decrease in the heat output per unit area. It therefore follows that the twin design criteria sometimes used for these systems of the customer deciding how much he can afford to pay and how much land or roof area he has available for the collectors are often adequate. This conclusion does not contradict the argument used elsewhere in this book which states that because unglazed collectors have a high U value their performance is very dependent on operating temperature. A characteristic of solar systems is that for a fixed volume of storage and/or a fixed load the energy supplied per unit area of collector decreases as the area of collector in the system is increased. The effect is not linear since there is a maximum limit to the possible solar contribution to the energy requirement of any given load regardless of the area of collector installed; this follows from the fact that during any given day or other period of time there is a maximum temperature that can be attained – this is determined principally by the ambient temperature and by the peak irradiance level that is experienced. Figure 34 shows qualitatively how the solar contribution under any given weather conditions rises asymptotically to a level that is characteristic of the system type; simple swimming pool systems operate in the initial linear region of this graph during early spring but can approach 'saturation' as the pool temperature rises: negative feedback may be particularly strong in these systems during good midsummer conditions because the effective U values of both pool and collector increase with temperature, and the peak pool temperatures attained may be little influenced by (say) a doubling in the collector area.

The problems outlined in Section 2.4.2 become acute when fossil fuel boosting is used in swimming pool systems since this can shift the average $\Delta T/I$ values at which the collectors are required to work by a large amount with corresponding heavy penalties on the collection efficiency. In practice, an area of solar collector up to half the pool surface area should not produce any serious loss of efficiency due to the generation of excessive temperatures provided, of course, that solar energy is the only source of heat for the pool. The principal benefit from a larger system would appear to be a longer comfortable swimming season, but if this is not required then there may in fact be little point in the collector area

exceeding a quarter to a third of the pool area, assuming the latter to be well insulated.

One interesting design limit on the size of large industrial or power-generation solar systems may be mentioned; it does not follow that a solar system may be extended indefinitely if it is to supply heated fluid to a central sink because the collectors that are remote from the sink have to transmit their heat over a long distance and losses can be unacceptably high. For the sizes of systems that may be contemplated for use in the UK however, the flow distribution problems outlined in Section 3.1.1 are likely to be far more important.

4.3 Flowrates and pump sizing

Calculation of which size of pump to use in a given solar circuit is a straightforward matter but one to which insufficient attention is sometimes given. The usual application for pumps in single-family dwellings is as part of a central heating system where wide variations in flow rate can be tolerated; often the pump is chosen simply on the basis of the number of radiators it has to serve or on the size of the boiler and is 'balanced' by adjusting the flow control until the system appears to operate satisfactorily and without undue noise.

Solar systems can be more sensitive to incorrect pump sizing than are central heating systems for several reasons. If an oversized pump is used then the true efficiency of the solar system may be degraded because of the waste of expensive on-peak electrical power; the same fault in a central heating system merely simulates a small amount of electric resistance space heating, and is unimportant because space heating is (of course) required when the central heating system is operating. In a solar system flow rates that are too high can result in undue pump hunting, whilst insufficient flow will decrease the collector efficiency.

A reasonable flow rate per unit area of collector may be derived by considering the average conditions under which a solar panel might be expected to operate. For a small domestic hot water system the minimum collection rate will be around 50 W/m² (below this there may be little justification for running the pump, see Section 3.7.1), with a seldom realised maximum of perhaps 700 W/m². An estimated average energy collection rate is therefore probably in the range 200–400 W/m². The temperature difference that can be tolerated across the solar collector may be estimated to lie in the range 3–10°C, but because of the negative feedback effects that operate in solar water heating systems, it is not immediately apparent whether a high temperature difference (corresponding to a low flow rate) will be a significant disadvantage. However, it is possible to estimate the maximum flow rate that could conceivably be used to real advantage; with a retained power level of 500 W/m² and a temperature difference of 3°C the required flow rate for water is 0·04 l/m²s.

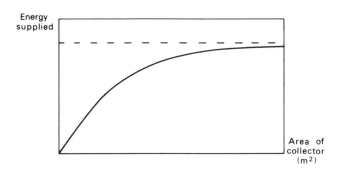

Figure 34 The energy supplied by a given solar system reaches a maximum for any set load and weather patterns, irrespective of additional collectors being installed

Experience however indicates that a flow rate of this magnitude need only be used in a swimming pool system (where retained power levels in excess of 500 W/m² are common), and for domestic water heating systems a rule of thumb is 0·014 l/m²s, which is the metric conversion of the old design rule of 1 gallon/sq ft hour.

It is the author's opinion that a flow rate of between 0·014 and 0·03 l/m²s should prove quite satisfactory for domestic water heating systems that use an aqueous-based heat transfer fluid. Claims that significantly better performance can be obtained with higher flow rates may indicate that either the flow distribution in the collector array is at fault (see Section 3.1.1), or that the collectors are of a type that is unduly affected by operation under laminar flow conditions. Good selectively coated collectors will need a lower flow rate than cheaper units because a rise in temperature of a few degrees will have less effect on their heat loss rate: it is here assumed that a value of 0·016 l/m²s is adequate, but in practice a slight increase may prove beneficial if high antifreeze concentrations are used.

Choosing a pump entails calculating the total flow rate required (0·016 times the number of square metres of collector for an aqueous heat transfer fluid), and calculating the pressure drop in the chosen type of pipework (see next section). A suitable pump from the range available will be one that can achieve the desired combination of pressure head and flow rate at a high setting of its flow control. The position of the pump in the circuit can be important in ensuring satisfactory operation (see Section 3.4.1).

If other than aqueous-based fluids are used the pump manufacturers should be consulted in order to determine whether a unit designed for duty on water circuits will work efficiently with other liquids: it is suggested that flow rates for non-aqueous fluids should be typically 0·025–0·05 l/m²s in domestic systems (see Section 3.6.2). It should be noted that under laminar flow conditions pumping power increases approximately as the square of the flow rate and under turbulent flow conditions as the cube of the flow rate. For any system the power requirement may be calculated from the product of the flow rate and the total head: for water the equation is

Power (watts) = 9·81 × flow rate (l/s) × total head (metres of water).

In a typical domestic solar system the requirement will be about 2 W, but a suitable centrifugal accelerator pump will consume about 30 W of electricity.

Probably the two cheapest methods of checking the flow rate in an installed system are to use either a variable-area flowmeter or one of the combined balancing valve-flow indicators that are now available.

The characteristics of variable-area meters have been discussed by the author elsewhere[94]; an additional cautionary note is that they should be well protected from frost damage.

Some of the combined valve-indicator units have pressure tappings either side of an orifice plate (to which a suitable manometer may be connected) whilst others incorporate a direct readout of flowrate.

Whilst any type of flow metering equipment may be considered to be an optional extra on a small domestic solar system it may prove useful as an indicator of simple faults such as air-locking.

In multi-array systems inexpensive flowmeters may be used to indicate the correctness or otherwise of the flow distribution, and, for this reason alone, may be considered an asset. For this application, calibration for the particular fluid to be used is usually unnecessary because the principal function of the meters is to indicate whether the flowrate in each array is the same: a single calibrated meter may be used to determine the total flow rate.

4.4 Pipework

The flow of liquids in pipes is a complex subject but for most applications the data can be reduced to a number of tables giving the pressure loss for various flow rates for sizes of pipes commonly available. Since pressure loss increases approximately as the square of the flow rate (for turbulent flow conditions) linear extrapolations cannot be used, and any temperature dependence of viscosity usually results in an increasing flow rate with increasing temperature[106, 107].

The starting point for any calculation is however a determination of the fluid velocity that will result from a given total flow rate, and in small pipes this should be kept below 2 m/s[107], and preferably below 1 m/s, if all risks of both noise and erosion are to be avoided.

Corresponding flow rates and velocities are given in Table 3 and it is evident that for solar systems in houses 12 mm or 15 mm pipe or similar may be suitable.

However, small diameter pipes show a greater head loss than might be anticipated because a greater proportion of their cross-sectional area is occupied by the boundary layers that are a feature of most fluid flows. For this reason the use of 12 mm tube for small domestic solar systems is not as attractive as Table 3 might suggest.

Table 3 Showing the relationship between flow rate and velocity for standard sizes of copper pipe to BS 2871 Table X. The figures in brackets are the number of square metres of collector that could be served assuming a flow rate of 0·016 l/m²s

Nominal pipe size (external diameter) mm	Fluid velocity = 1 m/s	Fluid velocity = 1·5 m/s
12	0·092 (5·7)	0·137 (8·6)
15	0·145 (9)	0·218 (14)
22	0·321 (20)	0·381 (30)
28	0·539 (34)	0·809 (50)
35	0·835 (52)	1·25 (78)

Table 4 The equivalent length in metres of various fittings for standard pipe sizes. The figures are approximately correct for water between 20 and 40°C and assume turbulent flow

Pipe size (mm)	Gate valve	Right angle bend	Compression elbow (sharp right angle bend)	Capillary elbow (soldered sharp right angle bend)	Stopcock
12	0·18	0·18	0·37	0·25	3·1
15	0·24	0·24	0·49	0·33	4·0
22	0·40	0·37	0·80	0·54	6·5
28	0·55	0·52	1·1	0·74	9·0
35	0·72	0·64	1·4	0·95	11·5

Once the proposed layout of the system is known the total pipe length can easily be determined but before the total pressure drop can be calculated due allowance must be made for the number of bends, valves and other fittings. The easiest way of allowing for these is to use published data which gives the equivalent length of a fitting, that is, the length of straight pipe that gives rise to the same pressure loss as does the fitting.

Table 4 has been compiled from reference 107 and is to be used as a rough guide only. For circuits where it is required to predict the flow rate exactly more accurate data should be used.

An example is given below to illustrate the use of the data in Table 4 together with that in reference 107. Suppose a solar collector of area 7 m² is to be installed on a large house and the total length of connecting pipework on the primary circuit is 10 m. (If the circuit is indirect an additional allowance must be made for the heat exchanger, here assumed to be a coil of 20 metres of 28 mm copper pipe). If the design flow rate has been chosen as 0·016 l/m²s then the total flow will be 0·112 l/s which precludes the use of 12 mm pipe if a 1 m/s velocity maximum is specified. The pressure drop in 15 mm pipe will be about 650 N/m²m and that in 22 mm pipe about 100 N/m²m. If 5 capillary elbows and 2 gate valves are to be incorporated in the circuit, then the equivalent lengths are 2·13 and 3·50 m for 15 and 22 mm pipe respectively. The total pressure drops for these two options are therefore 7·88 kN/m² and 1·35 kN/m², to which must be added 0·6 kN/m² for the heat exchanger (assuming it to be equivalent to 20 m of straight tube). Since the pressure drop with 15 mm tube is well within the capability of the smallest domestic circulating pump, this option is likely to be the most favourable. The above example ignores the flow resistance of the collector plates but for most designs this is very small and may be neglected; the principal reason is that the fluid velocity in any channel in these collector plates is usually much smaller than that in the connecting pipework. Collector plates incorporating a single length of small diameter tube may exhibit an appreciable pressure loss and the manufacturers should provide the appropriate data.

In draindown systems where the pump has to do work to lift water through a vertical height, this is equivalent to an additional working head to that calculated above. For example, if a pump has to lift water through a distance of 2 metres, this is equivalent to an extra pressure loss of 19 kN/m², and a higher head pump may need to be specified. This example illustrates what can be a serious disadvantage of some draindown systems – a high-head pump may be needed to start the circulation but if this is maintained to some extent by suction from the flow line an excessive flow rate can be produced; more complex systems use a high head pump for starting and switch to a smaller pump for running[108]. This refinement probably cannot be justified in domestic sized water heating systems, but use of two-speed pumps may offer a workable solution. The essential problem here is that centrifugal accelerator pumps are not ideally suited to this type of application.

5 Fixing solar collectors to buildings

5.1 Wind loading – approximate calculations

Perhaps the greatest potential danger in solar collector applications is the possibility that the collectors or some of their component parts may become detached in high winds and it is appropriate to consider the order of magnitude of the forces that these assemblies must be designed to withstand.

The following material is a summary of the author's design calculations for the solar system that was installed by BRE at a school in Tunbridge Wells early in 1976; details of the thermal performance of this system have already been published[109].

The system was to consist of a row of 4 collectors mounted on a flat roofed two-storey building; preliminary calculations showed that it would be advisable to build an enclosed A-frame structure so as to limit the wind loads and to site the collectors away from the edge of the roof where high suction forces were expected to be generated. At the time that these calculations were carried out the concept of weighting the collector assemblies down on to the roof was still being considered but subsequently it was determined that because of the limited strength of the roof it would be necessary to install rolled steel joists above the roof line and to mount the collectors on these.

The following calculations consider two principal questions that would be pertinent if a free standing collector assembly had simply been placed on the roof – whether the assembly would be in danger either of blowing over or of sliding across the roof.

The starting point for the calculations was the design wind speed V for the Tunbridge Wells area, 38 m/s. However, since the building was not in an excessively exposed position and because a 10 year design condition was considered acceptable this figure was reduced to 28·4 m/s from which the dynamic wind pressure, q, was calculated according to the usual equations[110]

$V_s = V S_1 S_2 S_3$ where $S_1 = 1·0$, $S_2 = 0·85$, $S_3 = 0·88$
$q = \frac{1}{2}\rho\, V_s^2$ where V_s = wind velocity
ρ = air density = 1·23 kg/m³

thus $q = 495$ N/m².

The force on a surface due to the maximum expected wind is given by

$F = q\, C_p A$ where C_p = pressure coefficient for the surface
and A = area of the surface

For an enclosed A frame located away from the edge of the roof the pressure coefficients were taken to be

C_p (windward) = 0·6
C_p (leeward) = −0·3 } For the whole structure

The angle of inclination of both sides of the A frame was taken to be 45° and the gross area of each side estimated at 9 m², (9 m × 1 m).

The forces on the A frame due to wind may be resolved as shown in Figure 35a.

The mass of the A frame was estimated as 180 kg, or 20 kg per metre length. For the purpose of calculations it was assumed that this mass was equally distributed between the two sides of the framework.

The mass of the collectors was known to be about 80 kg each (including glass and water), or 35·5 kg/m. The forces on a 1 m length of framework were calculated as shown in Figure 35b, assuming a north wind. Taking moments about edge A,

$R_B = 24·2$ kgf (1 kgf = 9·806 N)

It may be seen that with a south wind the corresponding reaction at A (with B as pivot) would be greater than 24·2 because the collectors are nearer to A than to B. Taking moments about B, $R_A = 42$ kgf. The net effective weight of the assembly under maximum wind load conditions is 66·2 kgf/m and the horizontal forces sum to 32·1 kgf/m. Thus, whilst there was little possibility of the A frame toppling over, a real danger existed that it could blow across the roof unless weighted down or otherwise restrained.

In order to calculate the localised forces acting on a small area of the structure, say one cladding panel, higher values of C_p were used; these values correspond to the high local forces that may be experienced – it is unlikely that the whole area would, at any one time, be subject to these forces. The pressure on a cladding panel was thus determined as 990 N/m², and the assembly was designed to withstand considerably in excess of this. The subject of wind loading is far more complex than might be supposed by the example given above, and the interested reader is referred to other BRE and BSI publications [111, 112, 113].

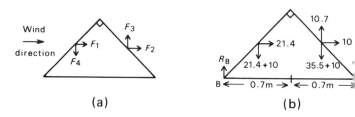

Figure 35 Wind loading on collectors: (a) Generalised resolution of wind forces on an enclosed A frame installation, (b) Calculated wind and weight forces for the installation at Tunbridge Wells School. Units: kgf

5.2 Fixing to flat roofs

A general conclusion that may be drawn from Section 5.1 is that it is not safe to assume that the weight of even very heavy solar collectors is sufficient to restrain them against wind forces when they are mounted on flat roofs.

The author knows of one case in which heavy steel collectors (similar to those used at the Tunbridge Wells school) were mounted on a flat garage roof in the UK in such a way that the roof membrane had to resist the wind loads; during high winds the collectors were torn off the roof, the connecting pipework was snapped, and the roof structure damaged. The collectors landed in the garden without causing injury but the consequences could have been serious especially as broken glass was scattered over the surrounding area.

If collectors are mounted on an open framework (as distinct from the enclosed A frame discussed in Section 5.1) it must be anticipated that the wind loads may be increased, principally because high pressures can be generated underneath the collectors. A satisfactory design must therefore ensure that not only are the collector boxes suitably anchored but that the cover glass is in no danger of being sucked out. It is possible to envisage conditions under which the rear surface of exposed collectors experiences a positive pressure and the front glass a negative pressure, and if the collector box has not been designed to minimise air leakage through its rear surface then under high wind conditions the net forces on the glass could produce a pressure of the order of 2000 N/m² (0·29 psi). In the absence of more exact data 2000 N/m² should constitute a reasonable design rule for collectors attached to open frameworks on moderately exposed flat roofs.

The second major problem in siting solar collectors on flat roofed buildings follows from the necessity to restrain them against wind loads and involves making good the almost inevitable penetrations through the roof surface.

If the roof decking is wood and is supported by wooden joists then carriage screws may safely be used to anchor the collector frameworks to the joists but care must be taken to ensure a satisfactory seal around the penetrations of the membrane. Screwing the collectors down to the decking itself cannot be regarded as good practice both because of the large number of screws that would be needed to ensure an adequate margin of safety and because any uplift on the collectors would tend to lift the decking off its joists.

For other types of flat roofs acceptable solutions are not so easily found but in some cases it may be possible to distribute the weight of the collector assembly on to the roof and to secure it with brackets taken over the roof edge; this approach has been employed successfully on the BRE solar laboratory but there will be many instances in which penetration of the roof membrane is the only feasible option. The weight of the assembly may be taken by the roof membrane only if it is strong enough and if highly localised forces are not produced. For example, it might not be permissible to place a collector assembly directly on to a felted roof that was covered with stone chippings because the few chippings that where in contact with the framework would be under high pressure and might be expected eventually to penetrate the waterproofing layers of felt. The solution sometimes adopted of installing several layers of felt or similar material between the chippings and the collector framework will certainly serve to distribute the load but there are other mechanisms whereby localised stress can be produced in a flat roof; these include the situation where a shallow pool of water resulting from a short shower lies in a slight depression whilst the surrounding area is heated by the sun. Evaporation of the water produces cooling of a localised area and a similar situation could be produced by parts of a roof being covered by a collector support framework; a substantial temperature difference could now be produced since the underlying roof would not be receiving solar radiation as would the water-filled depression described above. These potential risks are easily understood but whether they constitute a real threat will depend both on the detailed design and quality of construction of the original roof. BRE reports are available detailing the problems of flat roofs, and should be consulted for further information[114, 115]. It is however here emphasised that the mechanisms of failure can be complex, and it must not be assumed that a system is thoroughly proven just because it has withstood a couple of years exposure; one of the commonest mechanisms that can give rise to failure after a substantial period of time is the inability of many materials to exhibit true elastic behaviour, and failure in either compression or tension can eventually occur as the result of many cycles each of which produced a small net movement.

If the weight of the collector assembly is to be taken by the underlying structure of the roof without being transmitted via the roof membrane then the uprights which are passed through the membrane must be designed not only to take a vertical load but also to resist horizontal forces without exhibiting undue movement; any movement that does occur may tend to promote failure of the joints between the uprights and the roof membrane. Failure of these joints may also be anticipated if the action of cutting holes through the roof allowed some settling of the membrane to occur over a period of time. It is thought that this mechanism may be responsible for some of the problems that have occurred at the Tunbridge Wells school where water penetration of the flat roof occurred subsequent to the installation of the solar collector system. The failure of this roof occurred around two of the uprights that support the main RSJs and it was evident that considerable contraction of the roof surface away from the uprights had occurred subsequent to the initial sealing of the joints.

In general it must be realised that flat roofs are very prone to rain penetration problems and if solar collectors are to be installed then high standards of both design and workmanship will be necessary in order to ensure that problems do not subsequently occur.

5.3 Wall mounting

Wall mounting of solar collectors is not popular in the UK at the present time and this situation is probably the result of aesthetic disadvantages since in some other respects wall mounting may be preferred to the more usual locations.

Many of the solar systems installed to date on UK houses may be expected to exhibit problems in the longer term with rain penetration through the roof and it is shown in Section 5.4 that the requirements for a satisfactory roof mounted system are somewhat in excess of some current practice; whilst there is no doubt that any system of wall mounting will be more expensive than a very poor roof mounting for the same area of collector it is not apparent which of the two options would be preferred if both had to be carried out to a high standard of workmanship.

The principal requirements for wall mounting are that the framework to which the collectors are attached should be well secured to the building by using expanding bolts into brickwork (or other no less suitable heavy duty fixings) and should be adequately protected from corrosion: steel should be galvanised to BS 729[56].

Since the run-off from both collector and framework will be onto the underlying ground it may be advised that only stainless steel or other corrosion resistant fixings are used since stains from rusting iron and steel are very difficult to remove. Copper based alloys can also cause staining and the run-off from these can have a detrimental effect on other metals. Bimetallic and crevice corrosion between (say) the collector casing and the support framework may prove troublesome: Section 5.4 considers these problems in more detail.

Depending upon the height of the collectors the connecting pipework may be taken either through the wall of the house or directly into the loft space through the soffit board; in the former case the pipes should be angled in order to help prevent rain penetration and a small amount of flashing around the points of entry may be considered desirable. If pipes are taken through fire stop walls any damage must be made good[116].

The obvious disadvantages of siting solar collectors on walls are that they will detract from the smooth line of the building and may be overshadowed by nearby trees or other obstructions especially during the winter months. However, since the annual output of collectors used for preheating domestic hot water does not change substantially as their inclination is varied[104] an angle of only 30° to the wall should ensure a satisfactory thermal performance, provided that overshadowing is limited only to midwinter.

In addition, collectors installed at this relatively steep angle may be less subject to severe overheating in summertime and for many families where the house is vacated for several weeks in the summer they may offer an improved performance over roof mounted units.

Other practical advantages to accrue from wall mounting are that installation, maintenance and repair are brought within the scope of most DIY enthusiasts. Wall mounted collectors also have the advantage that they are more readily adapted to operation with gravity circulation systems (see Section 2) since the storage vessel may be placed in the loft.

It is probable that one of the most troublefree solar system designs for the UK will incorporate wall mounted collectors in an indirect gravity circuit but the potential for such systems on single-family dwellings will be limited by aesthetic considerations.

5.4 Fixing to pitched roofs

In introducing a detailed discussion of the problems of fixing solar collectors to pitched roofs it should be noted that this is one of the areas where a great many of the installations carried out to date in the UK may prove to be unsatisfactory within a time span that is much less than the 50–60 years that may be taken to be the expected troublefree life of a modern well constructed tiled or slated roof. Many cheap solutions to the problems of resisting wind loads and ensuring continued weathertightness have been put forward but it is considered that few if any are satisfactory, and the credibility of the solar industry in the UK requires its acceptance of the fact that installing solar collectors on the types of roofs most commonly found on UK houses will require high standards of both design and workmanship. Failure to appreciate these facts has already led to obviously unsatisfactory designs being introduced on to the market and if there are too many of these the inevitable backlash may damage the prospects for the UK solar industry for many years.

It is sometimes argued that since many solar collectors have remained both fixed to roofs and watertight for a few months or years the methods of installation must, therefore, have been satisfactory. These arguments are invalid for several reasons the most important of which is perhaps that the repairs to a roof that has been damaged by incorrect fixing of solar collectors can cost many times the value of the energy that may be saved annually by the collectors; since at the present time solar water heating systems are only marginally viable in the UK even when every argument and assumption is strongly biased in their favour it is clear that substantial maintenance costs cannot be tolerated. In addition, it is invalid to suggest that a few years' exposure is an appropriate test for the capability of a system to resist wind loads since peak forces in any given direction will only be generated very infrequently (typically once every 50 years); this is unfortunately no guarantee that they will not occur soon after the installation has been completed. Modern tiled and slated roofs in the UK are designed to withstand all but the most exceptional weather conditions and those that are initially constructed correctly have set a precedent of durability which must not be degraded by the activities of the solar industry.

The other common type of pitched roof construction consists of a sheet of (typically) 19 mm plywood laid over the rafters and covered with layers of waterproof felt. The problems of fixing solar collectors to this type of roof are relatively trivial compared to those encountered with the tiled or slated types since the weight may usually be taken by the plywood and waterproofing of bolt and screw holes may readily be achieved. The special design requirements for these roofs are discussed at the end of this section but most of the general principles that are outlined below for tiled and slated roofs may also be applied to those of all-wood construction.

In order that some of the recommendations given below may be fully appreciated it is considered worthwhile to outline the basic principles that underlie the design of tiled and slated roofs on single-family houses. The construction of most pitched roofs is either of the 'traditional' or 'trussed rafter' type and these have very different characteristics. Traditional roof construction often employed timbers of generous size and these were made an integral part of the house; rafters were laid on to substantial purlins and wall plates that were securely mounted on the brickwork and the completed roof could be expected to exhibit a high degree of robustness and tolerance of subsequent mistreatment. In houses with this type of roof the pitch was usually over 35° and it was normal practice to lay either the tiles or slates directly on the battens without any underlying felt or sarking. Water penetration resulting from rain being driven up the roof was limited because of the pitch, and few substantial problems were usually encountered. One of the most common long-term faults with roofs of this type was that they were constructed with either tiles or slates that were subject to lamination, a process where water freezing inside the tile or slate caused cracking. This problem was finally overcome with the introduction of concrete tiles which are usually guaranteed for 25 years, and may be expected to last for 60 years or more if properly installed.

Trussed rafter roofs comprise sections of timber which are far smaller than those usually found in traditional roofs but because of careful design the stresses can be kept to acceptable levels under all the predicted loading conditions. Trussed rafters may have little resistance to forces applied horizontally in the plane of the roof; sometimes the only resistance is given by the battens which are designed principally to take static snow loads in addition to the weight of the tiles or slates. A few diagonal braces in the plane of the roof are often incorporated and are a desirable feature[80]. If such bracing is found to be absent then it may be added prior to the installation of a solar system: if necessary existing bracing may be repositioned slightly but it must not be removed permanently. It may be advised that at no time should a trussed rafter roof be left without any diagonal bracing unless there is some alternative provision for ensuring lateral stability. With the advent of very low pitch roofs (in the range 17° – 27°) came the necessity to provide additional protection against driving rain since it was now readily possible for water to be driven between simple tile overlaps and into the roof space. The fashion for low pitched roofs in fact preceded the use of trussed rafters for housing

in the UK and was widely adopted as soon as interlocking tile designs which were reasonably watertight at these slopes became available. The waterproof felt or sarking which is almost universally used today in pitched roof construction was introduced originally as a secondary line of defence against wind driven rain and snow and whilst its more obvious benefit is perhaps to keep a considerable amount of dust out of loft areas the value of its primary function should not be under-estimated especially with very low pitch roofs.

The consequences of not adhering to satisfactory design and construction standards for trussed rafter roofs have recently been high-lighted by the collapse of a sports hall in Birkenhead[117, 118]; it is not improbable that damage resulting from inexpert installation of solar collectors could have similar results. Design faults in domestic trussed rafter roofs have recently been investigated by BRE[119].

Tiles and slates are held down on to a roof principally by gravity; concrete tiles have nibs which are hooked over the battens and in the absence of wind loads no additional fixing would be necessary. Slates have of course to be nailed to the battens because otherwise they could slide down the roof. Thermal expansion is easily accommodated since each tile or slate is free to move relative to its neighbours and in fact a considerable amount of thermal movement does occur since roof surfaces can reach upwards of 50 or 60°C under high solar irradiance. The weight of tiles is often underestimated by the layman but is in the region of 40–50 kg/m²; even so it is considered prudent to nail down all the courses in areas of prevalent high wind and every third or fourth course in less risk prone situations. Since high suction forces can be generated both near the edges of pitched roofs and around protrusions such as chimney stacks nailing all the tiles in these areas is advised[110, 120].

The suction force that can be produced on tiles is still the subject of research but is thought to depend partly on the tile profile – especially its depth – and partly on the pressure behind the tile, which is probably determined largely by the quality of the underlying felt. If the felt is poorly joined then the underlying pressure will be close to loft pressure but if airtight may be determined by the goodness of fit of the tiles themselves; large gaps can result in a high pressure region being built up between the felt and the underside of the tiles. These effects are illustrated in Figure 36.

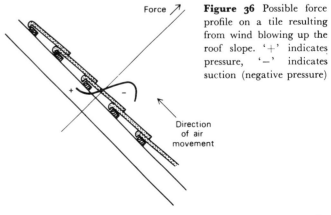

Figure 36 Possible force profile on a tile resulting from wind blowing up the roof slope. '+' indicates pressure, '−' indicates suction (negative pressure)

It may be seen that the most likely mode of failure is for the lower edge of a tile to be lifted by the wind whereupon it may either become displaced completely or drop back into position as the wind abates; repeated movement may be expected to result in breakage.

In the light of the above summary of roof design and behaviour it is instructive to consider some of the more obviously unsatisfactory methods that have been employed in the UK for fixing solar collectors to tiled or slated roofs; the examples that are used have been taken from reports that the author has prepared following inspections of solar systems installed on private houses. The principal defects of most of these installations were that the weight of the collectors was taken directly on the roof surface, the methods of securing the collectors were unsatisfactory, and the methods used to attempt to waterproof penetrations through the roof showed a lack of knowledge of basic good practice.

It is generally agreed that tiles or slates can withstand considerable point loading so long as the force is applied gently; lightweight solar collectors would therefore not be expected to cause immediate damage if they were laid directly on to the roof. However it must be anticipated that because neither the roof nor the solar collector will be perfectly planar there may be few points of contact and, therefore, that these points may be under considerable pressure; this applies especially to heavily profiled tiled roofs. If the rear surface of the collector box were compliant then an acceptable amount of load spreading might be achieved even with heavy collectors.

Three of the most unsatisfactory methods of securing collectors to roofs are shown in Figure 37; in the first method (Figure 37a) metal straps are pushed up under a tile and simply bent round the nearest batten inside the loft. The straps are then secured to the top edge of the collector boxes and the only fixing for the lower edge of the collectors is provided by the pipework. In the second method (Figure 37b) straps are used to secure the lower edge of the panels and the loads are again taken by individual lengths of the existing battens.

The most obviously unsatisfactory feature of both of these methods is that battens are not designed for taking high additional loads and should under no circumstances be used to secure solar collectors. The very minimum requirement for these methods is that additional larger battens should be installed on the underside of the rafters and the straps secured to these. The second unsatisfactory feature is that the straps are inserted under tiles or slates in such a way that gaps typically 4–6 mm wide are left either side of the strap and these can provide a passage for wind driven rain. Often no attempt is made to seal these gaps and since they are near the points where the felt is usually slashed in order to gain access to the underside of the tiles it is not surprising that water penetration into the loft has been experienced with these types of systems. This particular problem could probably be solved by sealing with a silicone sealant; there is no requirement that the sealant adheres well to the tiles so long as it remains in place and substantially fills the gaps.

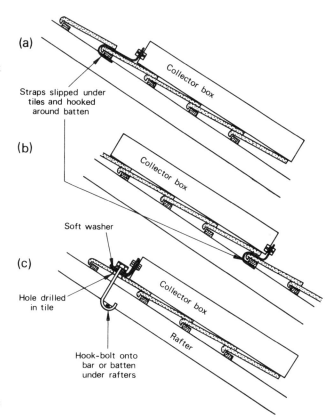

Figure 37 Three unsatisfactory but not uncommon methods of attaching collectors to tiled or slated roofs

In many cases the methods used to take pipes through the roof are also inadequate; in some installations inspected by the author crude holes had been drilled and chipped out of the tiles, the pipes pushed through and sealing attempted with a mixture of felt, mastic, putty, and silicone sealant. Often, the pipes had been installed in the valleys of the tiles so as to ensure a maximum potential rate of leakage.

Other unsatisfactory aspects of these installations are often that the straps are secured only to a part of the collector box that itself is not strong enough to take the weight of the rest of the assembly; in some instances straps have been fixed to parts of collector boxes that are secured only by a few small rivets, and in other cases to single bolt fixings through thin GRP (see Section 3.1.7).

A less obvious fault of both the above methods is that collectors should be properly secured along two opposite edges and the connecting pipework should not be relied upon to provide one of the fixings. Since high winds may give rise to suction forces especially on the lower half of collectors it should be anticipated that straps are unlikely to be able to resist these forces without bending and since this would cause the overlying tiles to lift the concept of strap fixings is unlikely ever to prove acceptable.

Figure 37c shows a system in which bolts are passed through the tiles and tightened down. This and similar methods of fixing have been advocated by other authors but they are here considered to be unsatisfactory: the principal faults are lack of proper waterproofing and high point loading of the tiles.

A thoroughly satisfactory system for collector mounting should incorporate consideration of the following criteria.

1 Each collector module should be restrained against movement both in and perpendicular to the plane of the roof. The greatest forces will occur down and on to the roof slope (due to the components of the weight of the collector) and upwards along the lower half of the collector (due to wind loading). In addition, smaller horizontal forces that tend to push the collectors along the roof may be experienced.

2 All penetrations through or under the tiles or slates should either be flashed using traditional and proven methods or should be enclosed beneath a weather-proof envelope. The latter solution is realised in designs which treat the collector box as a skylight and flash it into the roof, and by methods that use patent-glazing technology.

3 If collector boxes are placed directly on tiles or slates then provision should be made to prevent the generation of unduly high localised pressures.

In addition, provision should be made to prevent a build-up of leaves and other debris in the crevices between the underside of the collector box and the roof, and if the collectors are mounted on the lower region of the roof care should be taken to ensure that any rain falling on the upper part is either diverted around the collectors or can flow freely beneath them.

4 All the forces with the possible exception of the weight of the collectors should be transmitted through the roof surface and taken by supports attached to the rafters; it is not satisfactory to rely on the slates, tiles, connecting pipework or battens. These supports should be of such a design that the forces are not taken by one or two rafters (especially in a trussed rafter roof) but are distributed amongst the rafters underlying the collector assembly; this is particularly important where very heavy collectors are used.

5 The design should provide for reasonably easy replacement of any sheet of glass or other cover material and for removal and repair of any one collector module. This latter requirement dictates that each module should be fixed independently and should not rely on its neighbour for support.

6 If the sarking felt is damaged during installation of solar collectors it must be repaired to a standard that will ensure that water penetrating the tiles or slates higher up the roof will be channelled past the damaged area; this will ensure that the function of the felt is not impaired and is particularly important with low pitched roofs. Since it is normal for felt to sag between rafters the worst place to penetrate it is midway between any two rafters; however, damage adjacent to a rafter may need only superficial patching. If there is no alternative to holing the felt midway between rafters then the subsequent repairs must include provision for this area to be raised so that water entering higher up the roof may be channelled to either side of the damaged area.

7 Bimetallic contact in structures exposed to the weather should be avoided wherever possible. In designs where such contact does occur, for example, between metal collector casings, support frameworks, fixing bolts and flashing, only the more compatible combinations of metals should be used. A general rule for fixings is that they should be of a more noble metal than the components that are to be secured.

Stainless steel bolts and screws may be used in combination with many other metals, but not with aluminium in marine environments; in these situations only aluminium fixings may be used to secure aluminium components. Another problem with aluminium is that it may be slightly attacked by contact with new concrete roof tiles.

Generally, lead may contact either galvanised or un-protected steel but there is a risk of crevice corrosion of the lead (see below); relative movement of the two metals should be precluded in order to aid retention of the protective oxide film.

Copper may be allowed to contact lead, brass and stainless steel but should be isolated from aluminium, steel and zinc. The latter three metals may also be attacked by the run-off from copper or copper based alloys, and this should be avoided.

Expert advice should be sought whenever there is any doubt as to the suitability of a mixed-metal structure for exterior use.

8 Crevice corrosion, which occurs principally as a consequence of the oxygen gradient that can be set up in a layer of water trapped between two adjacent surfaces, may give trouble not only in mixed-metal structures but also where, for example, a galvanised steel collector casing is laid onto a galvanised support framework or where any metal component is installed in such a way that exposure to atmospheric oxygen is not uniform over its surface: laying metal cased solar collectors directly onto tiled or slated roofs clearly introduces many areas of potential oxygen depletion.

It is a curious fact that it is areas where the oxygen concentration is lowest that are attacked under these conditions: metals which rely on a passivating oxide film for corrosion protection can be particularly prone to crevice corrosion. A notable example is ordinary 18/8 (18 per cent chromium 8 per cent nickel) stainless steel: crevice corrosion in structures manufactured from this material may prove troublesome, especially in coastal areas, and consideration should be given either to eliminating crevices in the design or to using a stainless steel containing molybdenum.

9 Whenever timber is used externally to the building envelope it should be protected from decay and some treatments, notably water based products such as copper-chrome-arsenate, can give rise to corrosion of metals if direct contact occurs; aluminium, steel and zinc can be particularly heavily attacked.
In a few areas of the UK soft wood used inside roof spaces must be treated against infestation by the house longhorn beetle[121].

There would appear to be only a small number of acceptable solutions to these problems. The entire collector assembly may be flashed into the roof using either purpose-made or traditional lead flashings. A necessary requirement of this solution is that the joins between individual collector modules should be designed to accept flashing strips since water leakage cannot normally be allowed. Omission of the flashing along the bottom edge may be permissible in some situations but is preferably included to minimise wind effects; provision should however be made for ventilation of the collectors (see Section 3.1.2).

Alternatively each support bracket may be flashed individually into the roof and the collectors subsequently mounted on to these brackets. In addition, the flow and return pipes will usually have to be flashed into the roof either individually or as an assembly. Simple but satisfactory methods of taking small pipes through a tiled or slated roof do not yet appear to be available; as already noted some companies either drill through the roof and make little attempt at proper weatherproofing, or push the pipes up underneath the tiles or slates.

One possible solution would be to use a special moulded adapter in a standard vent pipe flashing; a longer term option which would be more satisfactory in some respects would be for manufacturers to produce special tiles with a preformed passageway in them: a suggested design is shown in Figure 38, but is of course not suitable for use with slates or plain tiles, both of which have to be

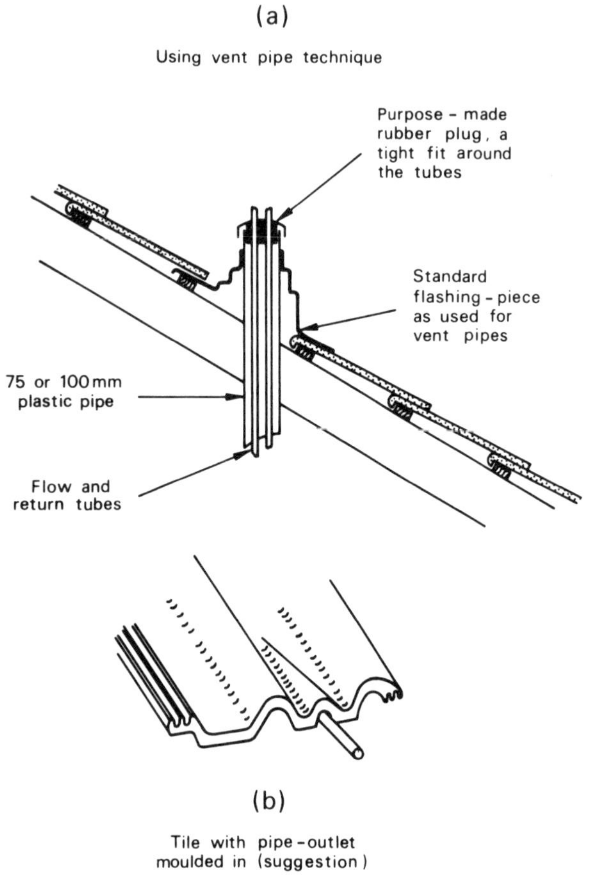

(a)

Using vent pipe technique

Purpose - made rubber plug, a tight fit around the tubes

Standard flashing - piece as used for vent pipes

75 or 100 mm plastic pipe

Flow and return tubes

(b)

Tile with pipe - outlet moulded in (suggestion)

Figure 38 Two suggested methods for taking small diameter pipes through tiled or slated roofs: (a) Using a vent pipe flashing, (b) Using a specially moulded tile

installed so that there are effectively 2 layers over any one point on the roof. Alternative and probably acceptable solutions in these cases are shown in Figure 39a and involve installing a specially made copper plate through which pass two short lengths of copper pipe. Stainless steel may also be used, and the junctions between the pipes and the plate brazed or welded. These simple designs can however introduce an unacceptably high heat leak into small systems; more sophisticated solutions involve using concentric tubes, but use of a thin stainless steel plate minimises the thermal leakage paths and simple designs may prove adequate.

Two universally applicable designs are shown in Figure 39b and make use of a lead flashing slate to which is soldered a tube of either copper or lead. The pipe(s) from the collector are then passed through this tube; in the design having a vertical tube a skirt attached to the pipe(s) provides weather-proofing.

It is likely that air locking will prove troublesome with many systems unless either an air vent is fitted externally (that is, at the top of the collector panels) or the flow pipe from the top of the collectors is installed so that it has a continuous rise into the roof space: in this design the pipe passes through the lead slate almost parallel to the roof and a weather-proofing skirt is no longer appropriate. If the lead tube is both of sufficient length (150 mm should be adequate) and is dressed down onto the pipe no rain or snow penetration should occur, especially if the joint is wrapped with waterproof insulation. Alternatively, a silicone (or even a foamed plastic sealant) could be used to fill the space between the pipe and the lead tube.

The magnitude of the heat loss introduced by any of these designs may be estimated very approximately by assuming an overall U value of perhaps 25 W/m^2 °C: for example, if the area of one flashing unit was 0·25 m^2 and the temperature difference between the transfer fluid and the ambient air was 20°C the loss rate would be 125 W, assuming that all the flashing was at the fluid temperature.

Since this condition will never even approximately be realised, except perhaps with thick copper flashing soldered to the pipework, the above calculation probably represents a near to worst case condition. It is therefore considered that the design concepts outlined above will prove satisfactory, especially with large systems, but in view of the expense of solar energy systems (and, therefore, of the energy that they supply – see Section 4.1) it is recommended that designs be used that minimise the heat loss, and some small additional capital cost to realise this objective cannot be considered inappropriate.

On some installations it may be acceptable to bring the pipes down the roof and through the soffit board into the loft; this should prove a satisfactory method, but if the collectors are located near the eaves provision to prevent rain water overshooting the gutter must be considered. A further complication is that air vents may have to be installed externally.

The third principal solution involves using patent glazing as the water-proofing envelope and installing the

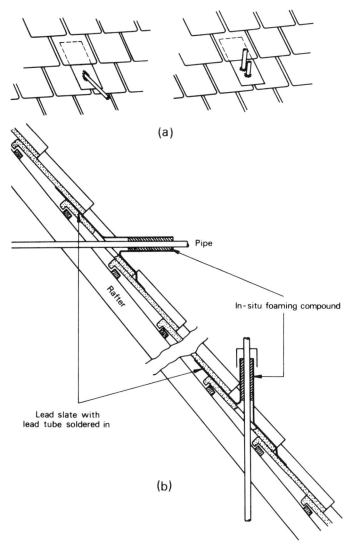

(a)

Pipe

Rafter

In-situ foaming compound

Lead slate with
lead tube soldered in

(b)

Figure 39 Four methods for taking small diameter pipes through tiled or slated roofs using sheet metal flashing: (a) Methods using thin copper or stainless steel sheet and suited for use with slates or plain tiles. Air-locking may be experienced in some systems if the design having vertical pipes is used, (b) Universally acceptable methods for either tiles or slates based on traditional lead flashing. It is suggested that the fluid pipes be thermally insulated from the flashing

size of collector plate for this type of application. An additional benefit is that lateral stability of a trussed rafter roof may be assured.

It would be advisable to incorporate a waterproof membrane in the construction so that any fluid leaking from the collector plates is prevented from entering the loft space; a sheet of polythene should be quite adequate if installed under a sufficiently thick layer of insulation such that a temperature of perhaps 40°C is not likely to be exceeded. Plastics and composites that will withstand higher temperatures are available and should be used if it is desired to place the membrane directly beneath the collector plates. Experience with these techniques in the UK is limited at present but one problem that has occurred results from the higher glass temperatures that are experienced when patent glazing is used above solar collector plates. It is shown in Section 3.1.5 that ordinary float glass should not be subjected to undue thermal stress, and whilst standard types of patent glazing are usually satisfactory when used in the situations for which they were originally designed it is apparent that some slight modification may be necessary to the clips which prevent the glass from slipping out of position; often these are of all metal construction and can induce a cold spot in the glass at a location that is already relatively highly stressed. Some thermal insulation between the clip and glass should solve this particular problem but in a few cases the thermal contact between the sides of the glass and the glazing bars may be sufficiently great to result in excessive thermal stress and it would seem prudent to select for solar applications those designs of patent glazing that incorporate some degree of thermal isolation between the edges of the glass and their supports. Under no circumstances should double glazing be used in a patent glazing system unless the design has been proved for use at sufficiently high temperatures. One additional problem that may arise in designs that use either a waxed cord or mastic bedding for the glass edges is that high temperatures can cause a softening of these materials – more load can then be thrown on to the retaining clips along the bottom edge of the glass.

collectors and pipework beneath this. The method has been cited as being more suited to new construction but is quite adaptable to most roof types provided that cost is not a primary consideration; for small areas of collector it seems unlikely that patent glazing will comprise the most economic solution unless undertaken by a firm specialising in small solar installations. A generalised design for a large patent glazed solar installation would involve removing the tiles and battens, and covering the rafters with 19 mm plywood; this can provide a suitable base on which to mount the insulation material, collector plates and patent glazing bars. If additional insulation is required this may usually be incorporated beneath the plywood. This design removes two of the objections that may be raised against installing solar collector plates between rafters; since the rafters may be subjected to high temperatures some movement may occur and the wide range of inter-rafter spacings that have been used militates against producing a standard

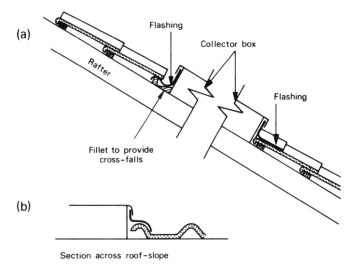

(a)

Flashing

Collector box

Rafter

Flashing

Fillet to provide
cross-falls

(b)

Section across roof-slope

Figure 40 Mounting collectors onto the roof surface and flashing all round

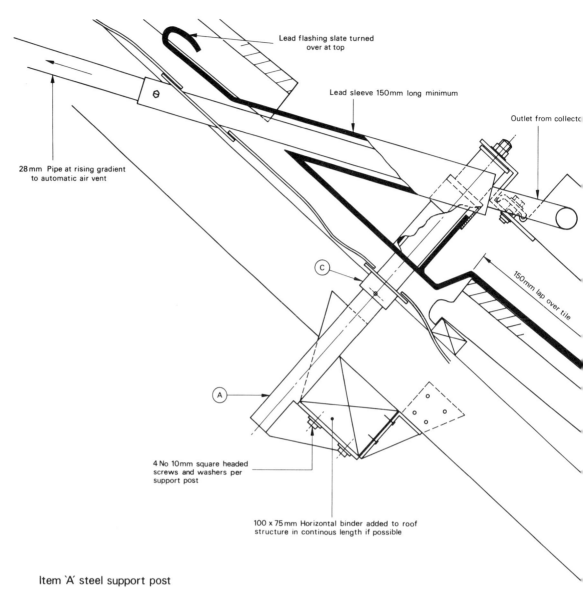

Lead flashing slate turned over at top

Lead sleeve 150mm long minimum

Outlet from collector

28mm Pipe at rising gradient to automatic air vent

150mm lap over tile

C

A

4 No 10mm square headed screws and washers per support post

100 x 75mm Horizontal binder added to roof structure in continous length if possible

Item `A´ steel support post

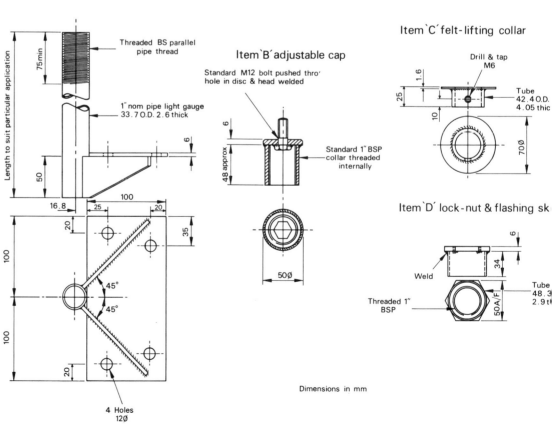

Threaded BS parallel pipe thread

75 min

1" nom pipe light gauge 33.7 O.D. 2.6 thick

Length to suit particular application

50

6

16.8   100

25   20

20

100

35

45°
45°

100

20

4 Holes
12Ø

Item `B´ adjustable cap

Standard M12 bolt pushed thro' hole in disc & head welded

6

48 approx

Standard 1" BSP collar threaded internally

50Ø

Item `C´ felt-lifting collar

Drill & tap M6

1.6

25

10

Tube 42.4 O.D. 4.05 thic

70Ø

Item `D´ lock-nut & flashing sk

6

34

Weld

Tube 48.3
2.9 t

Threaded 1" BSP

50 A/F

Dimensions in mm

Figure 41 A method for mounting collectors onto support posts fixed to the roof structure. This system was developed by BRE and BSRIA for fixing lightweight collectors to trussed rafter roofs, and is currently being evaluated. A considerable amount of load distribution can be achieved with this system, and it is considered suitable for most roof types: the dimensions of the main components and the exact detailing of the collector fixing points may need to be changed to suit any particular situation. The flow and return pipes may either be let through the roof with separate flashing (see Figures 38 and 39) or a dual-purpose flashing slate as shown here may be used. All the steel components are hot-dip galvanised; the only points of bimetallic contact are between the galvanised support posts and the lead flashing (which should give no trouble) and at the collector fixing points – depending on the type of collector it may be necessary to use insulating bushes and washers. All the screw threads external to the roof surface should be greased prior to final assembly

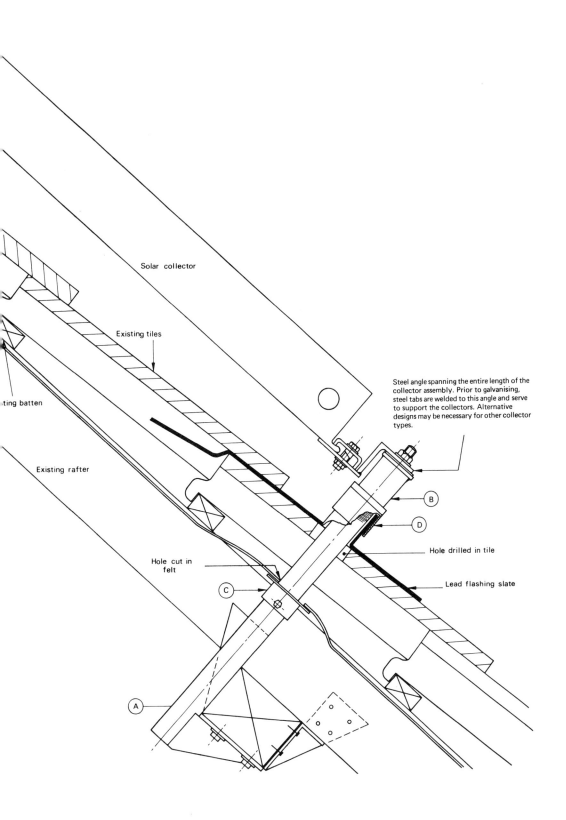

Solar collector

Existing tiles

Steel angle spanning the entire length of the collector assembly. Prior to galvanising, steel tabs are welded to this angle and serve to support the collectors. Alternative designs may be necessary for other collector types.

ting batten

Existing rafter

B

D

Hole drilled in tile

Hole cut in felt

C

Lead flashing slate

A

73

A cheaper method of installing collector plates inside the roof envelope has recently been tried on a private house fitted with a large solar space and water heating system[122]; the method has also been advocated elsewhere as a possible alternative to the expense of conventional patent glazing. The basic approach adopted is to adapt the existing rafters for the duty of supporting the glass and designs to date have used hardwood strips secured to the rafters as channels into which the glass is bedded using silicone sealant. It would appear that these designs rely heavily on the continuing dimensional stability of all the timber components and in view of both the frequency and magnitude of the thermal cycling that will occur some reservation concerning their long term reliability may be expressed, particularly if specially selected and treated timber is not specified.

There should be no difficulty in obtaining a satisfactory bond between the silicone sealant and the glass for a period that may exceed 10–15 years but the join to the hardwood strips would appear to be potentially less reliable and any fault is likely to result in a degree of water penetration. In summary, it would seem inadvisable at the present time for this type of construction to be incorporated into any large number of buildings except on a purely experimental basis.

Figures 40, 41, 42 and 43 show the main features of the four principal design solutions discussed above.

The special requirements in respect of fixing collectors to all-wood pitched roofs are few, and concern the methods by which fixings and pipes may be let through the external felt or felt slates. It should be satisfactory to bolt blocks of alloy, plastic, or preservative treated wood to the roof and to mount the solar collectors on these so that there is an air gap of at least 75 mm between the roof surface and the underside of the collector; this will ensure adequate ventilation of the felt surface but in view of the possible wind loading problems that may be induced all the felt around the collector installation should be held down with roofing nails. The blocks should be shaped at their upper ends so as to shed water and should preferably be mounted in a layer of bitumen. Alternatively, where

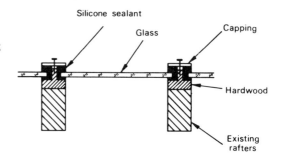

Figure 43 Fixing glass directly onto rafters to form a weatherproof envelope. The collector plates are supported between the rafters. This system relies heavily on continuing dimensional stability of the roof timbers

felt slates are used, flashing may be installed following the designs outlined above. Provision for load spreading in addition to that provided by the plywood may have to be made if a large number of heavy collectors are to be installed on an all-wood pitched roof. Measurements of load distribution in both traditional and trussed rafter roof constructions have recently been published by BRE[123, 124].

It must not be inferred that any of the methods discussed above are a perfect solution to all of the problems that have been outlined, but they are given here as a contribution to what is likely to be an area of continuing debate.

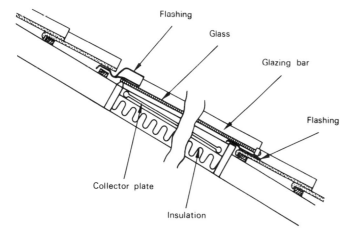

Figure 42 Installation of solar collectors under conventional patent glazing. The collector plates and insulation material are either supported between the rafters or laid on top of a sheet of plywood covering the rafters

6 Energy savings and financial considerations

6.1 General

When assessing the financial aspects of solar technology it should be recognised that the only benefit to accrue to the purchaser of a solar system is the energy saving that may be realised. This follows from the fact that with present technology solar energy cannot be expected to supply all the energy requirements for a process throughout the year and a back-up or auxiliary system capable of supplying the full demand will almost invariably be required under UK conditions. The only common exceptions to this rule are outdoor swimming pool installations but for the potentially more important domestic water heating type, there is usually no saving in the capital cost of the back-up system. This point has already been emphasised in Section 2.4.4.

It has been argued that use of solar energy should take precedence over other energy conservation measures simply because it makes use of 'free' energy. This argument is illogical; the correct method of assessment of any energy conservation system is to determine the amount of conventional (fossil or nuclear) energy that will not be consumed if the system is installed. It is shown later that application of energy conservation technology cannot necessarily be guaranteed to conserve fossil fuel reserves.

In a simple analysis the worth of a solar system may be assessed by the amount of conventional energy that it displaces and not by the amount of energy that it produces; a couple of examples are instructive. In the case of a system installed to heat an outdoor swimming pool only during the summer months the amount of conventional energy displaced is zero if the pool had previously been unheated and with a likelihood that it would have remained so if solar technology had not been available. In this case the installation of solar equipment actually results in a net increase in national energy consumption because the energy required to manufacture transport and install the solar system is never truly returned to the economy. The second example is more important since it illustrates a type of distortion that can accidentally be introduced into considerations of solar space heating system efficiencies. It might be claimed that solar space heating of dwelling houses could be a viable proposition in the UK and that large gains could be made by using either an 'active' or a 'passive' collection system (see Section 7).

However, simple calculations can be used to show that thermal insulation of a house is usually a more beneficial option than is application of solar technology (assuming of course that thermal insulation is technically possible)

and once the building is well insulated the heating season reduces essentially to the four winter months November–February, during which time there is little prospect in the UK climate of collecting a significant amount of solar energy with the type and size of systems that could reasonably be considered for incorporation into housing. In the absence of a viable system of long-term heat storage the solar contribution to the space heat load is therefore likely to be minimal during this period but can rise to much higher levels if it is conveniently assumed that the building must be kept at, for example, 20°C 24 hours a day during autumn winter and spring, and that the energy required to do this would have been derived from conventional sources in the absence of the solar system. The pertinent question of course is for what fraction of the autumn and spring periods would the house occupants have considered it necessary to run the conventional heating system, and the primary energy displaced by the solar system may be varied over a range of typically 10:1 depending upon the answer to this question. A grossly distorted result could be derived from an analysis which assumed that solar energy had usefully contributed to heating the house up to a higher temperature than would have been selected with a system using conventional fuel. The implications for calculation of the economics of solar space heating systems are obvious and it is emphasised that collected solar energy should only be assessed as financially beneficial if it has genuinely displaced conventional fuel.

Simple analysis is often used to determine the 'energy payback period' of a solar system and the only parameters sometimes considered are the energy required to manufacture the major components of the system and the likely annual collection of energy that might be accomplished by the complete system. Recent work[125] has indicated that energy payback periods for solar collectors used in water heating systems in the UK are in the region of 1 year and since this figure is far less than the financial payback periods determined by conventional analysis (see Section 6.4) it is helpful to consider briefly the possible reasons for this large discrepancy. One possibility is that the energy analysis may have omitted to consider all the processes that are a necessary preliminary to installing a solar system on a UK house, but even if the energy cost of the collectors is doubled (to allow for the pipework and storage vessels etc) there is still a marked discrepancy. The question therefore reduces to one of considering why the relatively simple manufactured components that comprise a solar water heating system are so expensive.

There are several possible explanations: the raw material costs may include a large non-energy component (which implies that they comprise a valuable resource perhaps none too appropriately used in relatively unproductive solar systems); the fabrication processes may be heavily capital or labour intensive; or the market price of the components may simply reflect large profit margins.

What is certain however, is that if the financial returns are favourable for any given energy conservation system, then so will be the energy returns, assuming only that the price of primary energy was the same for all the processes that preceded the production of the completed system. Since this latter condition is satisfied, at least to the accuracy of the present argument, financial analysis can be taken to be the more reliable indicator of the viability of any given project measured against the cost of all other resources.

This greatly simplified argument does not exclude the possibility that a system may be truly 'energy-effective' whilst not being 'cost-effective' under some given method of calculation, but in the case of solar water heating in the UK it would appear that a proportion of the large discrepancy noted above may be accounted for both by capital costs and by inadequate analysis of the energy costs of the complete systems.

6.2 Costs of component parts of solar systems

In view of the high prices that are sometimes paid for solar water heating equipment in the UK it is appropriate to consider briefly the cost of the individual component parts of such systems. The cost of a solar system to the consumer may be divided into hardware costs, installation costs, and profit margins. For convenience, a system of 4 m² will be considered since this may be taken to be a not unsuitable size for most UK houses (see Section 4.2). It will be assumed that the system incorporates an indirect solar cylinder and a sealed primary circuit – this represents one of the system designs that could be fitted to almost any type of house in any area of the country. The component parts of this system are listed below; the figures are based on 1978 trade prices of good quality hardware to BS Specifications where available.

	£
4 m² solar collector, excluding glass	264.00
190 litre copper indirect cylinder	110.00
Brackets and flashings to fix collectors to roof	80.00
Differential temperature controller and sensors	26.00
4 m² 4 mm float glass	28.00
Circulating pump (central heating type)	18.00
Sealed system equipment	15.00
Additional plumbing fittings and pipework	15.00
10 m × 19 mm closed cell pipe insulation	6.00
100 mm insulation jacket for cylinder	7.00
Antifreeze	1.00
	£570.00

To the sum of £570 must be added installation costs, overheads and profits, but since the figure of £264 already includes a considerable element of profit an addition of £150 would not be unreasonable giving a cost to the consumer of £720. No further element of VAT need be added since this is not payable on complete installations. It is strongly emphasised that the sum of £720 derived above is for a system that is engineered and installed to a much higher standard than is represented by some current practice in the UK, and it is interesting to estimate to what extent this cost could be reduced by future developments.

All the component costs listed above are for small scale purchases and quantity discounts of between 5 and 50 per cent are normally available but will not be assumed in this analysis.

The solar panels comprise at present the largest single component cost in most systems and it is pertinent to consider if any reduction on the price of £66/m² may be envisaged. A typical solar collector consists of an outer box, thermal insulation material, an absorber plate and glazing. The outer box may be manufactured in many different materials but if GRP or similar composites are considered then it is evident that the amount of raw material in a 1 m² box is of the same order as that in GRP products such as cisterns costing typically £8–£10; a figure of £10 is assumed below. All-copper collector plates with a surface finish that is claimed to be selective are currently available at between £20–£25/m² at trade prices but no significant reductions are to be anticipated because of the high cost of the raw material and the degree of production expertise already employed; a projected cost of £20/m² is therefore used below. The transparent cover may be either a durable plastic or glass and costs can range from about £4/m² for agricultural glass to £10/m² for some plastics and a median figure of £7, equal to that used above for 4 mm float glass, will be assumed. The thermal insulation material and cover supports may be expected to add about £3/m² giving a total projected cost of £40/m². There would seem to be little prospect that collectors to the above specification could ever be produced in small quantities at a trade price of less than £40/m² using 1978 data.

Replacement of the copper storage cylinder by a plastic cistern with a specially installed heat exchanger coil might save about £70 but some decrease in system performance could be anticipated. Replacement of the copper absorber plate by steel or aluminium might save £12/m² or £48 per installation but at the risk of introducing long term corrosion problems. Further savings that might be envisaged could include £40 on the collector fixing brackets once proven standardised designs become available, together with a substantial saving on present controllers, but in view of the fact that future designs may have to be more sophisticated to comply with recommendations on electrical safety (see Section 3.7.2) a saving of only £8 will be assumed.

Using all the above assumptions, the total system cost to the consumer of £720 reduces to £450, and for the type of system considered this may reasonably be taken as the minimum achievable cost assuming that the current situation in which the UK market is divided between many small companies will be maintained. If restructuring occurs then the increased scale of operation of the remaining larger companies might be expected to lead to a further reduction in the total installed costs.

6.3 Energy savings

The likely energy savings from a solar water heating system operating under UK conditions may be estimated either directly from the results of experimental work or from analysis of the behaviour of solar collectors under known irradiance conditions.

Since many dubious claims have been made in this area it is instructive to consider some of the basic facts concerning insolation in the UK.

BRE Current Paper CP7/76[1] contains data derived from measurements made at Kew meteorological station near London and may be used as a basis for estimating the likely output from a solar collector system; Table 5 below summarises this data.

A convenient starting point for analysis is acceptance of the fact that *net* radiation transfer can only take place between bodies at different temperatures; this follows from basic thermodynamic theory. Some theoretical difficulty is encountered when the bodies in question are not true 'black bodies' since their temperature in respect of transference of radiation energy is no longer easily defined. This problem can be resolved to some extent by assigning to each such body an 'effective radiation temperature' – often termed simply 'effective temperature'.

This approach is not without its difficulties because the effective temperature can depend upon the method of measurement[126] but the concept is still acceptable for many purposes. Further consideration of these topics may be found in text books on thermodynamics or heat transfer. A flat plate solar collector may be considered to have an effective temperature close to that of its outermost glass or plastic cover; since heat loss through the rear insulation is usually a small fraction of the total, this approximation is justifiable*. The sun may be considered to have an effective radiation temperature of about 5800 K whilst the lower atmosphere of the earth

behaves as an emitter of radiation with an effective temperature close to but rarely exactly equal to the air temperature. Usually the 'effective sky temperature' is a few degrees below ground temperature and this results in a net transfer of energy between the surface of the earth and the atmosphere. Under conditions of dense cloud cover very little net transfer takes place but a clear night sky can give rise to ground frosts even when the air temperature remains several degrees above 0°C.

Under normal operating conditions therefore, a solar collector will receive radiation from the sun and from the atmosphere and will return some radiation to the atmosphere. In addition, during those periods when the collector is hotter than the surrounding air, it will lose heat by conduction and convection. These effects are illustrated in Figure 44.

Under steady state conditions:
$$S+A=C+L+Q$$
$$\therefore Q=S+A-C-L$$

Since the temperature of the outer glass or plastic cover is usually higher than the effective sky temperature, the term L is greater than A and the only source of potentially useful energy is therefore S.

It is sometimes argued that the outer glass or plastic cover could be made 'selective' in that it could absorb A but only emit a small amount of L thus giving a net gain of energy. Unfortunately this is not possible because the wavelength spectra from sky and collector are similar and it is a fundamental law of thermodynamics that the absorptivity of a body at any given wavelength and temperature is equal to its emissivity. There is thus no prospect of producing selective covers with properties as useful as those of the selective surfaces discussed in Section 3.1.10; the best that can be achieved is to limit term L to a value very close to A and this is possible using infra-red-reflecting coated glass (see Section 3.1.4). The numerical values of A or L may be calculated using the Stefan-Boltzmann Law[127]: at 300 K (27°C) blackbody radiation is 459 W/m² and rises to 1451 W/m² at 400 K (127°C).

In summary, the only significant net energy input to a solar collector derives from term S which, from Table 5, amounts to about 3575 MJ/m² year or 993 kWh/m² year under optimum conditions at Kew. Systems installed elsewhere in the UK will of course experience a different climate but any effect on their output is likely to be

Table 5 Total solar radiation incident on 1 m² of south facing collector at different angles to the horizontal (averaged from Kew data 1959–1968). Units: MJ/year

Horiz	30°	45°	60°	Vertical
3275	3575	3530	3300	2500

* Some types of plastic sheets have such high transmissivity for long wavelength infra-red radiation that this approximation is invalid.

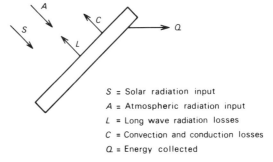

S = Solar radiation input
A = Atmospheric radiation input
L = Long wave radiation losses
C = Convection and conduction losses
Q = Energy collected

Figure 44 Simplified steady-state energy balance of a solar collector

relatively small, except in Scotland where some considerable decrease might be anticipated because of both the reduced insolation levels and the lower ambient temperatures. It should also be noted that the energy supplied by systems installed in industrial areas may be expected to be slightly below that calculated using insolation data from rural areas.

The fraction of the incident solar energy that reaches the collector plate is limited by several factors the most important being reflection from the cover, absorption in the cover, and absorption by deposits on the cover surfaces. Taken together these losses amount to about 20 per cent under favourable conditions and give an energy absorption on the collector plate not exceeding 80 per cent of 993, or 794 kWh/m² year: using average Kew data this is the maximum output that could be achieved if heat losses from the collector plate were always zero. The actual output that may be achieved is usually very much less than 794 kWh/m² year because for much of the operating time L exceeds A, and C is strongly positive; work to date in the UK has estimated the heat output from solar panel systems used for preheating domestic hot water at between 200 and 500 kWh/m² year*; the upper figure is credible only for systems incorporating well engineered selectively coated collectors which operate at low temperatures, and will not be achieved by much of the equipment currently on the UK market. Since the actual useful output will depend strongly on the collector type, the size of the system related to the water usage, and the quality of the installation work, it is not possible to quote precise figures. No thoroughly reliable data on the performance of sets of solar systems under real-life UK domestic conditions is yet available but ongoing BRE research is aimed principally at obtaining this information[6].

It should however be noted that future developments in other areas may decrease the output to be expected from solar systems of the type outlined in Section 2.2.2. Perhaps the two developments most likely to affect the design of domestic hot water systems are a greater economy in the use of hot water (for example, by increased use of showers instead of baths), and possible application of waste water heat recovery techniques. Some preliminary work in this area has already been outlined[6] but the cautionary note given here is that application of any water or energy conservation measure is likely to decrease the benefits from a solar system: many energy conservation technologies are in fact mutually exclusive in the sense that application of any one can worsen the prospects for another.

It is sometimes argued, in respect of either domestic or industrial systems, that application of heat recovery technology will enhance the prospects for solar collectors because they will be able to supply a greater percentage of the then reduced load. A little thought will show that whilst solar energy may meet an increased fraction of the load the heat output per unit area of collector will almost

certainly be decreased, and it is the latter quantity that alone determines whether economic viability will be achieved in a system in which year-round back-up is required – the importance of this qualification is explained in Section 6.1.

6.4 Cost-effectiveness

The subject of cost-effectiveness analysis for capital intensive projects is complex and there is no universally applicable method for the calculation of solar collector economics.

Many factors need to be considered by a potential purchaser; amongst the most important for a household are the number of years that the family expects to reside in the same house, the expected rate of increase of fuel costs, inflation, and any repairs that might be necessary to the solar system. In addition, the availability of a mortgage for the system and the rate of tax paid by the potential purchaser are important considerations as is any likelihood that the installation might add to or subtract from the value of the building or increase its rateable value. A factor not often considered is the possibility that the energy supply industries could introduce seasonal tariffs whereby winter consumption was heavily penalised. Such action could have catastrophic consequences for solar systems that supply most energy during the summer months.

At a practical level, it is important that every component of a solar system is designed so that it may be expected substantially to retain close to its initial level of performance; economic calculations used to justify the purchase of a system often assume a constant level of performance over the expected system lifetime. Simple tests that might be developed for checking systems installed in single-family houses are outlined in Section 2.2.1, and elsewhere attention is drawn to many areas of system design where concern may be expressed regarding what is current practice: the most important areas would appear to be the functioning of control systems, basic good plumbing design, and the effects that chemical pollution and weathering in general might have on the performance of collectors. Long term testing under UK conditions of cover materials (especially those coated with selective films) and of collector plates would appear to be necessary before any truly reliable assessment can be made of the potential long term energy savings realisable from widespread use of solar energy systems in the UK.

Given however that these practical aspects are expected to be satisfactory the internal rate of return (a measure of cost-effectiveness) may be calculated. The results of some internal rate of return (IRR) calculations are given below: it is emphasised that all costs are in real terms and net of general inflation. Internal rate of return calculations for many of the possible energy conservation measures that might be applied to domestic buildings are to be published by BRE[128].

---

* These units may also be expressed as W/m²; the corresponding values are 23 and 57 W/m², and represent average power outputs per square metre of collector.

In view of the current uncertainty concerning the likely heat output from solar systems operating under UK conditions calculations are presented for a 4 m² system that displaces either 400 kWh/m²year (5·75 GJ total) or 250 kWh/m²year (3·60 GJ total).

The annual maintenance charges of £10 are taken to include the cost of running a circulating pump: it must be realised that this probably represents a best case condition and many systems may incur far larger maintenance costs if they are to continue to function satisfactorily.

Fuel costs to the consumer for on-peak electricity, off-peak electricity and gas are taken to be £7.62, £3.58 and £1.45 per GJ respectively. The figure for off-peak electricity assumes that all the consumption for water heating is during off-peak hours, and all the figures are net of standing charges. A seasonal gas boiler efficiency of 65 per cent is assumed. If storage and distribution losses are taken to be zero this is equivalent to assessing the solar energy delivered to the hot water as a contribution to the *useful* energy. (See Appendix III)

The assumption of a 65 per cent efficiency for a gas boiler needs to be explained in the light of other recent BRE work[101] which found system efficiencies of typically 30 per cent for fossil fuel boilers running under summertime load conditions. It is here assumed that the use of better insulation, especially on the storage vessel, combined with a control system that prevented short-cycling, could raise the system efficiency to this higher level. Furthermore, it is here considered that as both these measures should have

been taken prior to purchasing a solar system the figure of 65 per cent is not unreasonable; use of a much lower efficiency figure would improve the apparent economics of the solar system, perhaps to the levels attained in the 'off-peak' examples.

The IRR calculations use a discrete economic model in the sense that returns are evaluated annually; it may be noted that in the examples shown in Tables 6 and 7 where the IRR is negative, the system does not displace sufficient fuel over its lifetime to repay even the initial capital investment.

There are however further complications in a national assessment of the potential usefulness of energy conservation equipment. For example, a BRE analysis of the consequences of thermal insulation of dwellings has shown both that part of the theoretically realisable energy savings were taken up by increased comfort levels, and that true primary energy savings can only be properly assessed when allowance is made for the primary energy input to the goods that may be purchased with the income that results from a lowered fuel bill[129].

Two examples are sufficient to illustrate the thesis that installation of solar water heaters may, in some cases, result in only a minute reduction in national energy consumption.

If a householder installs a solar water heating system he will, if the system works, need to purchase less fuel for water heating purposes. For a householder paying tax at a very high rate (and therefore, by implication, being a

Table 6

Capital cost of system (£)	720	720	720	450	450	450
Auxiliary fuel	Gas	Off-peak	On-peak	Gas	Off-peak	On-peak
IRR† (5·75 GJ displaced) 0%	−17	−10	−1	−15	−6	+4
3%	−10	−5	+3	−7	−1	+9
IRR† (3·60 GJ displaced) 0%	*	−17	−6	*	−15	−2
3%	−17	−10	−2	−15	−7	+2

* In these cases the saving is less than the maintenance charge.
† Internal rate of returns (per cent) assuming:
  (a) 20 year life with no fall-off in thermal performance.
  (b) £10/year total maintenance.
  (c) Fuel price rises of 0 and 3 per cent/year in real terms.

Table 7

Capital cost of system (£)	720	720	720	450	450	450
Auxiliary fuel	Gas	Off-peak	On-peak	Gas	Off-peak	On-peak
IRR† (5·75 GJ displaced) 0%	−37	−25	−12	−33	−20	−5
3%	−30	−21	−8	−26	−16	0
IRR† (3·60 GJ displaced) 0%	*	−36	−20	*	−33	−14
3%	−48	−30	−16	−46	−26	−10

* In these cases the saving is less than the maintenance charge.
† Internal rate of returns (per cent) assuming:
  (a) 10 year life with no fall-off in thermal performance.
  (b) £10/year total maintenance.
  (c) Fuel price rises of 0 and 3 per cent /year in real terms.

person well able to afford a solar energy system) the consequent financial saving may be taken to be equivalent to a tax-free income since the capital investment in the solar system, large as it might have been, will probably no longer be considered.

With this additional income, the householder may decide to increase his 'standard of living' by purchasing extra goods or services, and some of these may be energy intensive. A plausible scenario is that an increased amount of central heating oil may be purchased using the 'income' from the solar system.

Suppose the system displaces 1000 kWh of on-peak electricity annually. At 27 per cent generation efficiency this is equivalent to a primary energy saving for the country of 3700 kWh or 13·3 GJ.

Assuming a cost of 2·8 p/kWh for on-peak electricity the financial saving is £28/year which would purchase 68 gallons (310 l) of central heating oil at an assumed cost of 41p/gallon. The energy content of most hydrocarbon fuels is about 47 GJ/tonne, or 42·3 MJ/l assuming a specific gravity of 0·9. The energy content of the purchased fuel is therefore 13·1 GJ which is uncomfortably close to the figure of 13·3 GJ derived above, and in this example the solar system would save the country only 0·2 GJ annually. The saving would be negative if gas were to have been purchased (because £28 would buy 19·3 GJ), but would of course be greater than 0·2 GJ if off-peak electricity had been displaced.

The second example applies to a greater number of consumers: if the solar system were purchased not for cash but by instalments by a householder paying tax at the standard rate then there would be a net *loss* of income because the monthly repayments would be greater than the value of the fuel savings. In this case the system not only saves 3700 kWh of primary energy annually but, because the standard of living of the householder is depressed, further savings may easily result.

These examples, however simple, starkly illustrate the fact that the net national impact of energy conservation measures cannot be reasonably projected unless included in a full economic planning framework that reflects income and price effects on energy consuming lifestyles.

7 Monitoring of solar systems

Determination of the thermal performance of a solar system, whether it was designed for space or water heating, is a topic which seems often to be the subject of some confusion, and it is therefore perhaps not surprising that not all of the work undertaken to date in the UK may be considered wholly satisfactory.

The following brief synopsis of the basic principles of thermal performance monitoring is to be regarded as an introduction to the subject; it is anticipated that a more complete discussion will be published subsequently.

There are two distinct methods that can be used to monitor solar system performance; these may be termed 'absolute' and 'comparative', and are not mutually exclusive in their application.

The absolute method involves the collection of data, usually from temperature and heat-flow transducers, that may subsequently be processed to yield information on the thermal behaviour of each of the components of interest within the energy-handling and supply systems. For complex systems, the cost of the necessary instrumentation can become a limiting constraint on the whole experiment and data must either be collected by automatic logging equipment or by a mini-computer, which may also serve to process the data. The latter approach has been adopted in the BRE low energy house laboratories and has been described elsewhere[130].

The comparative method involves measuring the 'overall' performance of several solar or solar assisted energy systems together with several 'control' systems which derive their energy wholly from conventional sources. The complexity of the necessary instrumentation can be far less than is required for absolute methods and useful results can often be obtained very simply. The principal disadvantage of a comparative method is usually that no 'fine structure' may be obtained which would give an insight into the detailed behaviour of equipment. If the loads on both the solar and non-solar systems are identical then only one of each type of system need be monitored but if, as more usually occurs, the experiments are conducted in occupied buildings, then because of the variability of the loads imposed on the individual systems it is necessary to measure the performance of several of each type in order that statistically meaningful results can be obtained.

Since the aim of comparative monitoring is usually to determine the solar contribution to the total energy demand by deduction rather than by direct measurement the whole scheme must be carefully designed so as to prevent spurious or misleading results being obtained. A couple of examples will suffice to show the type of distortion that can accidentally be introduced into such experiments.

If it is desired to determine the solar energy contribution from a particular solar water heating system then a reasonable experiment would be to incorporate the systems into at least 20 houses and to compare the annual water heating bills of these houses with those of nominally identical houses in which the water heating was performed wholly by conventional means. (For convenience it will be assumed that electricity is used.) The monitoring would consist simply of measuring the electrical consumption of the immersion heaters in both sets of houses and comparing the average annual consumption in the 'solar' houses to that in the 'control' houses.

If this experiment were conducted on a large enough scale then the answer would be meaningful but because of the large variation in hot water usage between households occupying nominally identical houses it would be sensible also to measure the hot water usage of each household. A more meaningful result – the average amount of electricity needed to heat each litre of hot water consumed in both sets of houses – could now be computed.

The system as outlined still suffers from several inadequacies but is sufficient for present purposes in that it demonstrates the principles of the comparative method. It should be noted that a crucial condition that must be fulfilled if a simple comparative method of this type is to succeed is that the addition of the solar system to (say) half the houses should be the single biggest difference between the water supply systems of those houses. If, for example, the hot water cylinders in the solar houses were better insulated than those in the control houses then (from Section 2.3.7) it may be surmised that there could be a sizeable difference in energy consumption between the two sets of systems which could not correctly be attributed solely to the existence of solar equipment in one of the sets. Of course, the difference in energy consumption attributable to the insulation could be estimated and a due allowance made in the calculations, but since any such estimation is subject to considerable error the accuracy of the final results is thereby unalterably degraded.

Similarly, if the effectiveness of a solar space heating system is to be assessed using largely a comparative method the overriding design consideration must be that the control houses or other buildings must be as similar to the solar-assisted buildings as possible and, insofar as is consistent with the basic building designs, should have equal amounts of thermal insulation in the floors, roofs and walls.

Exceptions occur where a roof or a wall is an integral part of the solar system but the similarity of the rest of the building should be maintained whenever possible. In extreme cases, where the whole building structure is to play a part in collection or storage of solar energy then a comparative method can yield little information about the performance of any element of the structure, and may be considered inappropriate. These strictures are especially important in assessments of solar space heating systems in the UK because the installation of (say) additional thermal insulation in the solar houses (if houses are being considered) could lead to a much reduced fuel consumption which could then be attributed erroneously to the solar hardware; since solar energy is inherently unsuitable for space heating in the UK (because of the lack of appreciable amounts of high intensity sunshine during the 'real' winter months of November–February) it is possible that additional insulation could make a greater contribution to reducing the space heating load than could the solar system. As a direct consequence of this, even if the effect of the insulation were calculated the inherent errors could be as great as the true 'solar' savings and the potential for producing distorted results is obvious.

Unfortunately, schemes in which solar houses are better insulated than the corresponding control houses have already been built in the UK and it has been stated that the solar houses are expected to save at least 50 per cent of the energy consumed by the normal houses. These statements may be perfectly reasonable predictions, but it would be appropriate if it were made somewhat clearer what percentage of these savings were expected to accrue from the relatively expensive solar hardware and what percentage from the relatively cheap thermal insulation.

The first problem for any proposed experiment is to define the quantity or quantities that are to be measured or deduced; the quantity that is often of most interest for solar systems delivering energy in the form of heat is *the useful heat supplied by the system*. Some care is needed in defining this term: useful energy is the energy required to perform a certain task and differs from net energy by an amount equal to the flue and other losses of the system. For a space heating system the useful heat supplied by the solar system may be thought of as the amount of heat delivered to the load which would otherwise have had to be supplied by an appliance consuming auxiliary (conventional) fuel.

In the general case where space heating is used in a building the requirement for energy may be termed the *demand*, and this may be satisfied by a combination of *supplies* as shown in Figure 45.

The solar contribution to the demand is the useful heat supplied by the solar system. So:

Solar + Aux = Demand.

It must be made clear at this stage that not all of the term *Solar* may have been derived from solar energy; some further analysis is needed to clarify this point. A solar heating system can usually be broken down into its functions of collection, storage, and subsequent distribution of solar heat.

In Figure 45 the incident solar radiation S is received by the collection system and this entails the expenditure of auxiliary energy A_1 and usually results in a substantial loss of energy L_1.

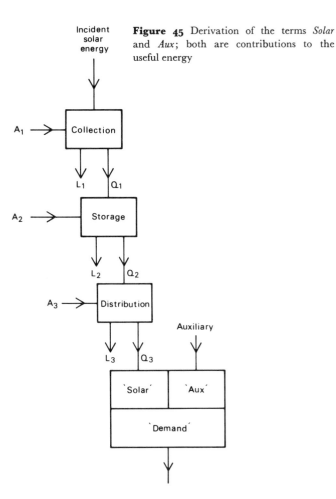

Incident solar energy

Figure 45 Derivation of the terms *Solar* and *Aux*; both are contributions to the useful energy

The amount of energy transferred to storage is clearly $S + A_1 - L_1 = Q_1$. Once in storage the energy (usually heat) can be lost with the passage of time and this loss is termed L_2. Some auxiliary energy may have to be supplied to keep the storage system itself functioning correctly (this requirement is unusual but does occur) and the amount of energy passed to the distribution system is $Q_1 + A_2 - L_2 = Q_2$. (It is assumed here that L_2 is lost in such a way and at such a time that it cannot be usefully employed but there are systems for which this is not true.)

Once passed to the distribution system Q_2 needs an input of A_3 in order to encourage it to pass to the load and in this process L_3 is lost. The final transfer of heat to the load is Q_3 and this quantity equals the term *Solar* if all of L_1, L_2 and L_3 are truly lost. In most space heating systems L_3 may be added to Q_3 since if space heat is not required the distribution system is inoperative and if it is required (and if the distribution system is within the load space) then all of L_3 is useful. In water heating systems however L_3 may only be useful when there is a time-coincident space heating demand*.

These equations must be used with care when defining system efficiencies or similar quantities – it would be nonsense to say that over a certain time period the system efficiency was zero because Q_3 was zero or, conversely, to say that the efficiency was 99 per cent just because

---

* Strictly, L_3 would only be a contribution to the useful energy requirement – see Appendix III.

$Q_3/S = 99/100$ over another time period; the amount of stored energy must always be included in the calculations.

To illustrate the use of this method of analysis a simple space heating system will be considered in which L_1, L_2 and L_3 are all true losses. It will be assumed that A_1 and A_3 are both electricity – as is most likely, and that A_2 is zero – as is usual in simple storage systems. The net result over a suitably long time period is therefore that an amount of energy equal to $S + A_1 + A_3 - L_1 - L_2 - L_3$ is transferred to the load for the expenditure of an amount of electricity equal to $A_1 + A_3$ ($= A$). For convenience it will be assumed that the efficiency of the power station + grid system is 25 per cent (the actual figure as given in reference 65 is 27 per cent), that the auxiliary fuel is natural gas which is burned with an effective efficiency of 65 per cent, and that natural gas has a zero energy overhead. Furthermore, it will be assumed that the quantity *Solar* is equal to 50 per cent of *Demand*. An analysis of the primary energy used in the total system is therefore as shown in Figure 46.

The scale represents the order of magnitude of losses that can be expected in a solar space heating system in the UK; the exact values are not important here but it should be noted that a situation can arise in which the primary energy used in generating A is greater than that in the gas that could have been used to satisfy the other half of the demand. In this case the system would have used *less* primary energy if all of the demand had been met by burning gas than in the situation depicted in which there is a sizeable solar contribution. The basic physics of this situation is easy – the solar energy needs so much electricity to get it delivered to the load that it would have been better (in primary energy terms) not to have installed a solar system at all.

The above discussion has been included in order to emphasise the importance of designing a monitoring system correctly, and whilst it is outside the scope of this book to detail the various types of instrumentation that are available it should already be obvious that every component of an energy handling system should be considered in the light of its effect on the overall energy balance. Unfortunately however, real systems are rarely as straightforward as the idealised situation analysed above; for example a pump used in a domestic hot water preheating system may give part of its input energy to the water and the rest of it to the atmosphere. The latter portion contributes to L_1 (and may be useful heat in winter) but all of the former may not necessarily be counted as useful in the sense of its being worth money since in the absence of the temperature rise consequent upon this energy input the solar circuit would have functioned more efficiently and would have been able to transfer a greater fraction of S to store.

These more complicated effects are often insignificant but in some systems, notably those using air handling equipment which is trying to extract heat from a low temperature source, they may become more important.

For a combined water and space heating solar system a method of analysis that has proved instructive is to subtract from the total observed energy savings an estimated component for water heating alone. For example; if a 40 m² collector system saved 3000 kWh annually then it may be considered that 6 m² dedicated to water heating might have saved 1500 kWh – itself quite a modest output for a good system.

It follows therefore that the remaining 34 m² must be justified on the basis of their supplying 1500 kWh/year for space heating – an output of only 44 kWh/m² year. If this figure is equated to a primary energy saving of (say) 60 kWh/m² year then using recent analysis[125] the collectors would need to operate for 15 years even to repay the energy expended in their manufacture.

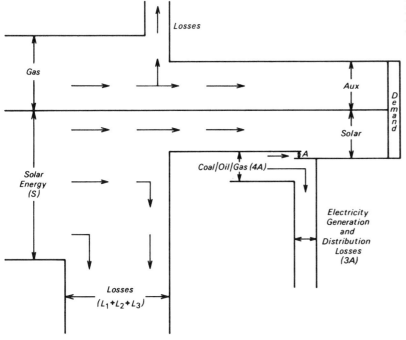

Figure 46 Primary energy analysis of a solar assisted space heating system. The terms *Solar* and *Aux* are the resulting contributions to the useful energy

Appendix I

Aspects of legislation affecting solar collector systems

This section should not be taken to comprise a complete or authoritative summary of all the legislation that can affect the installation or subsequent use of solar energy systems in the UK.

Any solar system affixed to a building to which the Building Regulations[121] apply must in itself comply* with those Regulations and its installation must not impair the ability of the building structure to continue to comply with the Regulations.

The other principal requirements are that the system complies with the local water byelaws (often identical to the Model Water Byelaws[18]) if it is connected to a system supplied with mains water, and that it has received planning permission if this is required by virtue of its intended position; these two requirements apply even if the system is not to be affixed to a building. In addition, electricity supply regulations must be considered.

Since the rigour with which byelaws and planning regulations are interpreted and enforced may vary between different regions of the UK the best general advice that may be given at the present time is that any person intending to install a solar system on his property should first obtain the views of the local building inspector, the planning authorities, and the local water under-taking. It is likely that before permission to proceed is granted some technical details of the proposed system will have to be submitted and manufacturers and suppliers of solar energy equipment should be in a position readily to supply such technical details as may reasonably be requested.

In order to guard against any misunderstanding that may arise at some time in the future it is advised that the necessary permissions to proceed are obtained in writing before any final commitment to purchase the equipment is made; planning officers often write expressing agreement or approval, but these statements are not binding on the Local Authority until they have been formally endorsed by the Planning Committee.

Solar systems installed on industrial or commercial premises will be subject to the relevant industrial legislation including the Health and Safety at Work Act[131], the provisions of which require that the owner of the system take all due care to prevent any foreseeable danger from occurring; some provision against the generation of excessive water temperatures would therefore seem to be advisable.

The question as to whether the owner of a solar system has the right in law to continue to receive sunlight (and therefore, by implication, the right to prevent the construction of any new building that would obstruct such sunlight) has not been tested in the Courts but a recent interpretation of the Law of Ancient Lights suggests that such a right may exist[132], but probably subject to the condition of the system having been in place for a minimum of 20 years.

---

* Compliance in respect of the addition of a collector system to an existing building may only entail confirming with the Local Authority that the system is not deemed by them to be a structural alteration within the meaning of the Regulations.

Appendix II

Sample calculations of flow distribution in collector plates

It was shown in Section 3.1.1 that in the absence of significant Venturi effects or thermosyphon pressures the flow distribution in a header and riser panel design would be determined by pressure losses owing to the viscosity of the fluid.

If it is assumed that turbulent flow exists everywhere in the panel then the pressure loss along any unit length of pipe will be proportional to the square of the flow rate in that pipe.

It is therefore possible to write down equations for the flow in each section of pipe and to solve these iteratively using a computer. The mathematics will not be described below, but the program that has been used is a modified version of that given by Carnahan et al[133]. It should be noted that the results given in Figure 47 are not exactly correct because of the finite number of iterations used.

For convenience the calculations were performed using a total pressure loss across each panel of 100 N/m², and since the panels are of different sizes the resulting total flows do not correspond to any given flow rate per unit area; however, scaling of the results may be accomplished using two rules:

1   If the total flow is increased by a factor x then the flow in each riser is also increased by this factor. The *ratio* between the flow rates in any pair of risers thus remains constant.

2   If the flow is increased by a factor x then the corresponding pressure loss will increase by a factor x^2.

In Section 3.1.1 qualitative design rules for header and riser panels were given, and the examples shown here (Figure 47a–h) have been chosen to illustrate these rules: for example, the best flow distribution in these eight cases occurs in Figure 47d where a small number of long risers are coupled to large headers, and the worst case is shown in Figure 47e where a large number of short risers are coupled to small headers. The benefit of increasing the riser length (all other dimensions remaining constant) is illustrated most clearly by the improvement between the cases shown in Figures 47e and 47g, and that resulting from increasing the header diameter by Figures 47e and 47f: it is of course not coincidental that the largest fractional changes occur when an improvement is made to the worst design – that shown in Figure 47e.

It is realised that when collectors are used with low flow rates some or all of the flow may be laminar and analysis in this case is likely to be far more complicated because the pressure losses are then so low that thermosyphon pressures can become significant: as stated in Section 3.1.1 the only thoroughly reliable method of assessing the behaviour of an array of collectors is to determine the flow rates in each riser either directly or by inference using a technique such as infra-red imaging. It is here re-emphasised that just because a collector unit performs satisfactorily this may not necessarily be taken as proof of the satisfactory design of an array of these collectors.

As a guide to estimating when laminar flow will occur the Reynolds number, Re, may be calculated:

$$Re = \frac{u \cdot d}{v}$$

where u = velocity (m/s)
d = internal pipe diameter (m)
v = kinematic viscosity (m²/s)

The kinematic viscosity of water is usually tabulated in centistokes, and as a rough guide is 1·8 cSt at 2°C falling to 1 cSt at 20°C and 0·4 cSt at 70°C; conversion to SI units is accomplished by multiplying by 10^{-6}:

1 cSt = 10^{-6} m²/s

The internal diameter of 15 mm copper tube is about 13·6 mm and laminar flow can only be guaranteed in pipes when $Re \leqslant 2300$[134]. The critical velocity is therefore 0·169 m/s at 20°C, corresponding to a flow rate of 0·025 l/s. It may now be calculated that the collectors depicted in Figures 47a–h would be operating at least partly in the laminar region unless flow rates far in excess of 0·016 l/m²s were used. For example, in Figure 47g the area of collector is 5·4 m² and with 0·016 l/m²s the total flow rate required is 0·086 l/s, slightly above that depicted. Whilst the riser flows are all likely to be laminar* (which will alter the flow pattern from that shown) the header flow will be turbulent in those lengths where the flow exceeds 0·036 l/s.

For fluids other than water the kinematic viscosity can be considerably greater and this results in laminar flow being maintained to higher velocities: mineral (hydrocarbon) oils sold for solar systems typically have a kinematic viscosity of about 8 cSt at 2°C falling to about 2 cSt at 70°C, whilst silicone fluids have (usually) a viscosity between 10 and 20 cSt which is only slightly affected by temperature. As noted in Section 3.6.2 however the specific heat problem can be at least as serious as the increased viscosity.

In some texts absolute (dynamic) viscosity is quoted, and is related to kinematic viscosity by the formula

$$v = \frac{\mu}{\rho}$$

where v = kinematic viscosity (m²/s)
μ = absolute viscosity (kg/ms)
ρ = density (kg/m³)

---

* Establishment lengths for laminar flow have not been considered.

The units of absolute viscosity may also be written
Ns/m², but another unit, the Poise, is often used and some
texts give incorrect conversion factors. The correct
relationships are

100 cP (centipoise) = 1 Poise
1 Poise   = 0·1 Ns/m²

The absolute viscosity of water at about 20°C is
10⁻³ Ns/m² or 1 cP.

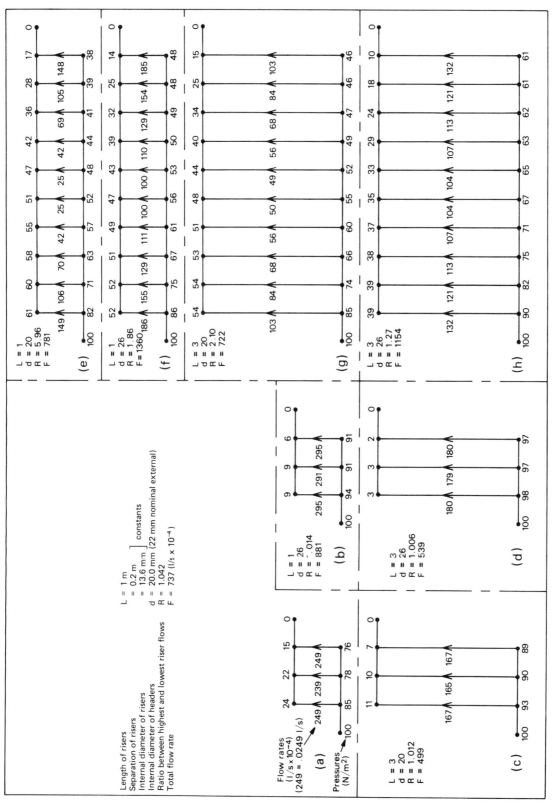

Figure 47 Calculated flow distribution for header and riser solar collector plates

Appendix III

Use of the terms 'net energy' and 'useful energy' in solar heating applications

The terms net energy and useful energy are often misused in solar energy literature; both are well defined quantities and it is shown below that only in special circumstances should collected solar energy be called either net or useful energy. This topic is discussed briefly in Section 7.

Useful energy is *the energy required to perform a certain task*, for example, the energy required to raise unit mass of water through unit temperature difference. If all efficiencies were 100 per cent and losses were zero only this amount of energy would have to be supplied to the heating system. In this book the term useful energy is used not only to describe the total required energy but also to describe contributions to the total required energy. (Strictly, the output from a system is termed useful only if it satisfies the full requirement for energy.)

Net energy is *the energy delivered to a consumer*; it is conveniently thought of as the amount of energy passing through a gas or electricity meter. Strictly, because both gas and electricity meters extract a minute amount of energy for their operation, the energy delivered to the heating appliance is very slightly less than the true net energy. The error is usually insignificant, and it is helpful to think of net energy as the energy reaching the heating appliance (point of use).

Figure 48 shows a typical layout of a gas-fired water heating system using a boiler and a separate storage cylinder. Net energy is delivered to the boiler and if all distribution losses are taken to be zero, the useful energy requirement may be calculated from the product $(T_h - T_c).V$ where V is the quantity of water drawn off

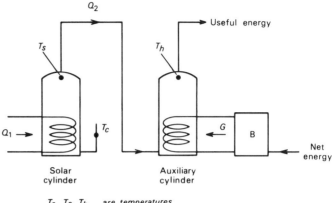

T_c, T_s, T_h are temperatures

G, Q_1, Q_2 are energy transfers

Figure 49 Layout of a solar-assisted gas-fired water heating system. G, Q_1 and Q_2 are energy transfers; T_c, T_s and T_h are temperatures

at temperature T_h, and T_c is the temperature of the cold feed to the cylinder; both T_h and T_c are here assumed constant. The energy transferred into the stored water by the heat exchanger coil (termed G in Figure 48) is neither net nor useful in the general case. In the absence of both cylinder losses and distribution losses, G may be called useful heat*.

Figure 49 shows a twin-cylinder solar-assisted hot water system in which the auxiliary fuel is gas. Solar energy, termed Q_1 to agree with the nomenclature of Figure 45, is transferred to the solar cylinder, and heat from the gas boiler is transferred to the auxiliary cylinder. However, because of the inevitable heat loss from the solar cylinder the quantity of heat supplied by the preheat system will be less than Q_1, and may be calculated from the product $(T_s - T_c).V = Q_2$ where T_s is the delivery temperature of the solar cylinder (here assumed to be constant). In gravity circulation systems all of Q_1 and Q_2 is obtained from solar energy.

If the heat loss from the pipe connecting the two cylinders is taken to be zero, then Q_2 clearly displaces some of G, but its worth may only be calculated on this basis if the auxiliary cylinder is kept hot continually: if this condition is not satisfied then the heat losses from this cylinder may be greater with the solar system installed than without it and, in the general case, the worth of a unit of Q_2 will be less than that of a unit of G. This has been discussed elsewhere[104].

Only when heat losses from the auxiliary cylinder are zero, and all distribution losses are also zero, may Q_2 be termed useful energy. If heat losses from the solar cylinder are also zero then all of Q_1 will eventually become a

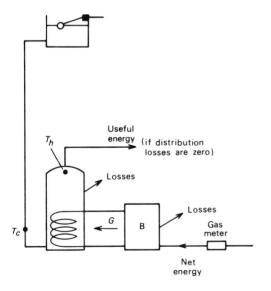

Figure 48 Layout of a gas-fired water heating system. Net energy is delivered to the boiler, which in turn transfers an amount G to the stored water. T_c and T_h are the cold feed and hot supply temperatures respectively

---

* If an electric immersion heater were to be installed in the cylinder in place of the heat exchanger coil then the net energy delivered as electricity would also be useful energy under conditions of zero heat loss.

contribution to the useful energy. It is suggested that Q_1 be called the solar energy transferred to store. Q_1 equals the solar energy collected only if there are no losses in the pipework linking the collectors to the store, and if there is no heat input from a circulating pump. It is suggested that Q_2 be called the solar energy supplied (by the pre-heat system).

However, the rather idealised arguments used above do not consider the possibility that the efficiency of the auxiliary heat source (here taken to be a gas boiler) may change when a solar preheating system is installed; if the efficiency does change then the worth of Q_2 may be reduced. Suppose that in a real system as shown in Figure 49, the auxiliary cylinder is kept hot continually*, and that 10 kWh have to be supplied each day to meet the load comprising the useful energy requirement and the cylinder losses. In the absence of the solar system (or in midwinter with no solar input), $G=10$ kWh/day and $Q_2=0$ kWh/day. If the average efficiency of the boiler under these conditions was 50 per cent then the net energy consumed would be 20 kWh/day.

If the load pattern was such that all the contents of the auxiliary cylinder were drawn off within a very short time, then without a solar system the boiler would be required to heat up a new batch of water from T_c to T_h, but with a solar system installed heating from T_s to T_h would be required. Assuming that the boiler efficiency was 75 per cent when the auxiliary cylinder temperature was in the range T_c to $\dfrac{T_h + T_c}{2}$ and only 37·5 per cent when it was in the range $\dfrac{T_h + T_c}{2}$ to T_h then, if the solar system was operative and T_s became equal to $\dfrac{T_h + T_c}{2}$, $G=Q_2=5$ kWh/day.

The resultant saving of net energy in this case would only be 6·66 kWh/day, as compared to 10 kWh/day with a constant boiler efficiency of 50 per cent.

This example is extreme in that the efficiency of a well controlled boiler would be unlikely to reduce from 75 per cent to 37·5 per cent, principally because the flame temperature would be well in excess of the average water temperature†, but serves to illustrate the difficulty of accurately predicting the true energy savings in solar-assisted systems: since the energy conservation potential of solar systems should be assessed on the basis of the amount of primary energy displaced – and not on the amount of solar energy collected or supplied – the importance of correctly ascertaining the amount of net energy displaced should be clear.

---

* This is clearly impossible unless the boiler has a near-infinite power output rating, and what is meant is that the boiler is not prevented from adding heat to the auxiliary cylinder if it wishes to do so. Under these conditions of operation the boiler will fire whenever the auxiliary cylinder temperature (assumed uniform) falls below T_h.

† If however a solar system were to be combined with existing heat reclaim equipment in which *all* the temperatures were of the same order, then the true worth of the collected solar energy might be near zero: the probable incompatibility of solar and heat reclaim technologies is discussed in Section 6.3.

References

1 **Courtney R G.** An appraisal of solar water heating in the UK. *Building Research Establishment Current Paper,* CP 7/76. BRE, 1976.

2 **Courtney R G.** Solar energy utilisation in the UK: Current research and future prospects. *Building Research Establishment Current Paper,* CP 64/76. BRE, 1976.

3 **Building Research Establishment.** Domestic water heating by solar energy. *BRE Digest,* 205. London HMSO. 1977.

4 **McNelis B.** Solar water heating – some economic and commercial aspects (Paper 7), International Solar Energy Society – UK Section, Conference C12, London, July 1977.

5 **Consumers' Association.** Solar heating, *Handyman Which?* London, August 1977, pp 448–453.

6 **Building Research Establishment.** *BRE News,* 46. Energy research and buildings. Winter 1978. p 8 and pp 12–13.

7 **Haig J M.** The householder's guide to plumbing. Stanley Paul 1974.

8 **Institute of Plumbing.** *Plumbing Services design guide.* 1977.

9 **Brinkworth B J.** Solar Energy for Man. Compton Press 1972.

10 **International Solar Energy Society – UK Section.** Flat plate collectors and solar water heating. 4th Edition, April 1977.

11 **McVeigh J C and Schumacher D C.** Going Solar. Natural Energy Association 1978.

12 **Yellott J I.** Utilisation of sun and sky radiation for heating and cooling of buildings. *ASHRAE Journal,* December 1973, pp 31–42.

13 **British Standards Institution.** Solar heating systems for domestic hot water. *Draft Code of Practice* document number 78/75355 DC. London, BSI, 1978.

14 **Heating and Ventilating Contractors' Association.** Solar heating for domestic hot water: Guide to good practice. London 1979.

15 **Building Research Establishment.** Durability of metals in natural waters. *BRE Digest,* 98. London, HMSO, 1977.

16 **Davey E T.** Solar water heating in Australia (Paper 4/71). International Solar Energy Society Conference, Melbourne, March 1970.

17 **Thompson P D and Hayden M B.** Corrosion problems in solar energy systems. *Materials Performance,* February 1978, pp 28–31.

18 **Department of the Environment.** Model Water Byelaws (1966 Edition). London, HMSO. 1966.

19 **Bloomfield D P and Fisk D J.** Seasonal domestic boiler efficiencies and intermittent heating. *The Heating and Ventilating Engineer,* September 1977, pp 6–8.

20 **Walker P C.** Private communication.

21 **International Solar Energy Society – UK Section.** Solar energy for heating swimming pools. Conference C10, London, January 1977.

22 **Milbank N O.** Energy consumption in swimming pool halls. *Building Research Establishment Current Paper,* CP 40/75. BRE, 1975.

23 **McVeigh J C.** Some experiments on heating swimming pools by solar energy. *JIHVE,* 39, 1971, pp 53–55.

24 **Hassan G.** A design procedure for calculating the size of a solar heat collector needed to warm an outdoor pool in Great Britain. *JIHVE,* 39, 1971, pp 56–62.

25 **Burberry P.** Building for energy conservation. Architectural Press 1978.

26 **Ballantyne E R.** Building design and solar energy. *Build International,* 6, 1973, pp 471–494.

27 **Page J K.** The optimisation of building shape to conserve energy. *Journal of Architectural Research,* No 3, 1974, pp 20–28.

28 **Wilberforce R R.** The effect of solar radiation on window energy balance. Paper 3.14. International CIB symposium on energy conservation in the built environment. Construction Press 1976.

29 **Building Research Establishment.** Environmental Design Manual. Part I. Design aids for summer conditions in naturally ventilated offices (to be published by HMSO).

30 **Maw R.** Polytechnic of Central London. Private communication.

31 **Department of Energy.** Energy Paper 16. Energy Technology Support Unit, HMSO, 1976. Chapter 4.

32 **International Solar Energy Society – UK Section.** Solar Energy for industry. Conference C14, London, February 1978.

33 **Meinel A B and Meinel M P.** Applied Solar Energy: An introduction. Addison Wesley 1976. Chapter 10.

34 **Duffie J A and Beckman W A.** Solar energy thermal processes. Wiley Interscience 1974. Chapter 7.

35 **Gillett W B.** Corrosion problems associated with the use of aluminium solar collectors. Paper 7.2. International Conference on Solar Building Technology. North East London Polytechnic, July 1977.

36 **Building Research Establishment.** Painting iron and steel. *BRE Digest* 70. London, HMSO, 1973.

37 **Building Research Establishment.** Painting in buildings: 2 – Non-ferrous metals and coatings. *BRE Digest* 71. London, HMSO, 1971.

38 **Duffie J A and Beckman W A.** op cit, Section 5.6.

39 **Meinel A B and Meinel M P.** op cit, Chapter 9.

40 **Close D J.** The production and testing of a selective surface for copper absorber plates. Commonwealth Scientific Industrial Research Organisation (CSIRO). Report ED7. Melbourne, June 1962.

41 **Riddiford C L.** Institute of Technology, New South Wales. Private communication.

42 **Dunkle R V and Davey E T.** Flow distribution in absorber banks (Paper 4/35). International Solar Energy Society Conference, Melbourne, March 1970.

43 **International Solar Energy Society – UK Section.** Practical aspects of domestic solar water heaters. Conference C13, London, October 1977.

44 Design and test report for transportable solar laboratory program. Honeywell, Incorporated. Report No NSF-RA-N-74-118, NTIS PB-240 609, October 1974. pp 3–76 – 3–82.

45 **Building Research Establishment.** Double glazing and double windows. *BRE Digest,* 140. London, HMSO, 1972.

46 **Building Research Establishment.** Condensation. *BRE Digest,* 110. London, HMSO, 1972.

47 **Department of the Environment.** Condensation. Property Services Agency Advisory Leaflet 61. HMSO 1976.

48 **Meinel A B and Meinel M P.** op cit. Chapter 8.

49 **Linsley G F.** Glazing flat plate collectors (Paper No 2). International Solar Energy Society – UK Section. Conference C13, London, October 1977.

50 **Fan J C C et al.** Transparent heat-mirror films for solar energy collection and radiation insulation. *App Phy Lett,* 25, (12), 1974, pp 693–695.

51 **Molzen W W.** Characterization of transparent conductive thin films of indium oxide. *J Vac Sci Technol,* 12, 1975, pp 99–102.

52 **Bruno R et al.** The Philips Experimental House. International Solar Energy Society – UK Section. Conference C8, London, April 1976.

53 'Glass in solar energy collectors'. Pilkington Environmental Advisory Service, St Helens, February 1976.

54 **Building Research Establishment.** Durability and application of plastics. *BRE Digest,* 69. London, HMSO, 1977.

55 **Building Research Establishment.** Cellular plastics for building. *BRE Digest,* 93. London, HMSO, 1974.

56 **British Standards Institution.** Hot dip galvanised coatings on iron and steel articles. *British Standard BS 729: 1971.* London.

57 **Building Research Establishment.** GRC. *BRE Digest,* 216. London, HMSO, 1978.

58 **British Standards Institution.** Specification for copper and copper alloys. Tubes Part 1. Copper tubes for water, gas and sanitation. *British Standard BS 2871 Part 1: 1971.* London.

59 **Hope A.** It's a wonderful idea, but . . . *New Scientist,* 1 June 1978, pp 576–581.

60 **International Solar Energy Society.** Sunspots, *Sun World,* 3, February 1977.

61 **Thomason H E and Thomason H J L.** Solar houses/Heating and cooling progress report. *Solar Energy,* 15, 1973, pp 27–39.

62 **Behrman D.** Solar Energy – The Awaking Science. Routledge and Kegan-Paul, 1979, Chapter VI.

63 **Minardi J E and Chuang H N.** Performance of a black liquid flat-plate solar collector. *Solar Energy,* 17, pp 179–183.

64 **Choda A and Read W R W.** The performance of a solar air heater and rockpile thermal storage system (Paper 4/48). International Solar Energy Society Conference, Melbourne, March 1970.

65 **Building Research Establishment.** Energy conservation: a study of energy consumption in buildings and possible means of saving energy in housing (Section 2). *Building Research Establishment Current Paper,* CP 56/75. BRE 1975

66 **Garg H P et al.** Design and performance prediction of a low cost solar water heater. *Research and Industry,* 17, (4), 1972, pp 125–129.

67 **Thau A.** Architectural and town planning aspects of domestic solar water heaters. *Arch Sci Rev,* 16, (1), 1973, pp 89–104.

68 **Jurisson J et al.** Principles and applications of selective solar coatings. *J Vac Sci Technol,* 12, (5), Sept/Oct, 1975, pp 1010–1015.

69 **Beekley D C and Mather G R Jr.** Analysis and experimental tests of high performance tubular solar collectors (Paper 32/10). International Solar Energy Society Congress. Los Angeles, 1975.

70 **Daniels G.** Solar Homes and Sun Heating. Harper and Row, 1976, pp 62–64.

71 **Speyer E.** Solar energy collection with evacuated tubes. *Trans ASME J Engr and Power,* 86, 1965, pp 270–276.

72 **Eaton C B and Blum H A.** The use of moderate vacuum environments as a means of increasing the collection efficiencies and operating temperatures of flat-plate solar collectors. *Solar Energy,* 17, 1975, pp pp 151–158.

73 **Buchberg H and Edwards D K.** Design considerations for solar collectors with cylindrical glass honeycombs. *Solar Energy,* 18, 1976, pp 193–203.

74 **Winston R.** Light collection within the framework of geometrical optics. *J Opt Soc Am,* 60, (2), 1970, pp 245–247.

75 **Winston R.** Principles of solar concentrators of a novel design. *Solar Energy,* 16, 1974, pp 89–95.

76 **Nelson D T et al.** Linear Fresnel lens concentrators. *Solar Energy,* 17, 1975. pp 285–289.

77 **Meinel A B and Meinel M P.** op cit. Chapters 5, 6 and 7.

78 **British Standards Institution.** Specification for light gauge stainless steel tubes. *British Standard BS 4127 Part 2: 1972.* London.

79 **Building Research Establishment.** Plumbing with stainless steel. *BRE Digest,* 83. London, HMSO, 1973.

80 **British Standards Institution.** Code of Practice for the structural use of timber. Trussed rafters for roofs of dwellings. *British Standard CP 112, Part 3: 1973.* London.

81 **British Standards Institution.** Specification for copper cylinders for domestic purposes. *British Standard BS 699: 1972.* London.

82 **British Standards Institution.** Specification for copper indirect cylinders for domestic purposes. Part 1. Double feed indirect cylinders. *British Standard 1566 Part 1: 1972.* London.

83 **Beale D.** Getting full value from the thermostatic radiator valve. *Heating and Ventilating Engineer,* October 1978, pp 16–20.

84 **Heating and Ventilating Contractors' Association.** Smallbore and microbore domestic central heating Part 1. Open vented systems, Part 2. Sealed systems: Guide to good practice. HVCA, 1974.

85 **British Standards Institution.** Code of Practice for Central Heating for domestic purposes, Part 1. *British Standard BS 5449 : 1977.* London.

86 **British Standards Institution.** Draw-off taps and stop valves for water services. *British Standard BS 1010 :1959.* London.

87 **British Standards Institution.** Specification for copper alloy globe, globe stop and check, check, and gate valves for general purposes. *British Standard BS 5154 : 1974.* London.

88 **Field A A.** Sealed Systems. *Heating and Ventilating Engineer,* March 1977, pp 5–9.

89 **British Standards Institution.** Ethanediol anti-freeze, type C. Sodium tetraborate inhibited. *British Standard BS 3152 : 1959.* London.

90 **British Standards Institution.** Ethanediol anti-freeze, type A. Triethanolammonium Orthophosphate and Sodium Mercaptobenzothiazole inhibited. *British Standard BS 3150 : 1959.* London.

91 **British Standards Institution.** Ethanediol anti-freeze, type B. Sodium benzoate and Sodium nitrite inhibited. *British Standard BS 3151 : 1959.* London.

92 **Anon.** Silicone as a heat transfer fluid. *Heating/Piping/Air conditioning,* July 1977, p 29.

93 **Institution of Electrical Engineers.** Regulations for the electrical equipment of buildings, 14th Edition. London.

94 **Wozniak S J.** Measurement in solar collector testing. International Solar Energy Society – UK Section. Conference C11, April 1977.

95 **British Standards Institution.** Specification for safety isolating transformers for industrial and domestic purposes. *British Standard BS 3535 : 1962.* London.

96 **Sharpley D E.** Control Systems. International Solar Energy Society – UK Section. Conference C13, October 1977.

97 **McAdams W H.** Heat Transmission, third edition, New York, McGraw-Hill, 1975. p 414.

98 **Brinkworth B J.** Active collection and use of solar energy (Paper 5). Construction Industry Conference Centre Ltd. University of Nottingham, April 1977.

99 **Webster C J D.** An investigation of the use of water outlets in multistorey flats. *Building Research Establishment Current Paper,* CP 4/72. BRE, 1972.

100 **The Institution of Heating and Ventilating Engineers.** IHVE Guide. Book B, 1970. B4–7 – B4–8. London 1972.

101 **Whittle G E and Warren P R.** The efficiency of domestic hot water production out of the heating season. *Building Research Establishment Current Paper,* CP 44/78, BRE, 1978.

102 **Morse R N.** Solar heating as a major source of energy for Australia. Paper 4.2–3. *Proceedings of the Tenth World Energy Conference, Istanbul,* 1977.

103 **Maw R.** Polytechnic of Central London. Private communication.

104 **Courtney R G.** A computer study of solar water heating. *Building Research Establishment Current Paper,* CP 30/77. BRE, 1977.

105 **Rosenfeld J L J.** Private Communication.

106 IHVE Guide, op cit. Book C. Section C4.

107 **Copper Development Association.** Design and Installation Guide for Copper Water Services in Building, Technical Note TN22, 1977.

108 **Esbensen T V and Korsgaard V.** Dimensioning of the solar heating system in the zero energy house in Denmark (Paper No 4). International Solar Energy Society – UK Section. Conference C8. London, April 1976.

109 **Wozniak S J.** Solar water heating at a Tunbridge Wells school. *The Heating and Ventilating Engineer,* July/Aug 1978. pp 10–12

110 **Building Research Establishment.** The Assessment of Wind loads. *BRE Digest* 119. London, HMSO, 1974.

111 **Eaton K J and Menzies J B.** Roofs, roofing and the wind. *Building Research Establishment Current Paper,* CP 75/74. BRE, 1974.

112 **British Standards Institution.** Code of Practice, Wind loads. BSI CP 3 : 1972, Chapter V : Part 2. London.

113 **Buller P S J.** Wind damage to buildings in the United Kingdom, 1970–1976. *Building Research Establishment Current Paper,* CP 42/78. BRE, 1978.

114 **Building Research Establishment.** Asphalt and built-up felt roofings: durability. *BRE Digest,* 144. London, HMSO, 1972.

115 **Building Research Establishment.** Built-up felt roofs. *BRE Digest,* 8. London, HMSO, 1970.

116 **Building Research Establishment.** Cavity barriers and fire stops. *BRE Digest,* 214. London, HMSO, 1978.

117 **Menzies J B and Grainger G D.** Report on the collapse of the Sports Hall at Rock Ferry Comprehensive School, Birkenhead. *Building Research Establishment Current Paper,* CP 69/76. BRE 1976.

118 **Building Research Establishment.** BRE reports on sports hall collapse. *BRE News 39.* Spring 1977.

119 **Building Research Establishment.** Early warning of building failures. *BRE News 44.* Summer 1978.

120 **British Standards Institution.** Code of practice for slating and tiling. *BS 5534 Pt 1 : 1978.* London.

121 **Department of Environment.** The Building Regulations 1976. London. HMSO.

122 **Armor M.** Solar energy installations: a new market for builders. *Building Trades Journal,* 22 April 1977. pp 26–31.

123 **Mayo A P.** Load distribution in timber roofs. *Building Research Establishment Information Sheet,* IS 16/76. BRE, 1976.

124 **Mayo A P.** Trussed rafter roofs – load distribution and lateral stability. *Building Research Establishment Information Sheet,* IS 24/78. BRE, 1978.

125 **Department of Energy.** Energy Paper 16. Energy Technology Support Unit, HMSO, 1976. Table 3.2.

126 **Meinel A B and Meinel M P.** op cit pp 41–42.

127 **Zemansky M W.** Heat and thermodynamics. McGraw Hill, 1968.

128 **Building Research Establishment.** Energy conservation: a study of the cost-effectiveness of some means of reducing energy consumption in buildings. A Working Party Report in Preparation.

129 **Fisk D J.** Microeconomics and the demand for space heating. *Energy*, 2, 1977. pp 391–405.

130 **Wozniak S J.** Measurement of system performance in the BRE solar house. International Solar Energy Society – UK Section. Conference C11, London, April 1977.

131 **House of Commons.** Health and safety at work, etc Act, 1974. *Eliz 2 Ch* 37, London, HMSO.

132 Allen and Another vs Greenwood and Another. Court of Appeal. As reported in 'The Times', 17 October 1978.

133 **Carnahan B, Luther H A and Wilkes J O.** Applied Numerical Methods. John Wiley, 1969. pp 310–318.

134 **Francis J R D.** A textbook of Fluid Mechanics for engineering students. Edward Arnold, London 1965. Chapter 13.

Acknowledgements

The IRR calculations in Section 6.4 were performed by Paul Freund and the analysis of flow distribution in Appendix II by Alan Penwarden, both of BRE.

The author wishes to thank colleagues at BRE with whom specialised parts of this book were discussed. The assistance given by the National Physical Laboratory in respect of Section 3.6.1 is also gratefully acknowledged.

Index

Produced in England for Her Majesty's Stationery Office
by Burgess & Son (Abingdon) Ltd., Abingdon, Oxfordshire
Dd.697657 K40 9/79